W9-CNF-547

The Versatile
Border Collie

The Versatile
Border Collie

by Janet Elisabeth Larson
illustrated by J. A. Johnston Aronoff

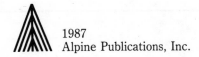
1987
Alpine Publications, Inc.

FRONT COVER PHOTOS
Upper Left—Munro owned by Susan Laymance.
Upper Right—O.T.Ch. HobNob Optimistic "Widget" owned by Janice DeMello.
Bottom—Australian Ch. Tullaview Temptress owned by William and Lynn Harrison.
BACK COVER PHOTO
Maurice MacGregor's "Floss." (Photo by Carole L. Presberg)

Design: Joan Harris
Layout: Susan Allard
Typesetting: Hope Guin, Artline

International Standard Book No. 0-931866-14-6

Printed in the United States of America.

Caora Con's Pennent U.D. - "Pendulum"
Photo: Janet E. Larson

Dedicated to the memory of "Pendulum," Caora Con's Pennent U.D. (1968-1978), who inspired me to write this book, and who taught me much about Border Collie character and training.

ACKNOWLEDGEMENTS

Grateful acknowledgement is made to Ronald A. Winslow Jr. and Rebecca Rule of the University of New Hampshire English Department for their helpful advice on the manuscript, also to the various Kennel Clubs and Border Collie Societies who provided needed information on dog shows, obedience trials and field trials.

Thank you also to Mrs. Gail Sanborn of the Lee Hill 4-H Club, who helped encourage me when I first started out, and to Edgar Gould and Maurice MacGregor who taught me how to train a working stockdog.

A special thank you to Judy Johnston Aronoff who did the fine illustrations, to Robert B. Harrison, Col. Willard A. Johnston, Patricia Ann Kuchma and others who provided fine photographs, and to Mrs. Anita Mundy who typed the manuscript.

CONTENTS

1. **Why a Border Collie?**   1
   Intelligence • Working Ability and Instincts • Characteristics • At Work • Buying

2. **Origin and History of the Breed**   9
   History • "Old Hemp" and Other Famous Lines

3. **Standard of Working Ability and Working Certificates**   17
   Standard of Working Ability • Working Certificates

4. **Choosing Your Border Collie**   21
   Registration • Where to Buy • Puppy vs. Adult • Male vs. Female • Spaying and Neutering

5. **General Care and Feeding**   25
   Feeding • Grooming • Exercise • Prevention of Theft • The Old Dog

6. **Basic Training**   33
   Training Principles • Equipment • Housebreaking • Socialization • Correcting Problems

7. **Formal Obedience**   43
   Training Simple Commands

8. **Training to Herd**   49
   Commands and Terms • Method of Training

9. **Health Problems**   59
   Infectious Diseases • Internal and External Parasites • Common Ailments • Inherited Diseases

10. **First Aid**   69
    Vital Signs • Emergencies • Adminstering Medication

11. **Breeding Better Border Collies**   73
    Genes and Chromosones • Breeding Program

12. **The Brood Bitch and Stud Dog**   81
    Selection • Mating • Problems

13. **Whelping**   87
    Feeding • Attending to Whelping • Problems

14. **The Puppies**   93
    Care • Orphaned Puppies • Selling • Feeding • Evaluation

15. **Sheepdog Trials**   101
    U.S. Trials • Great Britian Sheepdog Trials • International Sheep Dog Society • Trails in Australia and New Zealand

16. **Obedience Trials**   115
    Novice • Utility • Tracking

17. **Schutzhund Trials**   **121**
Origination • Requirements

18. **The Breed Standard**   **125**
Description of Standards • Comparison and Judging

19. **Dog Shows**   **137**
American • Australian • British • Training and Grooming

Glossary of Dog Terms   **141**

References   **145**

Bibliography   **147**

Index   **149**

INTRODUCTION

Many people today buy a Border Collie and then can't find any information on either the breed or its training. One dairy farmer purchased a well-bred Border Collie to herd his cows and expected the dog to train itself. It had plenty of instinct, for it kept driving the cows into a corner and holding them there all day long. The farmer thought the dog was "worthless" since it prevented his cows from grazing.

Other people are not familiar with the breed and consider the Border Collie to be some kind of a cross between a Collie and a Labrador or Spaniel. The Border Collie is not a cross-breed. It is actually the original working Collie—the ancestor of all the other collie and collie-type breeds. The Border Collie has been called by many names over the years: the English Shepherd, the Farm Collie, the Old Fashioned Collie, and "Scotch" Collie (to distinguish it from the more popular show Collie).

The Border Collie is not a rare breed, even though it is only listed in the American Kennel Club Miscellaneous Class. Border Collies are fully recognized for show purposes in Great Britain and Australia, where they are quite popular. In the United States, the Border Collie ranks with the Boxer in popularity, but most of these dogs are on farms and ranches. A drive through farm and ranch country confirms this. Almost every household has a nondescript black and white or tri-color, shaggy or smooth coated "farm" dog. Many of these farm dogs turn out to be Border Collies, not mongrels, as it is commonly thought.

It is my hope that this book will serve to fill in some of the gaps in information on the Border Collie, and help give the breed the recognition it deserves.

Janet Elisabeth Larson
1985

Why A Border Collie? 1

Hamish, a tri-color, male Border Collie trained for avalanche search. Hamish is also trained for stock work and recently won a started cattledog trial. He is owned by Mark R. Moderow of the Alaska Rescue Group. (Photo: Jim Hale)

As I sit to write, my gaze rests on a portrait of my first Border Collie, Pendulum. His alert black and white face with its soft amber brown eyes looks at me, almost as if he were watching. Looking into his eyes, I am reminded of a day many years ago.

An eleven year old girl is running down a country road. With her is her constant companion, Pendulum, who is exploring scents in the woods. A red sports car pulls up alongside the girl, and a man gets out and tries to grab her. She backs off, telling him to leave her alone! Again, he steps towards her, but at that moment Pendulum bursts silently from the woods, teeth bared as he lunges at the man. The man leaps for his car and slams the door on Pendulum—but not before the dog rips his pants. Momentarily, Pendulum has his front leg and tail caught in the door before the man opens it and kicks him out.

Until the day he died, Pendulum had a kink in his tail where it had been broken by the car door.

The Border Collie's intelligence and versatility is exceptional. A 1972 test in England involving eighty different breeds rated the Border Collie most intelligent; actually possessing the problem-solving ability of a twelve-year-old child. The English study tested the dogs in many different areas including reasoning ability, thought patterns, decision-making, abstract thinking, and more.

Their superior mental ability can be attributed to the fact that, unlike other breeds which are bred for points of conformation (such as the shape of their ears, coat color, etc.), Border Collies have been selectively bred for intellect and trainability. In the past, registries for Border Collies required all breeding stock to pass stringent tests of working ability and only the best working males were used for breeding.

Examples of Border Collie wit and ingenuity are legion. Commodore, owned by a shepherd in Arizona, exemplifies this unique problem-solving capacity. One day Commodore, after a long day of sheep herding, returned to the home corral carrying a felt hat in his mouth. After he had the sheep properly penned, Commodore pushed the gate shut with his paws and dropped the hat at the feet of the ranch foreman. The foreman recognized that both the hat and dog belonged to one of his herders, Leonti Soto. Commodore, pulled and tugged at the foreman's pant leg. The foreman obliged and followed Commodore to a distant pasture where they found his owner, Soto, badly injured and trapped by a rock slide.

In similar heroism a California dog named Tar received commendation after she swiftly grabbed a toddler by the seat of the pants preventing the child from tumbling to her death over the edge of a second story balcony.

Bryn, a tri-color bitch trained for search and rescue. To date she has three live rescues to her credit. She is owned and trained by David Riley of the English branch of the Search and Rescue Dog Association, Cumbria, England. (Photo: David Longford-Courtesy of Iris Combe)

A monument to the "working Collie" in Tekapo, Canterbury, New Zealand.

The Border Collie's intelligence is enhanced by his unwavering loyalty. A well-known example is the story of Tip. Tip's owner, an 85-year-old shepherd, went walking with her one day on the lonely English Moors. Both were missing for 15 weeks when searchers finally found the emaciated and feeble dog standing vigil by her dead master's body. A memorial stone stands at the site in Tip's honor.

In 1936, the body of a sheepherder was brought into Berton, Montana, to be shipped East by train for burial. Following behind was the dead man's dog, Shep. From that day on until his death in 1942, Shep met all incoming trains, hoping for his master's return. Shep never accepted a new owner and lived semi-wild on scraps left by the local townspeople. After he died, a monument to him was erected near the train station.

WORKING ABILITY AND INSTINCTS

"Apart from his work, there is not much to be said about the Border Collie," says A . Croxton Smith, leading British canine authority in the book, *The Sheep Dog, Its Work and Training*. With that statement, Smith cleverly understates the skill in which the Border Collie so excels. In a style unique to the breed, their working ability is foremost.

The trait that sets the Border Collie apart from most other breeds is his use of "eye." A crouching, snakelike movement with an intense stare used to hypnotize livestock is what characterizes eye. Using eye is so instinctive in Border Collies that even eight-week-old puppies have tried to eye and herd small animals. Young pups can be seen eyeing cats, chipmunks, and even blowing leaves!

Other inborn traits also appear in the Border Collie. As with many other herding breeds, the Border Collie heads-off, or circles around behind his charges to the side opposite his handler. This process of circling around behind the herd is called the "outrun," or "casting." Ideally, the outrun path should be wide and pear-shaped to prevent disturbing the animals. The close running dog who sporadically dashes toward his herd causes them to frighten and scatter.

The Border Collie, like many working breeds, is descended from the wolf, who is directly responsible for many of the dog's natural characteristics. For example, wolves hunt in highly organized packs. The faster, lighter individuals head off the prey and drive them back to the heavier wolves to be killed. These fast, lightly built wolves use a style very similar to the working Border Collie. The wolves circle wide around the prey (the outrun) so it cannot escape, pause, consider the best angle of approach and creep up to the animal with a fixed stare (eye), forcing the animal back into the jaws of the awaiting, more agressive pack members. As you can see, it is from the wolves' expertise in capturing game that the herding dog was developed.

Other modern driving breeds such as the Bearded Collie and the Rough and Smooth Collie, have been bred to assimilate the traits of the heavier, more aggressive wolf pack members who followed the herd, nipping and biting. Other wolf pack members excelled at tracking and flushing out prey as evidenced in our modern hunting dogs.

Wolves live and hunt in a fixed territory which they fiercely protect from predators, hence the origin of the dogs' instinct of protecting his master and property. Contrary to common belief, wolves are very social animals. Pack members obey a single pack leader, either a male or female, who has a dominant, aggressive personality. The remaining members of the pack have a social position as well, determined by their age, usefulness, and personality.

Wolves are monogamous animals, with both the male and female caring for the cubs. If one partner dies, the surviving mate remains loyal and rarely takes another companion. Similarly, the frequency of Border Collies mating for life is much higher than for other dog breeds. One of my own dogs refused to mate with any bitch except his chosen partner. When he was used at stud, the outside females had to be artificially inseminated.

In summary, many traits of our modern working dog can be directly attributed to his wolf ancestry. A Border Collie's loyalty to his owner is descended from the wolf's nature of faithfulness toward his mate and fellow pack members. Also, the dog's trainability results from the fact that pack members obey, and are disciplined by, the pack leader. Likewise, the Border Collie will obey and follow his human master. Over the centuries, the breed has been selectively bred to enhance these follower and trainability traits. Therefore, it becomes important for the owner or trainer to establish their role as pack leader. Border Collies that do not have a clearly defined, dominant person to follow may become neurotic and ill-behaved.

CHARACTERISTICS

In addition to the traits that originated in the wolf, many other attributes characterize the Border Collie. According to noted English dog trainer Jack Kenworthy, many of his fellow trainers are abandoning the breeds they have worked heretofore and are now turning to Border Collies because of their trainability. Kenworthy adds, however, that since they are a working breed, Border Collies are bored by inactivity; thus requiring the trainer to spend a good deal of time with the dog. To properly train a Border Collie the trainer should teach the basics in obedience, provide adequate exercise, and most importantly, give the dog some work to do.

Human companionship is very important to the Border Collie. Whenever practical, have your dog with you since they are much happier with people than when penned or tied up alone. Your kindness will be rewarded with undying loyalty. Once a Border Collie has chosen a favorite person he will follow him or her like a shadow, offering protection with his life if necessary.

Border Collies are extremely sensitive and must be treated with respect. For this reason, they should be treated gently in training. When a Border Collie is mistreated he behaves adversely and never forgets. Tara, a young pedigreed bitch, exhibited such carry-over behavior. Tara never had any passing interest in motor vehicles until one day when she saw her dam run over by a school bus. Following this incident, Tara became hysterical whenever she saw a motor vehicle. On one occasion she ran off and attacked a car, biting viciously at the front tires.

Firm, consistent discipline is also imperative. As previously mentioned, dogs only respect those owners who display a sense of authority and guidance.

THE BORDER COLLIE AT WORK

Herding

Border Collies are excellent herders and are used world-wide for this purpose. In Australia's vast outback they are indispensable. The Australian flocks are so huge that the dogs are trained to run along the backs of the sheep to get from one side of the flock to the other. This

Aust. Ch. Tullaview Temptress (Lindy), owned by Bill and Lynn Harrison of Australia, herding sheep.

A working Collie in the trenches - W.W.I

Caora Con's Pennent-U.D., a protection trained Border Collie, attacking on command. Note the hidden sleave. (Photo: J.E.L.)

technique called "backing" is especially helpful in stockyards for preventing sheep from getting into woolly traffic jams and injuring themselves.

In the United States Border Collies often herd turkeys on the large, mid-western farms. They are also commonly trained to work ducks, chickens, swine, goats, geese, and horses. More unusual uses include herding reindeer and red-deer in Norway and Scotland, respectively; and in South Africa, Border Collies have even been trained to herd ostriches!

The range of their herding ability is sometimes amazing. Roy, a Border Collie working on a western ranch, was instructed to herd cattle. But instead of returning with Guernseys or Herefords, he returned with 30 head of antelope! Antelope, known for their swiftness, travel up to fifty miles per hour.

In another case a Border Collie named Maid was competing at a sheepdog trial in Ireland. During the competition, an Irish Republican Army sniper terrorized the event by shooting wildly across the field. Meanwhile Maid calmly herded her charges. When Maid's owner, understandably shaken, picked himself off the ground he found her patiently awaiting his next command. In spite of the terrorist, Maid won the event, to the delight of the spectators.

On an English farm, Lass, who was too old to herd cattle, spent her time rounding up chickens. An ornery rooster from a neighboring farm would regularly sneak in to see the hens, but as soon as Lass would find him, she'd sort him out of the flock and chase him all the way home.

Military and Protection

During both World Wars Border Collies served as messengers, ammunition carriers, rescue, and mine detection dogs. According to British Col. Edwin H. Richardson, the Border Collie was preferred for this work. He said Border Collies' creeping way of movement enabled them to move from trench to trench without being seen. Their service and bravery was substantial. In World War II, a messenger dog named Roy, for example, aided the British and received two decorations for bravery. In one lauded case he saved forty trapped soldiers by stealing through a line of heavy fire.

During World War II, a sixty pound, black and white American Border Collie named Jigger made quite a reputation for himself as a demonstration dog for "Dogs for Defense." He was used to recruit dogs

Kim, a pedigreed Border Collie leads his team to victory in a sled dog race in Alaska. Today many Border Collie and Border Collie-Husky crosses are being used in sled racing due to their speed and bidability. Kim was owned by Keith Bryer. (Photo: Courtesy Judith Allen)

for the program, and to gain support for the organization. His trainer, Coy Franklin, said of him, "He was a natural attack dog. Sleeve-happy as they come." Franklin said that after his first week of training Jigger was biting so hard that the agitators had black and blue arms, despite the heavy padding. Jigger was also trained as a messenger, and demonstrated how dogs delivered messages over mock battlefields. During one demonstration, Jigger widened the act by nibbling at one of the "dead" soldiers, who promptly came to life. After the war, Coy Franklin took Jigger home. When Jigger died, he was given a military funeral by the American Legion and buried in a solid mahogany casket studded with 50 caliber hulls.

Guide Dogs for the Blind

While Border Collies are not generally thought of as guide dogs, they can make very effective leaders for the blind. Dr. Leon F. Whitney, prominent author, geneticist, and veterinarian, says that of all breeds the best prospect for guide dog training is the Border Collie or English Shepherd.

In order to become a guide dog, a Border Collie must stand at least eighteen inches at the shoulders, with twenty to twenty-four inches being ideal. (In England, larger dogs than this are also considered.) The prospective guide dog should be friendly, of stable temperament, and between one and two years old.

Those interested in pursuing guide dog training should contact Guiding Eyes for the Blind, Inc., Granite Springs Road, Yorktown Heights, New York.

Blaze, a guide dog, graduated from Guiding Eyes for the Blind, Inc. of Yorktown Heights, N.Y. in 1979. Blaze was bred by Caora Con Kennels. (Photo: J.E.L.)

Hunting

The Border Collie makes a superb hunting dog. British dog trainer John Holmes contends that the average Border Collie has a sense of smell equal to the typical gun dog, and can actually surpass the gun dog in tracking prowess. Holmes' own Border Collie, Judy, could point birds by using eye, retrieve on land or water, track humans and animals, and even attack on command.

Other examples of Border Collies used for hunting can be found. A friend of mine trained both of her dogs to retrieve ducks. One of my own Border Collies qualified in a local club's retriever trial but won no ribbons because she is not one of the six recognized retriever breeds.

A Border Collie in California uses his talent for hunting deer. The dog seeks out the deer and soon walks them unwittingly to the awaiting hunters. Although this technique is successful in drawing out deer, it is an illegal practice in some states, so be aware of your local laws.

A Border Collie retrieving a duck scented "dummy" from a salt marsh in November. This dog is an excellent duck and goose dog and loves swimming. (PAK Photo)

Track and Scent

For centuries the Border Collie has been required to track down lost, trapped, or missing sheep. Therefore, it is not surprising that many have received Tracking Dog degrees. In Scotland and in several other European countries Border Collies serve as mountain rescue dogs.

The United States Customs Department recently started to employ Border Collies as drug detection dogs. They were among the breeds chosen because of their natural inquisitiveness and retrieving ability. Border Collies are trained as bomb and drug detectors in Great Britain, and are increasingly used for the same purposes in the U.S. Armed Forces.

Sled Dog Racing

In the world of sled dog racing, the Border Collie is just gaining recognition. Several teams of Border Collies have already won major races while other sled dog owners are crossing Border Collies and Huskies to produce a faster, more competitive team. This practice is especially prevalent in New England where sled dog racing is popular.

Obedience

As an obedience dog the Border Collie reigns supreme. In England about ninety percent of the dogs competing in obedience today are Border Collies. The remaining ten percent is made up almost entirely of German Shepherds, Poodles and Shetland Sheepdogs.

In the United States, where AKC ILP Listed Border Collies are still rather rare, the few that are competing in obedience usually have spectacular success. Many have earned the coveted Utility Dog-Tracker title and Obedience Championship. Others have received the Dog World Award of Canine Distinction for earning their degrees in three consecutive shows with scores 195 or above out of a possible 200.

One of the first Border Collies to make a name for the breed in obedience was J.C. and Hazel Thompson's Rex U.D.T. He won hundreds of first place and Highest Scoring Dog in Trial awards. Many people seeing Rex work decided that they too wanted a Border Collie.

In 1978 the American Kennel Club instituted the Obedience Trial Championship, open only to those dogs with Utility Dog titles. Points are accumulated by winning first or second place in the open B or utility class. A total of 100 points must be won, including at least three first places in either class, under three different judges. The first Border Collie to earn the coveted title of Obedience Trial Champion was Pallison's Passion, a bitch owned by Pat Kaiser in 1978. Many Border Collies have since won this title.

Showing

The Border Collie is recognized for show purposes in five countries—Australia, Great Britain, New Zealand, South Africa and in the United States in the Miscellaneous Class. They can earn conformation championships only in Great Britain, Australia, South Africa and New Zealand, although they are eligible to earn obedience championships and titles in all five countries.

Many breeders hope that if the Border Collie does gain full recognition, the AKC will also recognize Working Certificates (see page 17) and make them a requirement for any dog to earn a championship in the conformation ring.

Television and Movies

You would think that being able to herd, track, hunt, guide and more would be enough for the versatile Border Collie, but no, he does even more. He can act, too. One of the most famous Border Collie performers was Clive, starring in the television show *Sargeant Cluff* with Larry Sands. Off-camera Clive was a pedigree Border Collie named Tuck, owned and trained by John Holmes. Tuck also appeared in the feature-length films *Casino Royale* and *Postman's Knock*.

King, a top trial dog owned by Charles Null of California, has also taken to the silver screen. A big, smooth-coated dog, King has been featured in the shows *Wild is the Wind* and *The Proud Rebel*.

Arthur Allen's Rock and Nicky starred in the Walt Disney movies *The Arizona Sheepdog* and *Border Collies in Action*. Border Collies have appeared in many other movies and television shows such as *Down and Out in Beverly Hills*, *Frankenstein*, *The Railway Children*, *Little House on the Prairie* and *Up the Creek*.

A protection trained Border Collie clearing the barrels. This is an agility exercise designed for Police dogs. (Photo: R.B. Harrison)

A Border Collie pulling his owner's cart. Note the special harness. (PAK Photo)

POINTS TO CONSIDER
BEFORE BUYING A PET BORDER COLLIE

The same superior and admirable traits that make this breed a great working dog often present a paradox for the average pet owner. As trainer Jack Kenworthy advises, because a Border Collie does not want to sit around idle, you should train and work with him every day. If a Border Collie becomes bored he will entertain himself, but often in an unacceptable way.

Recently, many people have been buying Border Collies as pets as a direct result of increased media coverage on such programs as *Little House on the Prairie,* where a white Border Collie is featured, and *Nop's Trials,* a recent best-seller by Donald McCaig. Many of these pet owners do not realize that this loving and extremely intelligent dog is also very energetic and may spend time chasing cars and children, chewing, and generally misbehaving if his energy is not expended in a positive manner. That is why it must be emphasized to all Border Collie pet owners that obedience training is absolutely essential.

A well-meaning family who owned a pet Border Collie puppy did not take the time to train him, so one afternoon while the family was out for several hours the puppy found other means of occupying himself. He ripped down the drapes and chewed the legs off a chair and tea table. When his owners returned home, the puppy's head was sticking out through a hole in the drapes, which hung around him like a garland.

Not all owners know how to properly handle these dilemmas. A farmer with a young Border Collie pup wrongly expected him to be able to work efficiently with no training or guidance. The dog drove the cows into a corner of the barn and refused to let them out. The farmer, not appreciating the dog's youth and lack of training, cruelly shot and killed the dog.

Of course, this is an extreme reaction to an owner's unpreparedness, but it also illustrates the point graphically. Border Collies are terrific dogs—loyal, loving, and incomparably smart. As owners we owe them respect and proper guidance.

Due to their great intelligence, Border Collies can be trained to perform a variety of tricks. (Photo: Robert Boyd Harrison)

Jake and some of the cast from "Up the Creek." (Courtesy S. Laymance)

A Shepherd and his Border Collie pictured on a wall in Dillon, Montana. (Photo: Judy Johnston Aronoff)

Origin And History Of The Breed

2

The Border Collie is one of the oldest existing dog breeds. The actual origin of the breed will probably never be known. We do know herding dogs have been used since man first domesticated livestock. The first definite Collie-like dog was described in 36 B.C. by the Romans Cato and Varo in their book on agriculture, *De Re Rustica*. They described a large, heavy boned, black, tan and white herding dog, with a rough (long) coat, or a smooth (short) coat. These big, fierce dogs, resembling today's Bernese Mountain Dog and Rottweiler, fought off predators and protected their flocks and herds from rustlers. These Roman herding dogs attacked and fought silently to prevent alarming their charges.

When the Romans invaded Britain in 55 B.C., they brought along dogs to herd and guard the livestock which were used to feed their armies. Once the Romans settled in the southern part of the British Isles, they took up agriculture. Their herding dogs became indispensable to help fend off wolves and other predators.

When the Roman Empire began crumbling, the Vikings from Scandinavia increasingly raided the British Isles. Finally, they successfully invaded Scotland and Ireland in 794 A.D. (See family tree of the Border Collie.) The Vikings settled in these areas, and with them brought their Spitz-type dogs to use for herding. The Viking Spitz weighed 25 to 35 pounds, and was usually black or sable in color with white markings. It had a short, dense double coat, prick ears, a foxy face, and often had blue eyes. Over a period of years, these small spitzes were crossed with the descendents of the Roman herding dogs eventually decreasing the size of the native sheepdogs. Modern descendents of the Viking Spitz include the Lapponian herder, Karelien Bear Dog and Finnish Spitz. These dogs are very similar in type to their ancestor, the Viking Spitz.

The smaller size and lighter bone structure was advantageous in the Scottish highland and Wales where the land was very rocky and hilly. In these areas, the shepherds found that a small dog, about 25 to 35 pounds was quicker on its feet and more agile, making them better suited to working wild mountain sheep. In the flat lowland areas of Scotland and Northern England, a taller, heavier dog evolved. These dogs, like their highland relatives, were usually black and white or tri-color, but averaged 50 to 65 pounds.

Today, the average Border Collie male weighs about 45 pounds and stands 21 inches tall, with females slightly less. Small dogs of the highland "fox" type and large dogs of the lowland "farm collie" type still occur today in Scotland and Northern England where the breed originated.

WRITTEN HISTORY

One of the earliest descriptions of the Border Collie was by the Welsh King, Hywel Dda, in 943 A.D. He described a black sheepdog taking a flock of sheep out to graze in the hills and coming home with them in the evening. The Welsh King was so impressed with the working sheepdog that he made a law stating that a good sheepdog was worth a prime ox. Back in those days, that was quite a sum of money!

Several centuries later, in 1486, in the *Book of St. Albans*, a shepherd's dog much like the Border Collie is described. The dog was called a "tryndel tayles," meaning long-tailed, to distinguish it from the bob-tailed cur dogs commonly used as a drover's dog in England.

In 1514, records show two lowland Polish Sheepdogs "Vallee Shepherds" were traded for sheep in Scotland. These dogs were bred to the local dogs developing a grey or blue merle, shaggy, bob-tailed breed that was undoubtedly the forerunner of the Scottish Bearded Collie and the bob-tailed Old English Sheepdog. It is also the probable origin of the grey and merle coat colors found in all the Collie breeds today. It is unlikely, however, that this cross had too much effect on the Border Collie, since the Vallee Shepherd looks like the Bearded Collie and Old English bob-tail, and works with a noisy, aggressive style (barking and biting at livestock's heels), not with the silent, intent style of the Border Collie (controlling livestock with lightening-quick dashes and a hypnotic stare).

An excellent description of the breed was made in 1576, by Dr. Johannes Caius in his book *English Dogges*. His description sounds like our modern, working Border Collie. He says:

> Our Shepherd's dogge is not huge, vaste, or bigge, but of indifferent stature and growth, because it hath not to deale with the blood thirsty wolf, sythence there be none in England, which happy and fortunate benefit is to be ascribed to the puifaunt Prince Edgar.....This dogge, either at the hearing of his master's voice or at the shrill hissing, bringeth the wandering weathers and straying sheep into the self same place where his master's will and wish is to have them, whereby the shepherd reapeth this benefite, namely that with little labour nor tyole or moving of his feete he may rule and guide his flocke, according to his own desire.

In 1700, Thomas Bewick mentioned the Border Collie in his book *The General History of Quadrupeds* as a "rough coated Collie, black with white tail tip.....this breed of dog appears at present to be preserved in the greatest purity in the Northern parts of England and Scotland, where its aid is highly necessary in managing the numerous flocks of sheep in these extensive wilds and fells." His book also includes a woodcut of a dog identical in appearance to a modern Border Collie. Sydenham Edwards also had a plate of three beautiful Border Collies and a bobtail "cur" dog in his book *Cynographia Britanica*, published in 1800. He titled this picture "The Shepherd's Dog and the Cur." Several other well-known British artists drew pictures of Border Collies. Some of the best known are John Constable's painting *The Cornfield*; G. B. Barber's *Noble, a Dog of the Highlands* (Noble is an example of the short-coated "smooth" type Border Collie); and T. W. Keyle's *Gypsie*, a portrait of Queen Victoria's first collie, a typical black and white Border type bitch.

The first Sheepdog trial of record was held in Bala, Wales, on October 9th, 1873. Many of the competitors and their dogs were Scottish, as was the winner, Mr. William Thomson, and his Scottish bred dog, Tweed. Tweed won despite the fact that his sheep at one point bolted over a stone wall into the crowds. Tweed, described as a medium-sized,

"The Shepherd's Dog and the Cur" from *Cynographia Britanica* by Sydenham Edwards, 1800. The "Cur" is described as a cross between the Shepherd's Dog (Collie) and the Terrier, and was considered as useful about the house as the Collie was among the hills.

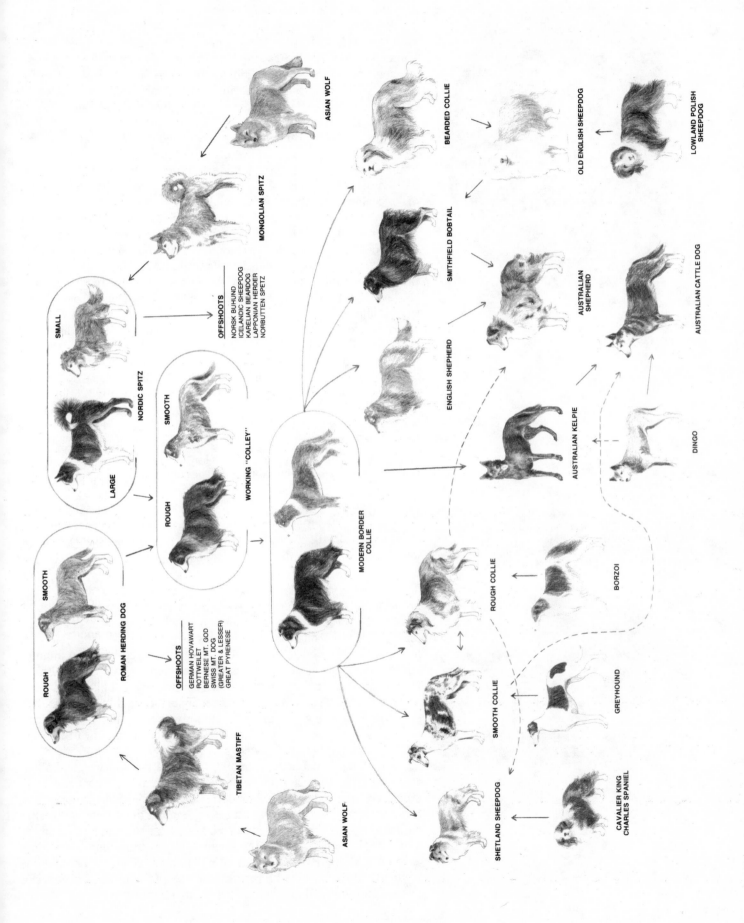

ASIAN WOLF

BEARDED COLLIE

OLD ENGLISH SHEEPDOG

LOWLAND POLISH SHEEPDOG

MONGOLIAN SPITZ

SMALL

NORDIC SPITZ

LARGE

OFFSHOOTS
NORSK BUHUND
ICELANDIC SHEEPDOG
KARELIAN BEARDOG
LAPPONIAN HERDER
NORBUTTEN SPETZ

SMOOTH

ROUGH

WORKING "COLLEY"

SMITHFIELD BOBTAIL

AUSTRALIAN SHEPHERD

ENGLISH SHEPHERD

AUSTRALIAN KELPIE

AUSTRALIAN CATTLE DOG

DINGO

SMOOTH

ROUGH

ROMAN HERDING DOG

OFFSHOOTS
GERMAN HOVAWART
ROTTWEILET
BERNESE MT. GOD
SWISS MT. DOG
(GREATER & LESSER)
GREAT PYRENESE

MODERN BORDER COLLIE

ROUGH COLLIE

BORZOI

SMOOTH COLLIE

GREYHOUND

TIBETAN MASTIFF

ASIAN WOLF

SHETLAND SHEEPDOG

CAVALIER KING CHARLES SPANIEL

11

The late Mr. Wm. Thomson, Winner of the first sheep-dog trial (Bala, Wales, October, 1873).

The Drover's Dog was generally a cross between the Colley and the Foxhound or Mastiff. The larger drover's dog was used to move cattle and large, vigorous sheep from place to place. (from *Illustrated Natural History*, 1865)

compactly built dog with a black coat and tan and white markings was also the winner of the beauty prize.

Because of the success of that first trial in Wales, trials were held all over the British Isles. They were introduced to Australia and the United States in the 1880's, and have continued through the years under the aegis of organized associations such as the International Sheepdog Society in Great Britain, the North American Sheepdog Society in McLeansboro, Illinois, and the American-International Border Collie Registry in Runnels, Iowa.

Over the years, Border Collies have been called by many different names. I am sure that you have probably met people who told stories of their boyhood collie, and "not one of those pointy-nosed show Collies like Lassie." Or you might have heard your father or grandfather tell of "old Shep," his "farm-type" collie who always went out to get the cows every morning and night at milking time. Some of the more common names used for the breed in the past were: the Shepherd's dog, Colley dog, Coally dog, and finally, just the Collie. The name "collie" was used to refer to herding breeds in general. There are numerous theories regarding the origin and meaning of the word. In recent years, the breed has been called the Working Collie, Old-fashioned Collie, Farm-type Collie, Scotch Border Collie, Irish, Welsh, and English Collie or Shepherd, to try to distinguish it from the popular show-breed the Rough or Smooth Collie. The show Collie is a totally different breed from the modern Border Collie, although they do share common ancestry.

Evidence suggests that the modern show Collie was developed partly with the aid of the Irish Setter and the Borzoi. The name Border Collie was applied to the old-fashioned working Collie in 1915 by James Reid, then secretary of the International Sheepdog Society. He inserted the name Border Collie into the registration forms of the Society. The name Border was chosen because the best working Collies came from the border counties between Northern England and Southern Scotland.

OLD HEMP

All modern Border Collies trace back to a single dog, *Old Hemp*, who was born in 1893. It is felt by some canine historians that very few herding breeds are free of Old Hemp's blood. He was bred by Adam Telfer of Northumberland, England. Hemp became a sensation when he began hitting the sheepdog trials at a year old. In his entire life he remained unbeaten, a record never equalled by any other dog. In the many trials in which he competed his spectacular speed and quiet, yet intense style, proved amazing. He could cover a trial course in minutes without exciting the sheep, and still keep them under control with his intense gaze, described by spectators as "the eye." This intent gaze, a characteristic today in all his descendents, seemed to hypnotize the sheep into following his demands. Hemp was so successful at making a difficult trial course look simple that the usually taciturn Scots described him as "bluidy marvelous."

Old Hemp stood approximately 21 inches tall and weighed about 45 pounds. He was black and white with a long, straight coat and semi-erect ears. He is the dog the modern Border Collie Standard was patterned after. Hemp's sire was an easy-going but unexceptional worker named Roy. His dam, Meg, was so intense that she had a tendency to hypnotize herself instead of the sheep, and was thus almost worthless as a worker. Hemp himself had all his parents' good points and none of their bad. He also had a remarkable ability to pass on his superior mental and physical characteristics to his offspring.

As a result of his success at the sheepdog trials, Old Hemp was widely sought as a stud dog. In his lifetime, it is estimated that he sired well over 200 sons and uncounted daughters. His offspring, like himself, proved to be superior workers and were sought out by people from as far away as Australia, Germany, France, Belgium, and the United States.

OTHER FAMOUS LINES

An early sire as important to the Border Collie is Old Hemp himself was Isaac Herdman's Tommy #16[1]. Tommy was bred by William Wallace of Northumberland, England. Tommy was a grandson of Old Hemp on his dam, Gyp's, side, and a great-grandson of Old Hemp on his sire Tweed's side. Tommy was of the "English Shepherd" type, black and tan with some white on his chest, neck, feet and tail tip. He was very strong boned and of medium size, with a rough coat. He had a gentle, easy going nature, but on stock was super keen and a bit hard to control. Had his handler been more skilled, experts who had seen the dog work feel he would have been a top trial dog. As it was, Tommy started four different familes of Border Collie. The fifth family of Border Collies started by Armstrong's Sweep, also carried Tommy's blood.

The first Tommy line was started by mating him to A. Brown's Old Maid, a tri-coloured bitch. This line contained the 1913 International Champion, T. P. Brown's Lad, and the 1929 winner, S. E. Bathy's Corby. The second family was produced by mating Tommy to G. P. Brown's Nell. This line contained the 1923 International Champion, G. P. Brown's Spot, the 1926 Champion, M. Hayton's Glen, the 1931 winner, J. Thorp's Jess and the 1935 Champion, J. Jone's Jaff II.

The third and most important line was produced by mating Tommy to Ancrum Jed. This mating produced the 1907 International champion, W. Wallace's Moss, who was later exported to New Zealand as "Border Boss." This line also produced the 1924 Champion, T. Robert's Jaff, J. M. Wilson's Fly the 1928 winner, J. M. Wilson's Craig, the 1930 Champion, and J. M. Wilson's Roy the 1934, 1936, and 1937 Champion. The J. M. Wilson dogs started many important modern bloodlines. The fourth "Tommy line" was started by mating him to J. Scott's Jed. This line produced Thomas Armstrong's Don, the 1911 and 1914 International Champion, and G. Whitig's Chip, the 1933 Champion.

Another early sire of importance was Thomas Armstrong's Sweep. Sweep was a grandson of Old Hemp, and himself International Champion in 1910 and 1912. He was quite large, very handsome, with a thick black and white coat. He was described as an outstanding, quiet, coolheaded worker, who had a calming effect on very wild sheep. He sired such famous dogs as S. E. Batty's Hemp II, the 1920 International Champion. Hemp II in turn sired James Bagshaw's Lad, the 1927 Champion. The Sweep line produced many champions among them Walter Telfer's Midge, Champion in 1919, and Walter Tefler's Queen, in 1932. A. Renwick's Don in 1906, J. Scott's Old Kep in 1908, Adam Tefler's Haig in 1921, and A. Miller's Spot, winner in 1925.

J. M. Wilson became one of the greatest sheepdog trial men and Border Collie breeders in the history of the breed. He produced an impressive array of champions. His first International winner was Craig, in 1930, J. M. Wilson's Roy, the 1934, 1936 and 1937 International Champion was Craig's most famous son. Roy apparently showed no interest in herding until he was two years old and was considered a dullard

Old Hemp, born September 1894. (Sire: Adam Telfer's Roy; Dam: Adam Telfer's Meg).

Adam Telfer's Haig, a tri-color male. William Wallaces Gen. James Reids Maddie. International Champion. English farmer's Champion.

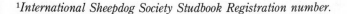

[1]*International Sheepdog Society Studbook Registration number.*

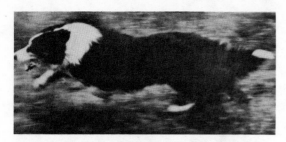

Imported Roy 8399—four times North American Supreme Champion. Only dog in America to win Supreme Championship four times. (Photo from "Border Collies in America" by Arthur N. Allen.)

The late Mr. Walter Telfer, winner of the first English sheep-dog trial (Byrness, 1876).

and a disappointment. It wasn't until Roy lost an eye in a fight with his half-brother, Jix, that he settled down and developed an interest in sheep. From then on Roy was described as a "marvel," and a "one eyed wonder." He was a very obedient, stylish, worker, and had great control over his sheep. Roy was a very popular sire and many of today's top winners trace back to him.

J. M. Wilson's wartime Cap #3036 was another very important influence on the Border Collie. Cap was a big, strong, black and white, rough coated dog, with a half-whited head and a lot of white on his body. He was a great all-round dog, with a natural outrun, and power to control both sheep or cattle. Cap's pedigree goes back to Old Hemp several times, and contains a red and white bitch, Wylie, in the sixth generation. This is significant, because most famous dogs today contain his blood through Wiston Cap. Cap was the sire of J. M. Wilson's famous Mirk, 1950 International Champion, J. M. Wilson's Moss second place winner, and J. M. Wilson's Glen, third place winner that year. Cap's great-grandsire, J. M. Wilson's Craig, the 1930 winner, also threw a number of red and white pups, the red (or chocolate) factor passed on to him from his sire, Hemp #153. Hemp's dam, Jed, was a daughter of the red and white Wylie.

John Richardson's Wiston Cap, the 1965 International Champion, is perhaps one of the most important modern pillars of the breed. Wiston Cap's pedigree goes back to J. M. Wilson's Wartime Cap sixteen times! Wiston Cap was born in 1963 and died in 1979 at the age of 15 ½ years. Cap was a big, handsome, tri-colour rough coated dog. He was very good natured and biddable, and had a natural wide outrun and good style. He has produced some excellent sons and daughters, including the 1971 International Champion, J. Murray's Glen, the 1972 winner, J. J. Templeton's Cap, the 1974 champion, Gwyn Jone's Bill. The 1976 winner, Gwyn Jone's Shep was his grandson, as was the 1978 winner Robert Shennan's Mirk, and the 1981 winner, E. Wyn Edward's Bill.

The wins of Wiston Cap's offspring are legion, however it has been noted that the champions he produced were from outcrosses with little or no J. M. Wilson dog's blood. Inbreeding with this line has caused decrease in size, loss of speed and stamina, and sensitive, moody temperaments. Also, a great many red or chocolate coloured dogs are cropping up. There have been complaints about lack of power in working large flocks of sheep and cattle. However, the outcross dogs have been truely outstanding, tough, hard workers on both cattle and large flocks of sheep.

John Gilchrist's famous 1947 International Champion, Spot #3624 produced another very famous line. Spot was sired by J. Purdie's Tam out of J. Purdie's Trim. He was black and white, rough coated, well marked, and of medium size. He was described as having real class, beautiful balance and was a treat to watch. His most famous grandson was J. Gilcrest's Bob #12684, the sire of the 1965 and 1966 Scottish National Champion J. Gilcrest's Spot #24981. Gilcrest's Spot was fairly large, rough coated, black and white dog with a half white face. This dog was known for his natural wide outruns, quiet, upstanding style and intense eye. His offspring have dominated the trial fields as have Wiston Cap's. Among the more famous offspring are the 1970 Irish driving Champion, J. Brady's Risp, sire of T. Flood's National Champion, Scott. Other dogs include J. Campbell's Cap (with his Nell) International Brace Champion in 1971, J. Gilchrist's Craig and J. Gilchrist's Roy and D. McTeir's Dave represented Scotland on the national team in 1967. G. Pritchard's Roy represented Wales in 1977. In 1978, James Gilchrist's Spot #59324 represented the Scottish team, and S. Donaghy's Nell III, the Irish team the same year. Raymond MacPherson's Tweed, a son of Gilchrist Spot, won the Open trial in Maryland in 1976, and Spot's daughter, Fleet, owned by Arthur Allen, won the North American Supreme Championship in 1970, 1971, 1972, and 1973. Spot's granddaughter, June, owned by W. Cormack won the Scottish National Championship in 1973, and his grandson's, Harford Logan's Jim won the Irish National Championship in 1974, and Capt. A. G. Jone's Tos won the Welsh National Championship in 1975. This line tends to produce a lot of predominately white dogs and some soft temperaments when linebred or inbred closely, however, most are known for their natural outruns, ease to train, and upstanding style of work. Red dogs have also been produced in this line, going back to J. M. Wilson's Wartime Cap.

The Shepherd's Dog or Colley from: "Dogs of Great Britian, America and Other Countries." By Stonehenge, 1884.

Robert of Brookfield-U.D. (Robbie) a male Border Collie herding cattle at the Brookfield Children's Zoo in Illinois as part of their "Animals in action" program. (Photo: Courtesy Gail Schneider and the Brookfield Zoo)

Standard of
Working Ability and
Working Certificates   3

Working certificates were first developed by the North American Sheepdog Society to preserve the herding instinct and intelligence of the Border Collie. Herding ability is a delicate balance of innate intellectual instincts that can only be determined by training the dog. For this reason, no breeder should consider using a dog or bitch for a breeding animal unless it has a working certificate. Breeders over the centuries have wisely bred for the Border Collie's working ability (his instincts to circle livestock and to control it with his intent gaze or "eye"). Without these instincts and his high intelligence, the dog cannot be considered a true Border Collie no matter how beautiful, or how closely he fits a written conformation standard.

The requirements necessary for a Border Collie to receive a working certificate are not complex. The dog does not have to be a trial dog. When the dog is adequately prepared, arrange for a recognized judge to watch your dog work. If you own no livestock, you may be allowed to use his. Once he has watched your dog, the judge will fill out and sign an application form which you should have previously obtained. Return the completed application to the *North American Sheepdog Society* or to the *Border Collie Club of America*.

STANDARD OF WORKING ABILITY
(Approved by the Border Collie Club of America, June 1978;
Amended June 1980)

General Characteristics   The Border Collie's unique style of working sets it apart from all other pure breeds of stockdog. This is the only breed of dog to work stock with its eyes, as though trying to hypnotize or outstare its charges. Unlike most other breeds of stockdog, the Border Collie is a "heading" dog, circling or heading around to the opposite side of the stock and driving it back toward its handler rather than driving them away. This breed works in a gentle, quiet manner, and the dog will use strategy rather than force to drive its charges. If force is necessary, the Border Collie will use it, but in most cases the animals being handled seem to realize this and don't put up much resistance.

Many Border Collie pups show a desire to work livestock as early as eight weeks of age, but in others it may take longer, sometimes as long as a year. Young pups and older dogs who have not been exposed to livestock often try to herd anything that moves, from blowing leaves

A Border Collie exhibiting strong "eye." (Photo: Reinke)

to automobiles. The dog will "eye" these moving objects just as it would livestock, and in many cases will even try to circle or head the object off.

Temperament   The Border Collie should give the observer the impression of an eager, alert, calm, well-adjusted, and highly intelligent animal. The expression should show keen interest in what is going on, and be alert and questioning. The dog should be responsive to command and be obedient, although it must show initiative when working out of sight or when the situation calls for it. A nervous, shy, stubborn, vicious or dull type temperament is undesirable.

Eye   This characteristic is found only in the Border Collie and breeds carrying an infusion of Border Collie blood. Eye refers specifically to the inborn power of the Border Collie to control sheep and other types of livestock with its keen and intent gaze. The dog's gaze seems to mesmerize or intimidate its charges into doing what it wants without having to resort to gripping or barking. The dog's legs are gathered under it for instant action should the animals try to break away. A dog who is "over-strong" in eye uses this power to excess, and tends to be overbearing and domineering. This may cause the animals it is herding to become nervous and rebellious. A "loose-eyed" dog on the other hand lacks concentration of eye, and cannot efficiently control its charges.

Style   The upstanding, free-moving dog is the most desirable type of worker. This type of dog stays on its feet most of the time, clapping and creeping only when the situation calls for it. The dog should be eager, obedient to command, and should show good speed and stamina. The tail should be carried low and in line with the curve of the hind legs when the dog is working, since this indicates concentration and intentness. A dog who carries its tail over its back or in a gay flip-flop manner is not concentrating on its charges, and in most cases indicates a "loose-eyed" dog. The dog should also have sufficient courage to stand its ground without flinching or turning tail if its charges show fight or attack it, however, force should only be used if absolutely necessary. A dog who constantly claps to the ground and creeps wastes time, and often takes an experienced trainer to get it on to its feet and working in the first place. This type of dog is considered "sticky," and in the extreme is when the dog's eye is so strong that it spends all of its time flat on its belly staring at the livestock, but is so intent that it won't get up. On the other hand, a dog that shows no concentration or caution while working is also undesirable. Such a dog will often rush back and forth barking and panic its charges. A well bred Border Collie should not bark while working, since this is not characteristic of the breed.

Gathering Ability   The Border Collie is by nature a heading dog, will instinctively cast or run wide around livestock in a semi-circle either to the right or left of the handler and end up opposite to him or her. The cast should be wide so as not to disturb the animals. Ideally, the dog should stop at twelve or one o'clock. The cast should be somewhat pear shaped (with the narrow end closest to the handler, widening out as the dog approaches the front of its charges during the cast or outrun). After completing the cast, the dog should stop and pause before coming onto its charges, or they can become frightened and scatter. The lift is the period after the dog has stopped which gives the animals it is herding their first impression of the dog, and allows the dog to assess the situation. After this the dog should quietly and calmly fetch the sheep and move them in as straight a line as possible toward its handler. The dog should naturally place itself at a moderate distance from its charges to keep them moving at an easy pace without scattering or becoming frightened. If the animals move out of line the dog should straighten them out by flanking (swinging back and forth) in the appropriate direction. A dog who does this naturally without command is said to be well balanced.

A close-run dog will often cause animals to scatter, or the dog may fail to see any strays further out in the field and inadvertantly leave them behind. Many dogs also tend to cut their casts short and come onto the sheep too soon. This can cause them to scatter and the dog will end up chasing them away instead of gathering them up and bringing them in. A dog who is over eager or aggressive may scatter its charges, while a sluggish or indifferent dog may lose contact and control of them. This type of behavior is undesirable, and often indicates poor breeding, or in some cases, poor training.

Driving   The Border Collie, unlike most herding breeds, is not by nature a driving dog. Most other herding breeds drive or chase stock away from the handler while nipping and barking at their heels. The Border Collie can, and is, trained to drive, but it works silently and calmly. The dog approaches the animals directly instead of casting in a circle, and uses his hypnotic eye to get its charges moving. Once they are in motion, the dog may flank the animals back and forth to keep them moving in a straight line. The dog should never bark and bite at the heels of the animals, but should work at a moderate distance in true, quiet Border Collie style. When working cattle, horses, swine, or goats, nipping at the heels of the animals is permissable when necessary.

Faults   Any deviation from these specifications is a fault. In determining whether a fault is minor, serious, or major, these two factors should be used as a guide: (1) The extent to which it deviates from the Standard; (2) The extent to which such deviation actually effects the working ability of the dog.

Disqualifications   Total lack of "eye"; lack of gathering or "herding" instinct; viciousness toward livestock; any dog which attacks or attempts to attack the judge or its handler; any dog who lacks the Border Collie's methods of working; any dog who scores less than 50 points:

A Border Collie driving sheep in an open field without the aid of a fenceline. It takes a lot of training to get a Border Collie to drive stock away from you, since his natural instinct is to round them up and bring them to you. (PAK Photo)

A Border Collie's instinct to herd is so strong he will even herd ducks in a pond! (Compliments of Sally Anne Thompson)

THE BORDER COLLIE CLUB OF AMERICA
WORKING CERTIFICATE PROGRAM
(January 1987 Ammendment)

Section 1. Working Certificate and Working Certificate Excellent. The Border Collie Club of America will issue a Working Certificate or Working Certificate Excellent for each dog, registered with either the ABCA, AIBC, NASDS or UKC and listed with this club, and will permit the use of the letters W.C. or W.C.X. after the name of each dog that meets these requirements.

Section 2. Certification. The dog must be certified by a recognized stock dog trial judge, at a recognized stock dog trial. The judge must be recognized as competent by the ABCA, AIBC, NASDS, or if from a foreign country, by the Sheepdog Society in that country. The person certifying the dog must not own or co-own the dog at the time of certification.

Section 3. Working Certificate. A purebred Border Collie shall be considered of proven working ability, and be awarded the Working Certificate (W.C.) when said dog, within the 15 minute time limit receives 60% of the available points, using typical Border Collie Style as outlined in the Standard of Working Ability.

1. Outrun, maximum 100 yards .... 20 points
2. Lift, five head sheep or other stock .... 10 points
3. Fetch, straight to handler .... 25 points
4. Turn, around handler .... 5 points
5. Drive, to post, no more than 25 yards .... 30 points
6. Pen, 12' by 6' with gate .... 20 points

Total 100 points

Section 4. Working Certificate Excellent. A purebred Border Collie shall be awarded the Working Certificate Excellent (W.C.X.) when said dog, within the 15 minute time limit, receives 60% of the available points, using typical Border Collie Style as outlined in the Standard of Working Ability.

1. Outrun, maximum 200 yards .... 20 points
2. Lift, five head sheep or other stock .... 10 points
3. Fetch, straight to handler .... 25 points
4. Turn, around handler .... 5 points
5. Drive to first panel-no more than 100 yards .... 15 points
6. Cross drive to second panel-no more than 100 yrs. .... 15 points
7. Pen, 12' by 6' with gate .... 20 points

Total 100 Points

Section 5. In the event the Border Collie is ever recognized for show purposes by the AKC or UKC, the AKC or UKC must also recognize the Working certificate, and no dog shall be permitted to become a Conformation Champion unless it is also certified as a working stockdog according to the above specifications.

NORTH AMERICAN SHEEPDOG SOCIETY & INTERNATIONAL SHEEPDOG SOCIETY WORKING CERTIFICATE.
Pass Mark is 60%, Time Limit 15 minutes.

1. Outrun, maximum of 200 yards .... 20 points
2. Lift, five sheep (or other stock) .... 10 points
3. Fetch, straight to handler .... 20 points
4. Drive, maximum 100 yards, past post .... 30 points
5. Pen 12' by 6' with gate .... 20 points

Total 100 points

For more information on Working Certificates, contact the appropriate organization. Addresses are listed in the Appendix.

Choosing Your Border Collie

Pendulum (left) and Mack (Right) in the tree house. These two Border Collies learned to climb ladders to join their young owners up in the tree house. (Photo: J.E.L.)

REGISTRATION PAPERS AND PEDIGREE

In order for a Border Collie to be registered, his pedigree (family tree) must be recorded in one of the official registration organizations for the breed. A registered dog is issued an identification number and certificate that includes his pedigree and official number. To qualify, *both* parents of the dog must be registered and the owners of both parents must sign a legal document known as the *Registration Application Form* attesting to the legitimacy of the mating between their two dogs.

Registration papers, however, *do not guarantee* that a dog is of good quality; all that is pledged is that the dog is a purebred. Before you buy your dog, be sure to receive a copy of his pedigree and the following information from the seller: the dog's registration and certificate, or if he is a puppy, the names and registration numbers of both the sire and dam, their owners' names and addresses, and the dog's birthdate. Obtaining this information protects you in the event that you don't receive the registration certificate within a month or two. Without this information, you have no specifics and the registry can't help you. The seller should pay for the registration for all puppies he sells. The buyer is responsible for transfer fees.

The following is a list of officially recognized Border Collie registration organizations:

The American Border Collie Association Inc. (ABCA)
Mrs. Patty Rogers, Secretary-Treasurer
Rt. 4, Box 255, Perkinston, MS 39573

The American-International Border Collie Registry, Inc. (A.I.B.C.)
J. Dean Kaster, Studbook Keeper
Runnels, IA 50237

The North American Sheep Dog Society (N.A.S.D.S.)
Rossine Kirsch, Secretary
RR 3, McLeansboro, IL 62859

The Kennel Club
I-4 Clarges St. Piccadilly
London, W1Y8AB, England

The International Sheep Dog Society (I.S.D.S.)
A. Philip Hendry-Secretary
Chesam House, 47 Bromham Road
Bedford, England MK40 2AA

The Australian National Kennel Council
Royal Show Grounds
Ascot Vale, Victoria, Australia

The New Zealand Kennel Club
P.O. Box 523
Wellington 1, New Zealand

The Kennel Union of Southern Africa
P.O. Box 562
Capetown, South Africa

The United Kennel Club
100 East Kilgore Rd.
Kalamazoo, MI 49001

Branches of the International Sheep Dog Society exist in almost every country of the world where sheep are kept, such as the South African Sheep Dog Society and the French Sheep Dog Society. All of the organizations are officially recognized. Many Border Collies are registered with more than one association.

Border Collies are not yet eligible for registration by the American Kennel Club, but AKC will issue an ILP number. The ILP, or "Indefinite Listing Privilege" is issued to dogs of any breed, even those of unknown parentage, provided they look like the breed they are supposed to represent. The ILP is used mostly for rare breeds, such as the Border Collie, and allows them to compete in the Miscellaneous Class and in obedience classes at AKC licensed shows.

Many clubs are specially devoted to the Border Collie breed, either on a national level, or on a local and regional basis. In the United States, the Border Collie Club of America (B.C.C.A.) and United States Border Collie Club (U.S.B.C.C.) are the national representative clubs devoted to the protection of the working Border Collie. The B.C.C.A. publishes a quarterly newsletter and is a clearing house for information of the Border Collie. The B.C.C.A. is not a registry. For their address and the address of the other Border Collie clubs, please refer to the appendix.

WHERE TO BUY

The best place to purchase a good Border Collie is from a conscientious breeder who really cares about the quality of his dogs. To insure that the dog you buy is a purebred Border Collie, find a breeder specializing only in Border Collies to negate the chance of any accidental mismatings with another breed.

Next, look around the place and make sure that all the dogs look healthy and are kept clean. The runs should be at least ten feet long by five feet wide, and the dogs should have shelter and fresh water. If the parents are advertised as being champions or having working certificates and obedience titles, *ask to see* the official certificate. Not every dog in a kennel is a champion, even if the person has a room full of trophies. Again, if you want a working dog, ask to *see* the parents working livestock—don't take the seller at his word.

The puppy should have been wormed twice—once at approximately three weeks and again at six weeks of age. He should also have had a distemper vaccination, which is usually a temporary "Measles vaccine," that prevents distemper until all maternal antibodies from the mother's milk dissipate. If the seller does not provide a health certificate, ask for a health guarantee and have the dog examined by your own vet.

A reputable breeder can usually be located by writing to one of the registries, Border Collie clubs or Sheepdog societies, or by looking through *Border Collie News* and *Dog World* magazines. Other good sources are advertisements in the farming and agricultural periodicals and your local newspaper.

A Border Collie and one of her young friends. If you want your dog to get along with children, you will have to introduce your puppy to as many well behaved children as possible. Teasing can ruin a puppy and turn it vicious, so supervise all get togethers. This particular bitch is attack trained, but was well socialized as a pup, and loves everyone unless told other wise. (Photo: R.B. Harrison)

If the kennel is far away, make sure it has a good reputation before buying. Does this person's dogs do well at the trials or shows? Do you know anyone who has purchased a dog from them; are they satisfied? Does the breeder guarantee his dogs, such as for working ability and freedom from inherited defects? When you buy a dog sight unseen, always see a photograph first to do some preliminary screening.

At this writing, the price of a six- to eight-week-old puppy ranges from $150 to $500. A registered purebred dog from a reputable breeder costs more than an unregistered dog. In addition to the bloodlines, you are paying for the shots, worming, advertising costs, food, stud fee, and veterinary care of the bitch and her puppies during the time the breeder has cared for them.

The older the dog, the higher the price unless he is of pet quality. If both parents are show or trial winners, you can expect to pay more for the puppies than if the parents are of poorer quality. Adult, trained dogs sell for between $500 and $5000, depending on the degree of training they have received and whether or not they are trial winners or champions.

The price of pet shop puppies is usually high and you will have no dependable information regarding the working ability or conformation of the parents.

Pet shop puppies sometimes come from pet owners who bred their females and couldn't sell the puppies. A wholesaler may buy up litters and ship them to retailers who then distribute them to the pet market. By the time the pet buyer brings the puppy home the animal may have changed hands several times, been exposed to diseases and stressed considerably.

Aust. Ch. Koshonee Cladach, owned by F.H. Marshall, and bred by Koshonee Kennels, Australia.

PUPPY VERSUS ADULT DOG

If you want a hand in creating a dog's personality, buy a puppy. The puppy should be between seven and twelve weeks old and training should begin immediately. A puppy older than twelve weeks that has not received human guidance and training (such as housebreaking, leash training, staying confined alone, playing fetch, etc.) becomes a problem. Research conducted on the mental development of dogs by the Roscoe B. Jackson Memorial Laboratory in Maine concluded that human contact and training is essential between the 49th and 112th day of life. Those dogs in the study that were only fed and watered until they were fourteen weeks old behaved like wild animals; conversely puppies taken away from their mothers before four weeks of age and placed in human care became aggressive toward other dogs and were often unable to breed later in life.

When buying an older dog, make sure he is fully socialized. Spend time with the seller to watch the dog work and to learn the code of commands. The vendor should assist you in training and learning the necessary commands as a prior stipulation for buying the dog.

Too many excellent working dogs have been ruined by a new owner's impatience or ignorance of proper working methods. Time must also be allowed for a mature dog to become settled and accustomed to his new surroundings.

Laird Sterling C.D.X. and his owner Judith Allen of Natomah Kennels. (Photo: Olan Mills)

MALE VERSUS FEMALE

The sex of your dog is a totally personal preference. Males tend to be more stubborn and often try fighting with other male dogs. They also tend to be more difficult to housebreak since they mark off their territory by urinating. On the other hand, female dogs may be shy and are more family oriented than males.

SPAYING AND NEUTERING

All dogs not kept specifically for breeding—male or female—should be altered. Contrary to popular opinion, altering either sex will not cause obesity and laziness. The only reason neutered dogs and spayed bitches become fat is through over-feeding and under-exercising which occurs just as often in "whole" dogs in a similar environment. All guide dogs for the blind are spayed or neutered, and as you know, they are not slovenly animals. Guide dogs are altered to prevent the female from coming into heat and attracting male dogs and to prevent the male from running away from his blind master after bitches in heat. In England, John Holmes has experimented with spayed bitches and castrated males as working stockdogs and has found no ill effects in their performance.

Another very important reason for spaying or neutering your dog (unless he is to be used for breeding and show or trial competition) is to help fight the pet population explosion. Every year in the U.S. alone, twenty-five million unwanted dogs and cats are abandoned to face starvation and other forms of destruction. Six million of these dogs, many of them registered purebreds, are killed annually in the U.S. by euthanasia in pounds and shelters. The number of Border Collies ending up in pounds and shelters is estimated at between 500 and 600 a year. Please don't contribute to this problem.

Neither female or male dogs should be altered until they are fully mature. Animals spayed or neutered too early do not attain their full physical or mental growth because they are deprived of certain hormones produced by the testicles or ovaries. However, there is *no* advantage to their siring or whelping a litter prior to being neutered.

Imported Sadghyl Shadow in Pepperland, owned by Leslie B. Samuels of San Angelo, Texas, and bred by Mrs. Edward Hart of Scotland. Shadow was a winner at the Crufts dog show in London shortly before Ms. Samuels moved to America. (Photo: Courtesy Leslie B. Samuels.)

General Care and Feeding

5

Scaling a ladder is part of the agility test given to police dogs. (Photo J.E.L.)

Today one of the most neglected aspects of the Border Collie is in their care and feeding. Many farmers still believe that a dog can be left chained all day in a dark, dank barn, standing in his often worm-infested feces like a cow or horse. Some even throw the dog's food on the ground, which is an ideal way to encourage a large and healthy worm population inside the dog. These same dogs are seldom wormed or de-fleaed. Food is often insufficient or poor in quality.

Proper nutrition is very important to the working dog. A poorly fed animal will lack stamina and not be as alert as a well-nourished dog. Studies of humans in refugee camps and developing countries indicate that malnutrition can cause mental retardation. If a healthy mother is malnourished while pregnant, her baby will be mentally retarded, stunted, and often deformed and if the baby continues to be malnourished during his first few years of life the retardation of mind and body becomes even more severe. Studies involving rats and dogs also show these results; so the significance to the working dog breeder should be obvious.

To breed or own a dog of superior intelligence, you must feed the dog a balanced diet and keep him free of parasites. To do this, modern kennel facilities and sanitation measures are needed along with a regular treatment program for internal and external parasites. A well-balanced and abundant food supply is also imperative for the growing pup and lactating female. Take a look at the top producing dairy herds. They are well managed—kept in carefully designed barns, wormed, vaccinated, and fed the best feeds. Why shouldn't working dogs be treated the same way? If we want to improve the Border Collie breed, it must be through proper care and management, just as with the major livestock breeds.

FEEDING

The Stomach and Digestion

The dog, like man, is a *monogastric* animal, meaning that he has only one stomach. Dogs cannot digest roughages such as leaves, stems and other plant materials unless they have first been cooked or broken down in the stomach of a ruminant cud-chewing animal. The dog's stomach serves several purposes. It holds food, then mixes it with gastric juice, which is mostly hydrochloric acid, water, and pepsin. The pepsin breaks down protein while the hydrochloric acid starts the breakdown of starches into simple sugars.

Next the food enters the small intestine where most of the actual digestion and nutrient absorption occurs. The pancreas secretes the fluids *amylase, lipase* and *trypsin* into the small intestine. Pancreatic *amylase* breaks down starches and complex sugars into very simple sugars that can be readily absorbed into the bloodstream. *Lipase*, along with bile salts secreted by the gall bladder breaks down fats, and *trypsin* breaks proteins down further into amino acids. There are also numerous tiny glands in the wall of the small intestine that secrete enzymes that help in the breakdown of proteins, fats and sugars.

The large intestine does not perform much active digestion. It does contain bacteria that breaks down any foods that were not broken down in the small intestine, but other than that mostly water is absorbed into the large intestine.

Diet

In the wild, canines generally eat the stomachs and intestines of their prey first. Next they will eat the heart, liver, and fatty membranes around the organs, and later, only if food is short, they will eat the muscle meat. Their eating habits supply adequate amounts of vitamin rich, predigested vegetable material and highly nutritious protein and fatty organ meats. Wild canines also eat bone marrow and bones for calcium and phosphorous. Therefore, don't be misled by dog food companies that claim that commercial meat is the dog's "natural food."

You may have noticed that your dog eats manure when he is near livestock. This is because manure contains predigested vegetable matter craved by the dog. Often dogs eat grass for the same reason and then throw up because they are unable to digest cellulose. These habits can usually be avoided by feeding cooked greens and grains, which most dry foods contain in the form of corn or alfalfa meal. The food must be cooked in order to break down the cellulose, like the rumin of the grazing animal does.

Border Collies were selectively bred by frugal Scottish shepherds for their inexpensive care. In their native Britain, they were often fed only oatmeal, bread crusts, and a few scraps. This is not a recommended diet, however. To get the most out of your dog as a worker or as a healthy pet, you should feed him a good quality commercial dog food. Also, the dog should be kept free of worms, or the food will be wasted on feeding the worms instead of the dog.

Most commercial dog foods are scientifically balanced for proper nutrition through extensive research by chemists and veterinarians at large dog nutrition research laboratories. Without a balanced diet, your dog will lack stamina and speed, his coat will be dull, and his mind dense. A good quality dry dog food should contain at least 21 percent protein, 7 percent fat, and 20 percent carbohydrates, and no more than 10 percent water. Canned dog foods, while providing balanced nutrition, are about 70 percent water and therefore are not economical to feed. Soft, moist dog foods provide adequate nutrition as well, but are also expensive to use.

Dry dog foods may be fed either moistened and soaked with water until soft (about 10 minutes), or with a tablespoon of bacon grease, or vegetable oil added for the dog's coat. Melted cooking lard may also be used, but not suet chunks because a dog's digestive tract cannot break down large chunks of fat. Bacon grease or lard must be refrigerated to prevent spoiling. Extra fat is needed in a dog's diet since dry dog foods are not packaged with a sufficient fat content. A high energy food, fat is especially important for the active working dog or lactating female.

Because an overweight bitch may have whelping problems, the pregnant female should not be fed extra food until the last week of her

A Border Collie holding his Christmas stocking. Border Collies like to be a part of the family and sometimes seem almost human. (PAK Photo)

pregnancy. After whelping, she should be fed a high calorie diet to aid in milk production—much the same idea as the feeding of a high production dairy cow. Bitch's milk is very high in fat, so supplemental fat is very important to ensure an adequate milk supply. The lactating bitch may also be fed a calcium and phosphorous supplement to aid in milk production. This should not be done, however, until after the birth of the puppies to prevent metabolic problems in the female. After the pups are weaned, the bitch should not be fed for a day. Afterward rations should be cut back to the normal amount to aid in drying her up.

Puppies should be fed a high protein, good quality puppy food starting at about three weeks of age until they are a year old. Until they are about four months old, puppies should be fed three meals a day and then two meals a day until about eight months of age, and finally one meal a day, preferably at night. Working dogs are fed at night to reduce the chance of gastric torsion from strenuous activity.

Food packages suggest that you feed your dog more than he really needs. A sixty pound adult Border Collie requires about three cups of dry food a day, a forty pound dog needs two cups, and a thirty pound dog requires one. On the other hand, puppies and lactating females should be fed all they will eat. You can tell if your dog is overweight by seeing if you can feel his ribs or spine. If you can just feel the ribs and top of the spine, then the dog is at the correct weight, but if you can't feel them or you feel a layer of fat over the ribs, the dog is overweight. Every "inch of pinch" over the ribs is equivalent to about ten pounds of extra weight. Like an overweight person, an obese dog suffers from stress to the heart and circulatory system, and if worked hard, can suffer from heart failure. Underweight can be due to parasitic infestations or other illnesses, and should be checked by your veterinarian.

Border Collie puppies look out at the world beyond their kennel. (Photo: J.E.L.)

GROOMING

Bathing

A dog can be bathed with baby shampoo as often as you like, providing the soap is thoroughly rinsed out and the dog is brushed to stimulate the natural oils in the skin and coat. A cream rinse can also be beneficial in helping to restore a shiny coat. After a bath, the dog should be toweled dry and kept warm—cold and drafts can make the dog catch a cold or pneumonia. Many people believe that frequent bathing is bad for a dog. One look at the beautiful coats of show dogs that are bathed every week during the show season proves that this is a fallacy. Rudd Weatherwax, Lassie's owner and trainer, bathes his dogs every day during filming, and Lassie has a beautiful, healthy, glossy coat.

Brushing

In order to properly groom your Border Collie, you will need a slicker brush (or carder), a bristle brush, a steel-toothed comb, and a pair of scissors. The slicker brush is ideal for brushing out matts, shedding hair, and general dirt. Brushing should be done daily to keep the skin clean, help circulation, and to spread the natural oils through the hair. The comb is used on the silky hair behind the ears only. It pulls out the undercoat and should be used on the body only during the shedding season or you will deprive the dog of his natural insulation against cold and heat. The bristle brush is used to fluff out the coat and to give the dog a once-over before entering the show ring or trial field.

The scissors can be used to cut out matts behind the ears. Before entering the show ring, you should also trim off the whiskers and trim

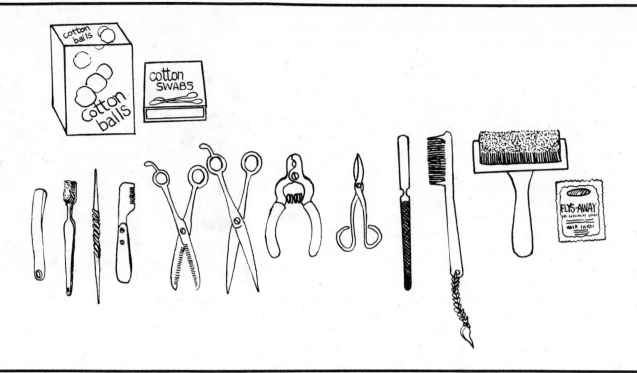

Grooming equipment. Cotton balls and Q-Tips for the ears, tooth brush and tooth scrapers, thinning comb and shears, scissors, guillotine type nail clippers, nail file, metal comb, slicker brush, Flys-Away insect repellent.

When filing or clipping your dog's nails, avoid cutting the quick. The quick is spongy tissue that will bleed if it is cut.

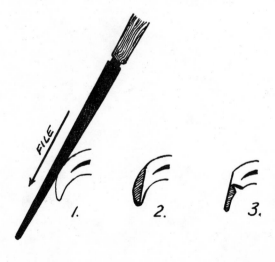

the excess hair on the feet, between the toes, and from the hocks down. This imparts a healthier look to the feet, legs and muzzle.

Ear Cleaning

The dog's ears should be checked periodically for accumulations of wax and for ear mite infestations. Wax can be cleaned out by using cotton balls or *Q-tips®* dipped in baby oil. Do not probe deeper than you can see. If the ears smell foul or have excessive secretions of wax, check with your veterinarian to see if the dog has an ear infection or ear mites. Be gentle and careful when working around the ears, since they are very sensitive organs. Always clean your dog's ears before exhibiting him in the show ring; to leave them dirty is an insult to the judge.

Nail Cutting

The nails should be trimmed about once a month unless the dog is exercised regularly on pavement. If you can hear the dog's nails clicking on the floor they are too long. It is best to get your dog used to having his feet handled as a puppy to avert difficulty trimming his nails later. Overly long nails can grow back up into the foot, causing lameness or splay feet, particularly in older and sedentary dogs.

Guillotine-type nail trimmers are the type which I prefer to use in cutting the dog's nails. Scissors tend to cause the nails to splinter. When cutting, only remove the hook and avoid the quick of the nail. The spongy quick will bleed when cut. The bleeding can be stopped by using a styptic pencil. The quick can be easily seen in light colored nails as a dark pink area; in black nails there is no distinction.

After clipping, a metal nail file can be used to smooth down the nails. Do not cut the nails the day of a dog show because the dog may become temporarily lame if you should accidently cut into the quick. It is therefore wise to cut the nails several days in advance of a show or trial.

Teeth

The dog's teeth should be checked every two or three months for tartar buildup. Tartar can be scraped off with a tooth scaler and the teeth brushed with a toothbrush and paste or soda. To keep your dog's teeth clean supply him with chew toys, large beef knuckle bones, or commercial bone substitutes every night.

It is best to start cleaning teeth while the dog is still a puppy so he can become accustomed to the idea. Be very patient and gentle, cleaning only a little at a time at first. To expose the molars you may have to place a piece of wood in the dog's mouth to hold it open. If the teeth are exceptionally dirty, the dog may have to be anesthetized by a veterinarian.

Show dogs should have their teeth cleaned regularly and brushed before the show.

Anal Glands

The anal glands, located on either side of the anus, secrete a lubricating substance when the dog defecates. This substance also contains a scent which helps the dog mark his territory. Some dogs are prone to impaction of these glands, causing great discomfort. The dog's manner of relieving this discomfort is to scoot along on his bottom, which many people think means he has worms. Sometimes the scooting does indicate tapeworms, but usually it is caused by impacted anal glands.

If you think your dog has impacted anal glands, take him to your veterinarian and ask him or her to show you how to empty these glands. It can be done by putting on clean rubber gloves and pressing the glands between the thumb and forefinger. A foul smelling, yellow liquid will be expelled relieving the impaction.

Exercise and Housing

The Border Collie is an active dog, bred for his speed and endurance while working sheep. As a result, the breed cannot be recommended for people living in an apartment or those with no yard. If you live in the city and still want a Border Collie, you must take the dog for long walks on a leash and play with him regularly in an open area.

Even in the country, Border Collies should not be allowed to roam unattended. Most Border Collie trainers agree that you should keep your dog confined to a pen when he is not with you. If you don't, you run the almost certain risk of having him killed by a motor vehicle. As the pup gets older and his herding instinct begins to develop, he will start chasing cars, eventually trying to turn a car as he would a sheep or cow. The result is often fatal.

Another problem that people have if they let their Border Collie roam is that he will chase deer and other people's livestock. The uninformed pet buyer assumes that Border Collies have an inborn kind-heartedness and an almost human desire to care for helpless animals. This is not true. As pointed out earlier, the Border Collie's herding instinct is merely a divergence of the wolf's instinct to hunt and when he is allowed to run unattended and untrained, he may even kill livestock.

Herding, or alternatively, obedience work, provide the best form of exercise for the Border Collie. If this is not possible, the dog can be trained to follow your bicycle and you can run him several miles a day. Allow the dog to slowly build up to the longer distances first, however, or he may become lame. Bicycling is a very satisfactory method of exercising both your dogs and yourself. Playing ball with the dog and having him retrieve until he is tired is also good exercise.

When you are not exercising or playing with your dog, and cannot have him with you, he should have a kennel run of his own. I do not believe in chaining dogs. Chained dogs are helpless and cannot escape from teasing children or other dogs, and can become entangled and even

"The Nose," or Border Collie antics. (Photo: J.J.A.)

29

choke to death. A pen, on the other hand, made with 6-foot high fencing and cement blocks around the edge to keep the dog from digging out (or other dogs from digging in) is safe and comfortable. A few dogs may need cement floors and a wire over the top of the pen to prevent them from digging or climbing out.

For one or two dogs, an area about 10 X 20 feet should suffice. The pen should be solidly made and should have a dog house large enough for the dog to stand up in. A house that is too big can't be warmed by the dog's body heat in the winter. A shade tree nearby or an awning over the pen will protect your dog from the hot summer sun. A constant supply of fresh, clean water should always be available.

PREVENT THEFT—TATTOO YOUR DOG

Every year thousands of dogs are stolen out of people's yards, kennels, and cars. Many of these dogs are purebreds, since there is a good market for them. Stolen purebreds are sold with falsified registration papers to "puppy mill" breeding farms, unsuspecting research facilities and unscrupulous individuals. Skins of certain breeds are used for coats in some countries like South Africa. Another use for abducted dogs is to use them as a form of bait for training pit bull terriers before they are used in illegal fighting competitions.

Dog theft is not a federal crime in the United States, however, stealing a branded animal is. A tattoo is considered a brand by law, and the FBI can be called in on any cases where branded animals are stolen. Dognappers do not like tattooed dogs and often release them as soon as they discover the tattoo. Commonly, a dog is tattooed with the owner's social security number on his inside right thigh or flank where the hair is sparse. Unlike ears that can be cut off easily, legs cannot be. Your social security number never changes throughout your life and can be easily traced to locate you.

The tattoo number should be sent to your state and local Humane Society with your name, address, and phone number so they can contact you if they find your missing dog. Many people also register this same information with the National Dog Registry, Box 116, Woodstock, New York 12498; phone (914) 679-2355. This organization is the only tattoo registry which is endorsed by Guiding Eyes for the Blind, Inc., as well as being recognized by numerous kennel clubs and the Humane Society of the United States. Registration is for a lifetime, and applies to every dog you may ever own. The National Dog Registry also sells stickers for automobiles and metal plackards for kennels saying "WARNING—TATTOOED DOG—Registered with the National Dog Registry."

It is also wise to keep a collar and identification tag on your dog at all times, even though you keep him on a leash or in a kennel unless you are there with him. If you are going to be gone for the day, lock your kennel run or put your dog in the house and lock the door. Free roaming dogs and those in parked autos are the most frequent victims of dognappers. If you do leave your dog in a car, put him in a locked crate, since you must leave the windows open to prevent him from getting heat stroke, and be sure to have a warning on your car window or crate that the dog is tattooed.

THE OLD DOG

Dogs, like people, eventually get old. But, with the proper exercise and nutrition they can remain healthy as they age. Because excess pro-

A good type kennel run should have a dog house, a floor with good drainage, and a fence at least six feet high unless it has a roof. A ten by twenty foot run gives one or two dogs ample area to exercise. The round stones provide drainage and help keep the feet in tight, working condition, unlike cement which can cause flat, splayed feet. (Photo: J.E.L.)

tein is not utilized by the inactive or older dog, their protein intake should be cut down by one-third and all high protein dog meal ceased. Too much protein can cause wear and tear on the kidneys, causing damage or even death.

Heart trouble in older dogs is common as many suffer valvular deficiencies and heart attacks. Overweight also can cause excessive strain to the heart just as it does in people, so do your dog a favor and keep him slim. Medication for heart problems is available from your veterinarian at only a few dollars a year. Heart pills make the dog look, feel and act younger, although you will have to prevent him from engaging in strenuous exercise.

Because the old dog feels heat and cold more easily, he should be well protected from the elements. He may find comfort in an old wool sweater tailored to fit. Other problems the older dog faces include loss of sight and hearing, arthritis, ear wax buildup and tartar on the teeth. He often loses control of his bodily functions and will thus need to be taken outside more frequently.

Old dogs often become smelly. When this happens, they must be brushed daily to remove dead flaked skin and hair. They should also be fed well-cooked green vegetables like green beans, spinach, or beet tops that provide chlorophyll to help eliminate flatulence and bad breath. Another feeding tip you may find helpful for the geriatric dog is one tablespoon of Gerital added to his diet. Brushing their teeth every week with a mild flavored toothpaste cuts down on tartar and improves their breath. To get rid of foul smelling ear wax, clean your dog's ears regularly.

The Border Collie's average life span is from 8 to 17 years. The breed tends to be slow maturing and long-lived if not over worked or neglected. When your dog gets older, perhaps becoming crippled, blind or suffering intensely from disease, it is better to have him put to sleep than to watch him linger in misery. Euthanasia is a difficult decision to make, but an alternative to watching your loyal, loving friend deteriorate and suffer. Remember him as an active playful dog.

A Border Collie retrieving over the high jump. Border Collies love to jump, and make obedience dogs "par excellence."

Basic Training 6

Now that you have an intuitive and intelligent Border Collie, you may think you can sit back and watch him train himself. Unfortunately, if you try this method you will end up with a canine delinquent. The smarter the dog, the more likely he is to find trouble. The original "Lassie" was a canine delinquent named Pal. His owners left him with Rudd Weatherwax for training and decided they didn't want him back. Pal went on to play in *Lassie Come Home* and other movies, and was one of the smartest dogs Weatherwax ever trained. He simply needed a job to do and an outlet for his intelligence.

A well-trained dog is a joy to own. He can accompany you safely anywhere. He will walk calmly by your side and not pull your arm out of its socket. He will lie down and wait for you outside while you go shopping. He will come when called, and wait to be let outside instead of charging through the door.

If you wish to remain on good terms with your neighbors, you must train your dog not to bark, jump on people or dig holes. These are very annoying habits and a sure way to lose friends. A dog who chews up furniture can even be grounds for a divorce. Rude behavior on the part of our dogs is totally uncalled for. Any dog can learn to be as well-behaved as a guide dog for the blind or movie dog.

Many people feel "training" is cruel and unnatural. This is not true. A dog is a pack animal and needs a leader to follow, obey, and respect. Without a leader, the dog can become neurotic, destructive and confused. Training cements the bond between master and dog. Many times I have seen a dog who appeared to adore one person, but once trained by another, switched their adoration and loyalty to their trainer. A trained dog is also more likely to risk his life for his master than an untrained dog because his bond of love is stronger. It is for these reasons you should try to train your own dog if at all possible. All advanced training from herding to police work and guiding the blind is based on the basic obedience commands given in this chapter.

If you already have an adult dog, don't despair. A well-adjusted, socialized dog can be trained at any age, contrary to the old adage, "You can't teach an old dog new tricks." My first dog was not obedience trained until he was four years old, and within six months he won the AKC's Companion Dog (C.D.) Obedience title in his first three shows with exceptional scores. He later went on to acquire the Companion Dog Excellent (C.D.X.) and the Utility Dog (U.D.) degree. This dog was also an accomplished cattle dog and was fully protection trained before his death in 1978.

Border Collies love to play, and need plenty of supervised exercise. Retrieving is an excellent form of exercise. Do not allow your dog to roam loose.

The correct way to put on the slip chain collar so it will release after a correction. Note that the end to which the leash attaches hangs down on the dog's right side. (Photo: Col. W.A. Johnston)

TRAINING PRINCIPLES

PRAISE - Energetic praise is as important as correction. Without praise, your dog has no incentive to learn. He even resents learning. You must not assume your dog "knows" when he is good. You must go out of your way to let him know you are pleased. Exaggerated praise with a happy tone of voice will convey your satisfaction and pleasure to your dog and make him all the more eager to please you in the future. Anytime you see an enthusiastic dog you can be sure the trainer is equally spirited when praising him. A lethargic, spiritless dog is one whose trainer is bored and uses a flat toneless voice when praising, or does not praise often enough.

Correctly timed praise must be given immediately after the desired action in order for the dog to associate it in his mind with what you are teaching him. Praise during the desired action is best of all. Before you start to teach the dog something new, make sure he is in a good frame of mind by first playing with him a little and praising him. It is also best to end each lesson on a positive note so the dog will always look forward to learning.

CORRECTIONS - In order for your dog to learn, he must also be corrected occasionally. Some dogs need more corrections than others. In order for a correction to be effective it *MUST* be *IMMEDIATE* or the dog will not associate the correction with the misdeed. If you wait more than two or three seconds, studies show the dog's brain cannot connect the punishment to the action, and you are being needlessly cruel. You may think the dog understands and is showing guilt when he hangs his head and cowers, but he is just reacting to your apparent anger and displeasure with him.

Different actions require different types of corrections. For instance if you catch your puppy making a puddle, a loud, gruff "No," accompanied by immediately placing him outside and then praising him when he does his stuff is adequate. If you catch your dog tearing up the couch, the crime is more severe, and requires a gentle shaking by the scruff of the neck and "mean talking" in a low, growling tone. This is similar to a wolf or bitch disciplining her young. In formal training, a quick, sharp snap on the training collar is used to get your dog's attention. The snap, done quickly and with enough force, pinches but does not harm. Try it on your own arm. The training collar should never be used to drag the dog or choke him or it could damage the dog's windpipe.

Another useful correction is a short section of lightweight aluminum chain about six inches long, or two or three small tin cans tied together. The chain or cans are thrown at the dog but do not hit him while he is "in the act," and are accompanied by a loud "No." The rattle and clang of the chain or cans startles the dog, and lets him know you can still punish him even when he is beyond your reach. The user should practice when the dog is not present to perfect his aim.

Do not hit or kick a dog! The dog learns to associate your hand or foot with unpleasantness and may learn that humans are unpleasant and not worthy of respect. You do not want your dog to associate corrections with you, but with his misdeed. Hitting and kicking often accompany rage and loss of control. If you feel the desire to hit and kick your dog, put him in his kennel until you calm down. You do not want a hand- or foot-shy dog, nor do you want a vicious animal who might one day turn on you. Most cases of dogs "turning on their owners" can be directly attributed to abuse of the animal and general lack of discipline. The dog disliked and disrespected the owner, and was allowed to assume the packleader position in place of the owner.

Slow corrections and loss of temper are the two worst mistakes committed by the beginner. You can practice corrections with the choke collar by putting it around a bannister, chair arm, or assistant's leg. Give a sharp jerk and immediately slacken the leash so the collar loosens. When you jerk the collar properly, you should hear a "zink" sound as the chain snaps. This sound accompanied by the quick pinch gets the dog's attention. A slow tugging correction can cause pain and resentment. Pull steadily on the training collar and watch your assistant start yelling and swearing. A series of snaps on the collar will keep the dog where you want him, and he will stay lively and cooperative. A steady pull will cause the dog to drag back or ahead and try his best not to cooperate.

EQUIPMENT

You will need a six-foot, soft leather or canvas web leash, available at most pet stores. Do not choose a chain leash because the constant rattle of the chain makes the snap on the training collar ineffective. It also causes chain burns on your hand and the weight makes the transition to off-lead work very difficult.

The training collar should be medium sized links. Large links prevent the quick snap and release, while a very thin link chain will cut cruelly into the dog's neck. A nylon training collar can make nylon burns on the dog's neck and it does not produce the snapping noise needed to get the dog's attention.

A ten-foot-long light weight canvas lead or cord tied to a snap is also needed in teaching distant control and in herding. Longer leads up to thirty feet are also available at pet shops. These are used for tracking and distance control in young dogs. Again, I prefer the canvas web to nylon, since nylon burns your hands if the dog pulls suddenly.

For the young puppy, a wire crate about two feet by three feet is ideal as a kennel. These are available at most pet shops. The crate serves as a bed and can be used for the rest of the dog's life. You can even take it with you when you travel. When you are too busy to supervise your dog, the crate keeps him out of trouble and out from underfoot. Later when he is an adult, you can put a rug or pad in the crate and leave the door open so he can come and go as he pleases. When he wants to be alone, your dog knows he is safe and secure in his crate.

Chew toys for the puppy are extremely important. They should be made of rawhide or hard rubber and be of sufficient size that they cannot be caught in the pup's throat and choke him. Large beef knuckle bones are also excellent chew toys and are nutritious as well. Do not use small bones, especially poultry or fish bones because they splinter and can kill your dog.

For herding you will need a ten foot bamboo cane pole, or a shepherd's crook. A small plastic shepherd's whistle is also very useful, and only costs a few dollars. For obedience work you will need a retrieving dumbell, which is made of two wooden blocks on the end of a dowel rod. The size of the dumbell depends on the size of the dog's head and jaws. Dumbells and scent articles are available from many dog equipment houses. Jumps can be made or purchased.

TRAINING THE YOUNG PUPPY

Housebreaking

Housebreaking can be easy if you use the right psychology. The most successful method I've found is to outsmart the puppy and always be one step ahead of him.

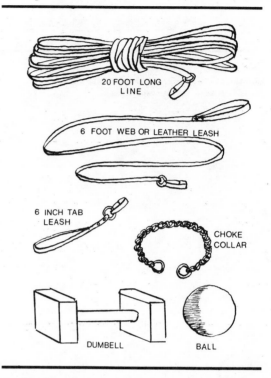

Equipment needed for obedience training your Border Collie.

House breaking aids. Spray bottle for vinegar/water solution, white vinegar, disinfectant, papertowels, housebreaking aid, newspaper.

To anticipate your puppy's actions, you must realize that what goes in must come out. As soon as your puppy has finished his food take him outside to play and let him do his duties outdoors. After he has relieved himself, offer praise and bring him inside. Since puppies can't yet control their bodily functions, it is very important to take them out every two or three hours to avoid any indoor accidents. When they occur, indoor accidents must be cleaned thoroughly or the pup will smell the spot and go there again. Instinctively, dogs are stimulated to relieve themselves when they smell excrement as a way of marking off their territory. Because dogs can smell one part urine (or any other odor) per billion parts water, a vinegar/water solution must be used to neutralize any odors.

Every morning, carry your pup outside or lead him directly out on a leash to prevent him from stopping along the way out to relieve himself. Most housebreaking problems occur because someone forgot to take a pup out first thing in the morning and within fifteen minutes of any meal. As an adult he may be able to hold his bladder and bowels all day, but this requires physical and mental control.

Older dogs who are not housebroken also must be taken out frequently and confined to a small area of the house, just like a puppy, until they develop mental discipline. Gradually, the length of time they can be left indoors may be increased. Moreover, be patient with an older dog since bad habits are more difficult to break than good habits are to form.

A playpen or crate prevents many housebreaking problems. Wolves instinctively do not like to soil their dens and similarly, Border Collies will not soil their crate or pen. When your dog is older and fully housebroken, he will learn that the whole house is his den. In the meantime, confine your dog to the pen or a small room. Baby protective gates in doorways can be used to help confine the puppy until he is more responsible.

If your dog still refuses to relieve himself outside and instead waits until you take him inside, it probably isn't his fault. He may have been trained by his breeder to go on newspapers only and thus doesn't want to soil the nice, clean grass. This is a simple problem to cure. Take some already soiled newspaper or commercial housebreaking aid and spread it outside. The puppy, smelling the odor of the excrement, will finally relieve himself outdoors as a response to his territorial marking instincts.

By using this method of training, you will find that your pup *almost* trains himself. As he gets older, you will be able to let him loose in the house for longer and longer periods of time without worry.

Socialization

From the first day you bring your puppy home you should work on socializing him. This is very important if your dog is to grow up into a well adjusted adult. Research done by Dr. Scott in Bar Harbor, Maine, for the Guide Dogs for the Blind, Inc. in San Rafael, CA, has shown that the period between seven weeks and sixteen weeks is very important to the mental development of dogs. Puppies that were completely isolated were incapable of being trained, let alone becoming companion dogs. The research proved that daily human contact is very important. Simple commands can be taught at this time, but the teaching should be in the form of games. The puppy can learn to walk on a leash, sit, lie down, come and fetch, but not in the disciplined manner of formal obedience.

Leash breaking is accomplished by allowing the puppy to wear a soft collar and drag a leash around, under supervision of course. Once he is used to the leash, pick it up and encourage the pup to follow you

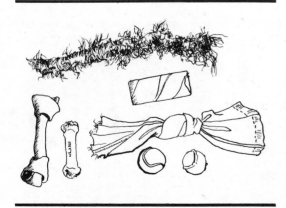

Puppy play toys. Burlap tug toy, paper towel tube, rawhide bone, nylabone, rag toy, balls.

around the driveway and yard. Make it fun; clap your hands; call his name; give him tidbits. Walking him around will familiarize him with his surroundings outside of the home and helps to build his confidence. It also builds his bond of trust with you, his handler.

"Come" can be taught by calling the puppy to you at feeding time and then praising him before you feed him. Whenever you call him at other times, make it a pleasant experience. Praise and fuss over him and give him a tidbit. He will begin to associate his name and the word "Come" with pleasure.

A common mistake many people make is to call their puppy to them and then punish him for some misdeed. The pup doesn't remember the misdeed, but the action of coming is fresh in his mind. He then thinks he is being punished for coming when called, and soon learns not to come.

"Lie Down" and "Sit" can be taught by gently placing the puppy in the desired positions and praising him. Do not worry if he wiggles about. This is not serious training. That must wait until he is six months old. Puppy training is simply to get him used to being handled and makes later training very quick and easy for both of you.

Retrieving is a great game for puppies, and is useful later on. Throw a ball or toy and encourage him to run out and pick it up. Then clap your hands and call him back to you. Make much of him, and repeat. This can be done throughout the day for fun and exercise. Remember that after exercise most pups will need to relieve themselves.

Once the pup has had his DHL shots and parvo virus shot at about three months, you should start taking him with you in the car to accustom him to riding. To prevent car-sickness you can give him a quarter of a *Dramamine®* anti-motion sickness pill. Do this about twenty minutes ahead of time. Also make sure he has relieved himself first. Take him to the park, beach, shopping mall and downtown and walk him around. Let people he meets pat him so he becomes adjusted to people. Take him out to meet and play with dogs that you know are friendly. This way he will learn not to fear strange people or animals. This training is especially important for any dog you plan to compete with in obedience trials, dog shows, or dogs to be trained for guiding the blind, police work or schutzhund.

Dogs raised in kennels or pet shop cages during these critical weeks are likely to become "kennel shy" as adults. They react with panic to anything new—new places, strange people, loud noises. Such dogs can never learn to take responsibility and they failed as guide dogs in the experiments performed at Bar Harbor. As adults these dogs were very nervous and shy, and many were neurotic. This critical time period has a lot to do with the adult personality. Genetics does play some part, since studies show shyness and nervousness do run in some families of dogs, along with other personality traits. The Bar Harbor experiments showed, however, that dogs from good genetic background can be ruined by improper socialization, while dogs from a background of shyness can be improved with careful socialization, but they will never be able to surpass their better bred counterparts.

If you think about it, this can only make sense. Imagine what would happen to a child raised in isolation (and there have been documented cases) from birth to ten or twelve years of age. If he never left his own home or met anyone outside his family, and then one day was taken away to a strange city with strange sights and strange people, this child would be terrified. The few cases of child isolation are sad, since the individuals usually took years to adapt to normal life, and some had to be institutionalized for life. A good well adjusted dog (or child) is no accident. He is the product of patience, dedication and work.

When socializing your Border Collie, remember to use the natural ability of children.

Make sure the puppy you buy is bright eyed, friendly and curious. Avoid the timid, shy types, since they tend to develop into fearful or poorly adjusted adults unless given lots of attention. (PAK Photo)

Teach jumping on leash at the lowest possible height. Never jump a puppy at full height until it is over a year old since the bones are not hardened yet, and deformities could result. (PAK Photo)

TRICKS AND GAMES

Fetch

Fetching is a trick that can be started at an early age. Throw balls and chew toys and encourage your puppy to chase and retrieve them. Be sure to praise any sign of interest in going to the thrown object and picking it up. Once he picks it up and carries it, clap your hands and run from him. This will excite the pup to come after you, hopefully carrying the toy. If he drops it, stop running, tell him to fetch and point to the toy. He will eventually get the idea.

When he is older, you can put him on a 10-foot cord, throw his dumbbell and command "Fetch." After he runs out to retrieve it, guide him back to you with the cord and teach him to sit in front of you. After he is sitting, reach for the toy and say "out." If he refuses to let go, take hold of the dumbbell and press the dog's lips against his teeth until he releases the object. Be sure to give plenty of praise and make this fun. Later you can work him off leash.

Discourage chewing of the item being retrieved, especially if you want to train him for bird dog work later. A person I know has a Border Collie who will get her pens and pencils while she is doing drafting and retrieve ducks when she takes him hunting.

Jumping

Jumping can be useful, expecially on a farm or ranch where fences abound. All one has to do is tell your dog to jump the fence instead of having to lift him over it. I teach all my dogs to jump, and most Border Collies love jumping. Jumping is also used in advanced obedience and schutzhund work.

Do not teach jumping until your dog is at least six months old, because the bones are still soft. When he is old enough, start with him on a short leash, and run up to a low obstacle (about one foot high) and jump over it with him, saying "Over." Make jumping fun by clapping your leg and praising your dog when he obeys. Your dog should soon be sailing over the jump when you walk up to it and command "Over." Tell him "Over Again" and guide him back over to your side with the leash.

Like any athlete, a dog must be started slowly. The height of the jump should be increased slowly over a period of time. Most Border Collies can easily clear a three or four foot high jump, and a six foot broad jump, after two months of training.

Speak

Barking is a useful command. It can be used when sheep are jammed up in loading chutes or when unloading sheep or cattle in trucks. It is used in the schutzhund search and bark exercise and is also a requirement for obedience competition in Australia. Chances are you won't have any trouble teaching your dog to speak.

The best way to train your dog to speak is to tie him up. Jump up and down, clap your hands, and try anything you can think of to excite him to barking. If this doesn't work, bounce a rubber ball or throw some food just out of his reach. When he is about to bark, say "Speak," praise him enthusiastically and give him a tidbit. To stop him from barking, gently clamp his mouth and soothe him to "Quiet." Again, praise him and give him a treat.

When your dog understands the command to speak, you can teach him to speak on a hand signal. I use a fist with my fingers closed around my thumb. As I say "Speak," I flick my thumb up. Soon your dog will catch the idea of barking when you flick your thumb without the voice command.

The bark signal could come in handy if you are ever threatened, or if you hear someone outside your home. The sound of a dog barking will frighten most people away.

Shake Hands

Shaking hands is a very simple trick to teach. Have your dog sit in a corner. Reach for his right foreleg with your right hand as you say "Shake Hands" or "Paw." At the same time, with your left hand, shift his weight over to his left side. If this doesn't cause him to start to lift his right paw, pick it up yourself. Then praise him and give him a tid-bit. Repeat this until he does it willingly.

To teach him to raise his left paw, say "Other paw" and shift his weight over to his right foot (with your right hand) so that he will lift his left paw. Again, be sure to praise your dog. This trick can later be modified to teach the dog to open gates with his paw on command. This is done by having the dog sit close to the gate while you are on the other side. Give him the command "Paw," "Open the Gate," and if necessary reach over and guide his paw so that it moves the gate open. Then praise him. Eventually he will get the idea.

"No Room" (Keep Out)

It is often convenient to teach your dog to stay out of certain rooms. You may think this sounds impossible or difficult. It isn't. All my dogs are trained to stay out of the living room and dining room, and they are very trustworthy. EVERY time your dog tries to cross an imaginary boundary into the forbidden room, run up to the doorway and point to the floor saying "No Room." If he has entered the room march him out by the collar saying "No Room." Then point to the floor by the entrance to the room and repeat "No Room." Be firm, but not hysterical. It will take several days for the dog to get the idea. To speed up the learning process, go into the forbidden room repeatedly yourself, and block him off as you go in, pointing firmly to the floor and telling him "No Room."

COMMON PROBLEMS

Chewing

Chewing forbidden items is best prevented by giving the pup plenty of chew toys and keeping a close watch on him. If you don't catch your pup in the act of chewing, you can't punish him. The best form of punishment if you do catch him is the "scruff shake." This is the exact form of punishment his mother would use. To do this, shake him by the loose skin of the neck and at the same time say "No" in a harsh tone of voice. You should not lift the dog totally off the ground or he could be hurt. Do not shout or yell.

Chew toys such as hard rubber balls, nylon chew toys, and boiled beef knuckle bones are ideal for teething puppies. Most dogs grow out of the chewing stage by the time they are a year old. If your pup has enough toys, he shouldn't need to exercise his jaws on the legs of your grand piano. When you do catch him in the act and he is too far away to reach, throw a magazine or newspaper and hit him from behind as you simultaneously yell "No." Chances are he won't see you throw the paper since his is preoccupied with his chewing. He will, however, hear the "No" and be shocked when he finds that the sky showers paper missiles whenever he chews. Practice your aim without the pup around so that you are accurate.

Border Collies will do anything for attention. (Photo: J.E.L.)

Surprise and quickness are the keys to punishment. If you are slow, your pup will soon train you. With a Border Collie, you *must* be the pack leader and earn his respect. Remember dogs are happiest if they have a pack leader to follow and obey. Border Collies have been selectively bred for the "follower" temperament for centuries. However, if you don't assume the role of pack leader, your dog will become neurotic or will be obliged to take over the role for you.

Barking

While you are asleep, your puppy decides he will howl. He has just been taken away from his brothers, sisters and mom. He thinks that howling and barking will attract his mom to rescue him. If you either cuddle him or yell at him, the pup will stop momentarily since his cries have gotten him exactly what he desired—company from a pack member in his distress. If you want to stop his whimpering you must steel your nerves and plug your ears. After a few nights he will realize that he isn't abandoned and that you will reappear every morning.

Barking in adult dogs is a learned behavior. Your dog has found that if he barks you will let him in the house or will decide to let him run loose instead of keeping him penned. Whenever you give in to him, he is winning a battle of wills and the behavior will be repeated. The best cure for a barking dog is the "tin-cans on the pulley" method. Put about ten tin cans on a string, and set up a pully system to the windowsill of a window in a room where you usually work. Whenever the dogs bark, open the window and yell "No—Quiet" while you pull the string, causing the cans to fall with a loud clatter. This startles the dogs and quiets them.

Barking is also a sign of boredom. Two dogs in a kennel run will play together and keep each other company. Giving them lots of play toys will help, too. I know of one delighted Border Collie with her own wading pool and large colored balls. She spends her day rolling the balls with her nose and splashing in her pool.

Jumping On People

You may have considered your puppy to be cute when he joyfully jumped up and planted his feet on you. Now that he is a full grown dog, he does this to all your guests. One day Grandma comes to visit and he knocks her over. Everyone's reaction is "He is a terrible dog!" But, if you analyze the situation, you can see that you are responsible. From the time a puppy is small you should say "No—Off" and push him down when he tries to put his feet on you. Now that he is an adult, you will have to give him a good hard KNEE in the chest, so as to throw him over backwards. Do not kick with your foot. When visitors come, put him on a leash, and if he jumps up on them, instruct them to give him the knee.

Chasing Cars

Car chasing is a real problem for any dog, and it is the number one killer of Border Collies. Many dogs learn to keep out of the way of cars the hard way. After being hit and nearly killed, they learn to look both ways before crossing the road, and move to the side whenever they see a car coming.

The best method I know to break this habit is to string groups of about ten tin cans together, then seek the aid of your friends. Have them drive by you and your dog, who is on a choke collar and check cord. When the dog goes after the car, the person in the passenger's seat throws the cans out the window, aiming for your dog's face. At the same

This Border Collie, Pennent II, has invented a game with two tennis ball at once! He has one in his mouth and one between his feet. Penn is owned by Guy and Judy Aronoff of California. (Photo: Judy Johnston Aronoff)

time, you must jerk him completely off the ground. He will be so shocked by the clattering cans landing on him and by the strange way he went flying through the air that he will probably never chase another car. Repeat this with several different cars until you are sure that he is cured. Although this seems cruel, it is far better than ending up with a dead or maimed dog.

Livestock and bicycle chasing can also be cured by using a check cord and tin cans. It is important to remember that if you plan to teach the dog to herd livestock, this type of training shouldn't be undertaken until the dog is fully trained for herding, otherwise you will stifle his herding instincts. In the meantime, just keep the dog on a leash when near a road or livestock.

Digging

Digging is usually caused by boredom. The best way to cure digging is to keep the dog busy. Train him to do some work and give him adequate exercise. Every time he digs a hole, place several tin cans tied together into the hole. When the dog starts to dig, the cans rattle and he should stop digging in that location. You may have to use a lot of tin cans, but he should eventually get the idea.

A Border Collie holds his master's crook while waiting for his turn on the trial field. Many Border Collies will fetch tools or messages for their masters after training. (PAK Photo)

Donna C. Lee of Ohio with two of her Obedience Border Collies, Donnalee's Deke C.D.X. (left) and Donnalee's Bradford U.D. (right).

Formal Obedience Training   7

Once your Border Collie has reached six months to one year of age, he is ready to start formal training. Formal training is not done earlier because the dog must be allowed to develop his personality and natural instincts first. In other words, he must grow up. I have seen pups fully trained much younger, but in every case once the dog became an adult, something snapped in the dogs mind, and he became a dull, spiritless individual. Guide dogs for the blind receive no formal training until one year. They are raised in a home by 4-H members to insure they are properly socialized for the first year.

Your training lessons should last about one-half hour, although you can have several lessons each day. Make sure you let the dog relieve himself before you train him, and do not feed him just before a lesson. Most adult working dogs are fed at the end of the day when the work is done. This helps prevent deadly gastric torsion (twisting of the stomach), and the dog is more alert. Do not train your dog if you are in a bad mood or angry for some reason. Wait until you calm down.

It is best to train your dog in comfortable sports shoes and casual, loose clothing. Do not smoke since the ashes might get in your dog's eyes and it is difficult to manipulate the leash and control the dog with a cigarette in your hand. Also do not carry a purse, since it would be in the way.

To start training, find a relatively quiet area with as few distractions as possible. Once the dog understands the commands you can practice in more distracting areas. Eventually you should be able to work your dog at a shopping mall, crowded park, dog show or anywhere.

Heel

"Heel" is the command which teaches the dog to walk on a leash without pulling your arm out of the socket. Heeling also serves the purpose of establishing a control base upon which all the other commands are built. It teaches the dog to pay attention to you and respect you.

The dog is trained to walk at your left side with his shoulder even with your left leg, and to sit automatically whenever you stop so he doesn't get in your way. The left side is the traditional side for the dog because most people are right handed and because hunters carry their weapons on the right side. It also leaves your right hand free to shake hands, open doors, or carry packages. Too much heeling work with the future herding or guide dog is undesirable, but the basics should be taught.

"Heel" position (side view). The dog's shoulder should be even with the handler's left leg.

"Heel" position (front view). The dog should watch the handlers face, sit squarely on its haunches, and the leash should be loose with a "J" in it.

First, make sure the training collar is properly fitted, and you have the correct type of leash (see Part I). Hold the leash in your right hand, thumb through the loop and one fold of slack in your hand (see diagram). Use your left hand to control the leash or to tap the dog's rump to make him sit. BE SURE TO KEEP A SLACK LEASH AT ALL TIMES. Never haul at his neck. Quick jerks on the collar, unexpected turns and instant praise are necessary. Try to make heeling fun. Say your dog's name and then the command "Heel" in an enthusiastic tone. Step off briskly. I do not feel it matters which foot you start with since the dog should be watching your face, not your feet. Talk to him encouragingly as you walk forward. If he runs ahead, snap him back sharply with the leash and praise him. If he crowds you, make a lot of quick left turns which will teach him to watch where you are going. If he heels too wide, snap the leash and briskly turn right so he has to hurry to keep up. Maintain a brisk pace and an enthusiastic voice tone. If your dog lags behind, give several quick jerks on the leash and run, forcing him to trot to catch up. Make heeling exciting and fun for the dog, otherwise he will quickly tire of it and become bored. Scatter halts throughout your heeling, but plan in advance. Before you halt, shorten the lead in your right hand. When you stop, pull up on the leash while simultaneously pushing down on the dog's rump; then praise him. Each time your start walking again, say the dog's name and command "Heel." Practice many turns, changes of pace and halts. Eventually he will sit automatically without aid from you.

If you plan to compete in obedience or schutzhund competitions you will want to make sure the dog sits straight whenever you halt. If he does not, take two steps forward and repeat. Make sure you shorten the leash enough to pull it up taut as you halt and push down on his rump.

A properly executed left turn is done by pivoting on your left foot and swinging your right foot around. The right turn is the reverse. To do an about turn, (reverse direction) you will need to hesitate on your left foot, shift your weight to the right, pivot, and step off on your left. The dog will have to travel around the outside. This is a right about turn. The left about turn is only used in Schutzhund. The beginning handler should practice turns without the dog until he has learned the correct footwork.

In the obedience ring you will not be able to talk to your dog except to say the dog's name and give the precise commands. No leg clapping, finger snapping or other signals are allowed, but they are useful for encouraging the beginning dog in practice sessions. If you plan to compete, slowly cut down on the extra signals and talking, but even in the competition dog, praise and encouragement during practice help keep up the dog's interest.

Sit-Stay

Your dog has already learned to sit during the heeling exercise. Now he must learn to sit and stay until you tell him to move. The sit command will be used later to teach the come command. To teach your pup to sit, pull up on the leash and push down on his rear as you command "Sit." Praise "Good Dog" in a soothing tone so as not to excite him. Then say "O.K.," which is the release command, and praise him enthusiastically.

When he is sitting automatically, you can teach him the stay command. Tell him to sit, and hold the leash short, with no slack, but not tight. Command "Stay," and hold the dog in place for several seconds. Then release and praise him. If he gets up, pull up on the leash, push down his rear, and say "No," "Stay" firmly, but softly. Wait a few more seconds and release him. After one or two lessons, start taking a step or two away, but extend your arm to keep the leash short and straight up and down from the collar. Return, tell your dog "O.K." and praise him. Then take a step or two to either side, until finally you can make a complete circle around him. Gradually build up the time and distance. Soon you will be able to step to the end of the leash, which should now be loose so as not to throw the dog off balance and force him to move. When he is reliable at the end of the leash, again start taking a step or two in either direction, until you can make a complete circle around him in either direction at the end of the leash. Always return to the dog's left side by going behind him. To prevent him from anticipating your release command, occasionally make him wait several seconds before you release him and praise him.

Remember to correct your dog immediately if he moves. Build up the time he must stay to two or three minutes. When he is reliable on a six-foot lead, put him on a twenty foot cord and gradually increase the distance. Circle him occasionally. Later, drop the cord and go further away. When he is reliable, you can start distracting him by running, hiding behind a tree or bush for a few seconds or rolling a ball. If he moves, correct him and put him back exactly where you left him the first time. Do not try too many distractions at once. It takes several weeks to reach this stage of training.

Down-Stay

The down is taught by pressing down on your dog's rear quarters so he is sitting, and then pulling his forelegs out from under him. Press sideways on his shoulders with the other hand if necessary. As you do this, command "Down" softly but firmly. Tell him good dog and stroke him comfortingly once he is down. Many dogs do not like the down because they feel vulnerable, so try to make your dog feel relaxed about the down position. The down command is very important to the herding dog, and it is the most comfortable position for the dog if he is expected to stay in one place for any length of time. The down is one of the most useful of all commands. It is useful in stopping an overeager young dog from exciting or harming livestock. It can also be used to stop a dog that is about to cross a road in front of traffic.

Some trainers advocate stepping on a dog's leash and forcing him to the ground. To me, this is a bit harsh and can cause resentment. I see no reason to use such a harsh method unless correcting a fully trained dog who is deliberately disobeying.

Come

To teach the come, put your dog on a sit-stay and walk to the end of the leash. Wait about 30 seconds, then say his name and "Come" in a happy tone of voice as you run backwards, reeling him in like a fish, and saying "Good Dog" enthusiastically. If the dog is slow or tries to run to the side, a series of short jerks while you are reeling him in will help. Praise him as he is propelled toward you after each jerk, so he knows that is what you expect of him. When he is almost in front of you, tell him "Sit," and praise him. Be enthusiastic or he will think coming is a bore and learn to take his time.

When he has learned to come, stop, give the command to sit, and then make him sit in front of you. If he does not sit, pull up on the leash and push down on his rear.

Your dog should come to you anywhere at any time. When he comes quickly and sits in front of you without being told, put him on a thirty foot cord. Once he is reliable on the cord and is fully trained in all the other exercises, he is ready to learn an off-lead come. It is best to start off-leash exercises indoors or in a fenced enclosure. Later the dog should

Teaching the recall exercise, or "come" on command. Take in the slack, and back up a few steps to encourage the dog to come in. (Photo: Col. W.A.J.)

be worked in many different places—indoors and out. Be sure to work him on leash the first time in each new location.

Once he has mastered these basic commands (heel, sit, down, stay and come), you have a farily well trained animal. If you praise your dog enthusiastically every time he comes, and make training fun, your dog will be obedient and eager. My Border Collies have always come at breakneck speed when I call them. This is especially impressive in the "recall" exercise at dog shows.

Stand-Stay

The stand is another exercise performed in the obedience ring. However, it is also practical. A dog that will stand and stay is easy to groom and easy for a veterinarian to examine. The stand is used instead of the "down" in herding trial work, since excessive "dropping" is considered undesirable. The stand-stay is one of the more difficult exercises. To teach it, put your dog on a choke collar and lead. Shorten the leash, and as you say "Stand," block his right hind leg and hold it gently with your left hand to keep him standing. After a few moments, release and praise him. Repeat this until the dog gets the idea that he is supposed to stand on command. Then introduce the "Stay." At first, stand the dog for only a few seconds. Be ready to grab his hind leg and hold him up if he tries to move. Gradually move further away as he gets steadier, just as you did with the sit and down.

When your dog will stand reliably without moving his feet for a minute, start examining him while he stays. Look in his ears, run your hands down his back and sides, and lift his tail. Later in training you can run your hands down his legs, and lift his lips to examine his bite.

This exercise can also be modified into a trick. Place a fully trained dog on a stand-stay while you have another dog jump over his back. Then tell the second dog to stand and have the first dog jump over him.

Heel Off Leash

Do not attempt off-leash heeling until your dog is reliable on all on-leash commands, even in very distracting places. When he is dependable on lead, go back to your own yard. Tie a light nylon cord about two feet long to the ring on the collar and also snap on the leash. Heel for a few minutes, then unsnap the lead. Your dog may think he is free and try to run off. If he does, he is in for a big surprise! His collar will tighten instantaneously as you give a snap on the leash, and he will find you still have an invisible connection to him. After a few days if all goes well, stop using the string, but carry the leash in your right hand. Later drop the leash entirely. Be sure to use lots of praise and encouragement and walk at a brisk pace with plenty of turns, changes of pace and halts to keep things interesting.

Finish

The "finish" is an exercise used in obedience trials in which the dog returns to heel position from a sit in front. To teach this exercise, put your dog on a lead and have him sit in front of you. Say his name and "Heel," step back and jerk his collar so that he is forced to move beyond your left side. Then step forward, giving a quick jerk on his collar to bring him to heel position. Pull up on his collar and tap his left (outside) hip with your left hand so that he sits in heel position. Praise him lavishly and do a few steps of regular heeling. Repeat several times each lesson. Eventually you can discontinue the backward and forward steps and the jerks on the collar, and remain motionless. Many Border Collies enjoy this exercise immensely and always make a flying leap or

Teaching the "stand-stay" for examination. Hold the dog's collar and place your arm under the dog's belly to keep him from sitting down. (Photo: Col. W.A.J.)

spin as they go into heel position. At a dog show, a flying finish is a real crowd pleaser. At one show I saw a Border Collie get so carried away with the flying finish when the crowd clapped that he repeated it five more times, and started to bark, too! This was great fun for him, but it resulted in points off his score that day.

Hand Signals

Hand signals are easily taught. Give the hand signal at the same time as the voice command. After several repetitions the dog will pick up the idea. With praise and practice, soon he will respond to the signal alone.

Hand signals are used in Utility obedience classes, by movie performers, military and police dogs. I do not advise teaching hand signals to a herding dog, since they force the dog to watch the handler, not the livestock.

The signal for "Stay" is to show the dog the flat of your palm, like a policeman giving the halt signal. "Down" is signaled by raising your hand above you head and dropping your hand and arm downwards as if pushing the dog to the ground. The "Sit" command is given by having your hand at your side, and then raising it upward from the elbow. "Heel" is a swiping motion of the left hand by the left leg. "Stand" is given with the right hand, while the dog is at heel, the fingers extended, palm toward the dog.

Whistle Commands

Whistle commands are taught the same way as hand signals except the whistle is given immediately after the voice command. I use a shrill "whee-oo" for "Down," "tweet" for "Stand," "ta-weet ta-weet" to walk on up to sheep, "bob-white" to circle left, "cheer-ee-oo" to circle right, and "ta-ta" to slow down. A plastic shepherd's whistle costing only a few dollars can be purchased for this purpose. To use it, hold it between your lips and blow into the folded side. Do not cover the open side with your lips. With practice you should be able to play a tune. The advantage of whistle commands is that the dog can hear them from a distance of several miles, wind permitting.

Donnalee's Bradford-U.D. working scent articles. He will select the article with his owner's scent from a pile of identical articles with the steward's scent on them.

Directed jumping (bar jump) is an exercise in the Utility Level of Obedience. A potential obedience puppy should be friendly, active and alert.

47

"Way to ME"

Training To Herd 8

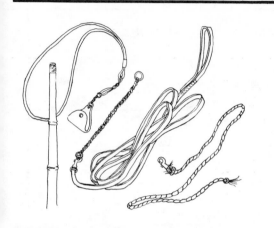

Equipment for training the herding dog. Crook, shepherd's whistle, choke collar, longline, and drag line.

Although it might appear that teaching a Border Collie to herd is a complex task, it really is not, providing you buy a well-bred dog from a proven working line. A dog from non-working parents may lack herding instinct, and therefore be untrainable. Alternatively, some people think that any intelligent dog can be trained to herd like a field trial Border Collie, but that isn't true either. A Border Collie with inborn herding instincts will circle livestock and control them with an intent, almost hypnotic gaze. He will try to outguess his charges' every move, and head off any that try to break away. He will work livestock quietly. A dog without these natural instincts will never learn to work like a trial Border Collie.

Many herding breeds are driving dogs, or "heelers," like the Australian cattle dog, Welsh Corgi and the German Shepherd. Their style of working is entirely different—they nip at the heels of their charges and bark, which is known as "heeling." Instead of circling around behind the flock and bringing them to their handler, they run back and forth on the same side of the flock as the handler and drive the animals away from him.

A few Australian Shepherds, Collies, Shetland Sheepdogs, Bearded Collies and Belgian Sheepdogs have heading instinct to some degree along with driving instinct, but they lack the strongly inbred gaze called the "power of the eye" found in the trial-bred Border Collie or Kelpie.

It is very important to understand your dog's natural instincts and capabilities before you start training. Every breed, and every dog, is different. Some purebred Border Collies have no herding instinct and will never become effective herders. With any breed, the inherited ability from a line where instinct is tested and proven with every generation is the best guarantee of success.

The method of training outlined in this chapter is not the only method of training a working stockdog. Almost every successful trainer has his or her own method that works well. The method outlined in this chapter was devised for the person with limited experience working alone. For the best results, find an experienced Border Collie stockdog trainer in your area and have him or her help you train your dog. Most Border Collie people are very willing to help the beginner. If you can attend a Border Collie Stockdog Training Clinic in your area, do so. It will be well worth your time and money. For a list of Border Collie Stockdog clubs in your area, see the appendix.

Many top Border Collie trial trainers do not require the dog to know any formal obedience before being introduced to livestock. Some trainers say it ruins a dog's initiative and causes him to watch his handler instead of his charges. I have seen Jack Knox, an outstanding trainer and

Commands and Terms

DOWN	The command to drop instantly to the ground.
DRIVING	The sheep go away from the handler with the dog behind them. This is not natural to the Border Collie or Kelpie, and must be trained.
EWE	A female sheep.
FETCH	The sheep are driven to the handler with the dog behind them.
FLANKING	Circling the sheep from the right or left to keep them in a bunch or change their direction.
GATHER	The dog collects the sheep from their scattered grazing positions to a compact group.
GO BYE	The command for the dog to circle to the left.
HEELING	The dog nips and bites at the feet and legs of livestock to move them. Often accompanied by barking.
LIFT	The pause between the outrun and start of the fetch.
MODERATE EYE	A dog who has enough eye to control sheep effectively, but not so much as to be overbearing.
OUTRUN	A pear-shaped or semi-circular course taken by the dog to get to the far side of the flock without alarming them.
SHEDDING	Separating certain animals from the flock or herd.
SINGLING	Separating one animal from the flock or herd.
STAND	The command to stand on all four legs without moving.
STAY	The command to remain in place until commanded to move.
STEADY	The command to slow down to a creeping walk.
STRONG EYE	A dog which stares intently at stock. Sometimes to the point of becoming rooted to one spot.
THAT WILL DO	The command releasing the dog from his charges.
WALK ON UP	The command to walk toward the sheep.
WAY TO ME	The command for the dog to circle right.
WEAK DOG	A weak dog will turn tail when faced with an aggressive animal. It will never be able to effectively work tough sheep or cattle.
WEAK EYE	A dog that lacks concentration on his charges, and lets his gaze wander. This type of dog cannot control his charges well, and is usually not an effective worker.
WEARING	When the dog holds the flock up against the handler by running back and forth on the opposite side. The dog will bring the sheep after the handler wherever he may walk or ride with no additional commands. It is also used to mean holding back animals who have been separated from the main flock.

"Down" the dog when he reaches the opposite side of the flock. The dog should know basic commands like Down, Stay and Come before introducing him to livestock. (Photo: Col. W.A.J.)

The author demonstrates how to teach a dog his "sides." Keep the dog back off the stock using the round pen, your body position and the cane. Use the cane as an extension of yourself to block the dog's path if he tries to cut in close. (Photo: Col. W.A.J.)

Most Border Collies will circle instinctively to the opposite side of the penned flock from the handler. This instinctive desire to circle or "gather" will be used to teach the flanking commands.

trial man take an untrained biting dog into an enclosure off leash- and have the dog circling well back off his stock, changing directions and stopping in a short time. He does not use any artificial devices such as collars, leashes, ropes, whips or fencing to protect the stock. He relies entirely on body language, and tone of voice to encourage or correct the dog. His knowledge of both dogs and sheep goes back to his childhood on the Scottish hills and moors with his father. If you can find a trainer who utilizes the dogs natural instincts to gather and control livestock rather than mechanical obedience, you will end up with a far better working dog.

FIRST STAGE - THE ROUND PEN

When your dog is very obedient, and knows how to walk on a leash, down, stand, stay and come, you are ready to try working him around livestock. (See Chapter 8 for basic training.) Most trainers work with ducks or gentle lambs until the dog understands directional commands. You will need a cane or bamboo pole about ten feet long, and a small round pen. The cane pole is used only as an aid to keep the dog wide and give directions. Never use the cane pole to strike the dog for he will become afraid of it and it will be of no use when you need it later. Border Collies tend to remember bad experiences, and I know of good dogs who were ruined in one quick burst of temper. If you feel your temper going, stop and end the lesson.

The round pen will be used to teach your dog his flanking commands around the outside, while protecting the ducks or lambs on the inside. Many young dogs are a bit rough when first introduced to livestock. The pen saves the animals and also makes the trainer's work easier.

Walk up to the pen with your dog on leash. Tell him to "Down-Stay." If he refuses, practice his obedience near the pen until he obeys. Then he is ready to learn his flanking commands.

Flanking Commands

The flanking commands are "Go-Bye" (circle to the dog's left) and "Way to Me" (circle to the dog's right). The Border Collie's instinct is to stay on the opposite side of the flock or herd from you, his pack leader. Since the animals are in the pen, he should keep running to the opposite side of the pen from you. Any well bred Border Collie will do this with no training whatsoever, even as early as six weeks. (I use the round pen to test all my six week pups for herding instinct and natural ability.)

Some strong-eyed dogs will remain fixated on the ground, staring at the animals. This type of dog is difficult to train. Pull him to his feet and force him to circle the pen. If he still does not move freely after many repetitions, you may have to resort to other methods to get him moving freely.

The best way to get a strong eyed dog moving is to have fast moving sheep in an open field. Chase them by the dog and scatter them. Hopefully the excitement will cause the dog to get up and circle them so they bunch up. This same trick will sometimes arouse instinct in dogs that appear totally disinterested in livestock. Once the dog is moving freely, go back to the round pen.

One bitch I know remained fixated on the ground despite all efforts by the handler to get her on her feet. The handler became so frustrated that he booted her in the rear. She was so intent on the sheep that she did not see her owner, and was totally surprised. She then shot around the sheep and had them bunched in a minute.

To teach the "Go-Bye" (circle to the left) command, down the dog and leave him. Then reapproach him, walking in the direction you want

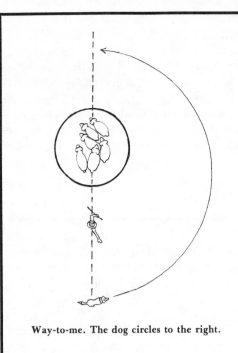

Way-to-me. The dog circles to the right.

Go-bye. The dog circles to the left.

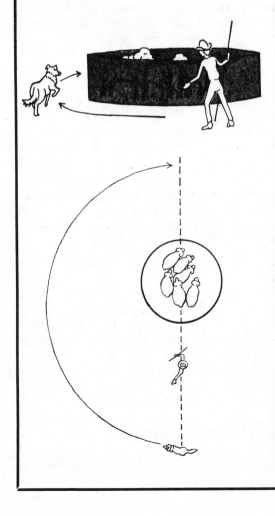

him to go. You should reach a critical position where you can see the dog wants to move around the stock to keep his balance. Command "Go-Bye." He should then break the down and run to the right. If he is too obedient to break, give an "O.K." and then "Go-Bye." Praise him as he runs so he understands he is pleasing you. Then drop him on the opposite side of the pen.

Approach the dog again, and repeat the whole process until he associates the command with the action.

The "Way to Me" command is taught in the same manner as "Go-Bye," however the handler and dog circle to the right instead.

The "Go-Bye" and "Way to Me" commands should be alternated so the dog doesn't anticipate either command. You must remember the dog will move away from you by instinct. Over a period of time, decrease the number of steps you take until finally you can remain in one place while you command the dog back and forth on the far side of the pen.

The command "That Will Do" should be taught from the first day you work near stock. When you are finished with the lesson or want a break, command "That Will Do," jerk on the cord, and firmly lead the dog away from the animals. You can even alternate training with "That Will Do." The dog must learn that this command means to leave the stock alone.

Outruns

The outrun is very similar to flanking, and utilizes the same circling instinct. Once you have taught the dog his flanking commands, you can do outruns. Down the dog about thirty feet from the pen. If you want him to do a right hand outrun, place yourself on the left of the center-line, midway between him and the pen. Your position will cause him to go right, but hold your cane pole to the right to force him to run wide. As he goes by you, walk to the centerline. Drop the dog when he reaches the 12 o'clock position.

If the animals were not penned, a dog who cuts in too close would cause them to scatter. That defeats the purpose of the outrun, which is to quietly gather the sheep or cows without alarming.

The left hand outrun, "Way to Me," is taught in the same way as the right hand outrun, except that you position yourself to the right of the centerline, with your pole pointing left. Again, take a few steps to reach the centerline as the dog goes by. This helps force him wide and puts you in the six o'clock position which is exactly balanced to the twelve o'clock position where you will drop him. Slowly position yourself closer to the centerline and the dog at the start of the outruns. Eventually you will be able to send the dog from your side without moving at all.

Driving

The driving commands should not be taught until the dog knows his flanking commands well, and can execute a miniature outrun around the round pen. The reason for this is that driving is contrary to the Border Collie's natural instincts, and can confuse the dog totally, or even ruin him. Trainers who do not understand this natural instinct in the Border Collie become hopelessly frustrated trying to train them. Most stockdog breeds drive livestock away from the handler naturally, while the Border Collie and Kelpie go to the opposite side and drive them back to the handler.

I heard about a farmer who wanted his cows out of the barn. His pup kept driving them back into the barn, both dog and man working at counter-purposes. The man was so angry and exasperated that he called the breeder, who advised him to go and stand where he wanted the dog to put the cows. The pup then drove the cows out of the barn to the pasture where the man stood. The man soon found he could walk anywhere, and the dog would force the cattle to follow him.

A man who only wants a drover's dog might find a breed such as the Australian Cattle dog more satisfying than trying to force a Border Collie or Kelpie to fit his needs. This does not mean a Border Collie cannot make a useful driving dog, since many are excellent.

To teach driving to a Border Collie takes patience. Put the dog on a leash, and command "Walk On Up" as you walk toward the pen. Stop every few feet and command "Stand-Stay" or "Down-Stay." It is best to alternate the two commands. There are many situations where it is best for the dog to remain standing, instead of dropping to his belly. Be sure to keep practicing flanking and outruns or the dog will become bored and confused. If the dog lets his gaze stray from the animals while he is doing the "Walk On Up" command, point to the pen and in a low whisper hiss out the command "Watch." Then do some more flanking or command "That Will Do," and repeat the lesson. Remember, do not overdo driving.

The command "Steady," which means to slow down to a creeping walk, is another very useful command, especially when working excitable sheep. You must slow down, hunch over, and take tiny, short steps. The dog will do the same in order to imitate you. Start alternating the "Walk On Up," "Steady," and "Stand-Stay" commands as you approach the pen. When your dog understands the commands, let him drag the lead. If he tries to circle, step on the leash and repeat "Walk On Up."

SECOND STAGE - THE FIELD

In the second stage of training the dog knows all of the basic obedience and herding commands and he is ready to work in a small field or paddock area, without the round pen. In the beginning he should be trailing a ten-foot light cord or clothesline from his collar. This makes it easier to correct the dog if he gets out of hand or to give him guidance.

Wearing

A dog that keeps livestock following you is said to be "wearing" the animals. A Border Collie will do this naturally without commands, but commands are useful to keep control of the situation. Wearing requires a dog with natural balance and the instinct to hold stock up against the handler. A dog without caution must be constantly commanded to stop and start to keep him from exciting his charges. Obviously a dog who doesn't need constant commands is preferable. Many young dogs are over-enthusiastic but develop caution with practice and age, so be patient. Eventually your dog should be able to keep the sheep or cattle following you no matter how far you walk or ride on horseback.

Make sure the animals you are using are calm and gentle. Lambs accustomed to being handled by dogs or at least humans are best. Ewes with lambs or rams can be very aggressive, and should not be used. Neither should cattle. A bad experience with rough stock could ruin a young dog.

The first thing you must do is test your dog's obedience on leash. If he doesn't obey your commands to down, come, stand and heel, you will have to practice with him in the enclosure until he does. After he has heeded your commands, walk up to the sheep, which should be near the fence lines and tell him "Down—Stay." Next, walk around to the opposite side of the sheep and tell him to "Walk on Up," and back up yourself so the sheep will feel free to move away from the dog. The

Teaching "walk on up."

Teaching the "walk on up" with a "stand-stay" instead of a "down-stay." Excessive clapping is undesirable in trial competition, so teach the dog to stand as soon as possible. (Photo: Col. W.A.J.)

53

Wearing the sheep to the handler. The handler backs up, and the dog forces the sheep to follow. Most dogs will do this instinctively. Encourage him by saying "walk on up" as you start to back up.

dog will get up and come toward the sheep when he sees them drifting away from him toward you.

Do not let the sheep run past you. Use your pole to help slow them down. If the dog comes on to the sheep too fast, drop him. Then after the sheep settle down, tell him "Walk on Up," "Steady." Command "Stand—Stay" if he starts hurrying again, or if he is too excited, drop him instead. Try to avoid dropping him and use "Stand" whenever possible, since excessive clapping in a sheepdog trial is undesirable. Standing also looks more natural. Keep repeating this until the dog keeps the sheep following you at a walk. Running livestock should be avoided, since it can cause abortions in pregnant animals, weight loss in meat animals and heat exhaustion in hot weather. Aggressive dogs that work too fast are responsible for giving herding dogs a bad name.

Practice the "Steady" command by walking slowly backward, holding back the sheep with your pole. If the dog does not slow, tell him to "Stand" every few steps. He should have learned "Steady" while working in the round pen.

Soon you should be able to turn your back and walk around the field with the sheep following and the dog bringing up the rear. Watch carefully and stop your dog if he works too fast or has trouble with the sheep. If one of the sheep decides to fight the dog, throw a small stone or pebble to startle it. The sheep will not know what hit it, and assuming the rock had something to do with the dog, it will usually give up and rejoin the flock.

Flanking Commands

Practice training the flanking commands, "Go-Bye" and "Way to Me" as you did previously with the round pen. You will need the cane pole again, as an aid to keep the dog from crowding the sheep. The best way to start practicing flanking commands in an open area is with the sheep against the fence. Have the dog "Down" behind you and the sheep. Allow the sheep to drift down the fence line and place yourself midway between the dog and sheep. Hold the cane pole out from the fence and command the dog to "Go-Bye" or "Way to Me," depending upon which way the sheep are traveling. At first do not allow the sheep to travel more than fifty feet from where you left the dog. Distance can be built up over a period of time.

Remember "Go-Bye" is to the left and "Way to Me" is to the right. If you have trouble remembering which way is which, put a piece of tape on the back of each hand and write the commands on it. Use the pole to force the dog out wide, and if necessary take a few steps in toward him as he runs by. Drop him when he reaches the 12 o'clock position next to the fence.

To do the "Way to Me" (circle to the right) command, step in between the dog and the sheep, tell him to "Stay," and cause the sheep to drift down the fence line about fifty feet. Place yourself at the halfway point with your cane out, and command "Way to Me." Force the dog wide by stepping into him as he goes by. Drop him again at 12 o'clock. Then back-up, tell him to "Walk on Up" and do some wearing to keep up his interest. If you do not allow him to wear sheep into you every now and then, he will become bored with the whole process, since it accomplished nothing.

Periodically tell the dog "That Will Do." He should already know the command means to leave the stock alone. If he does not do so, step on the cord he is trailing, firmly lead him away, and praise him. This gives both livestock and dog a breather.

Teaching "Way to Me" using the fence line. Handler will force the dog out wide with his cane if the dog tries to cut in close.

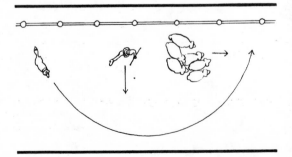

Once the dog is reliable on his flanking commands and wearing along the fence, begin working away from the fence. If you have problems, go back to working along the fence line until you and the dog are more confident. A half-hour lesson on a hot day, or at most one hour in cooler weather is sufficient. Several short lessons each day are far better than one long lesson, since long lessons tend to bore the dog and tire the sheep.

If the sheep bunch up in a corner, an inexperienced young dog will probably be unable to move them because he is afraid to go into the cramped space between the fence and the sheep. To cure this fear, leash the dog and accompany him into the corner, forcing the sheep out. Next, down your dog and make him stay. This exercise keeps the sheep out of the corner and lets the dog know that the sheep won't try to crush him.

Until a dog is confident and experienced, do not force him into corners or any cramped areas unless you accompany him because he could be injured and develop a fear of sheep. One of my dogs was pinned into a corner as a six month old pup. I felt she had progressed enough to work by herself, but she was butted and dragged by an angry ewe, and she has since been reluctant to approach aggressive sheep.

The Outrun and Fetch

When your dog fully understands the commands, "walk on up," "stand," "down," "stay," "steady," "way to me," "go-bye" and "that will do," he is ready to work on outruns in the small field. The outrun is where the dog circles wide behind the sheep and then hesitates before the fetch, where he brings them in to you.

To begin training, put a 10-foot cord on the dog and down the dog at one end of the enclosure with the sheep at the other, no more than fifty to one hundred feet away. Next, walk about midway between the sheep and the dog, and to the left of the centerline. Hold your cane out to the right in the direction you want the dog to go. Tell him "go-bye" and, as he circles, force him wide by moving to the centerline. If he cuts too close, move into his line of travel and force him wider. If he tries to circle the wrong way, block him off with your body and cane and steer him back in the correct direction. This should not happen if you are correctly positioned with respect to the dog and sheep, because it is contrary to the Border Collie's instinct to run toward you while working sheep. When the dog reaches the opposite side of the sheep, down him at 12 o'clock.

Once the dog is down behind the sheep, you can tell him to "Walk on Up." Direct the dog to bring the sheep to you with the same commands you used in wearing. Then back up to the opposite side of the field as the dog brings the sheep to you. This exercise is the beginning of the "lift and fetch."

As your dog begins to understand your commands, stand further and further away from the sheep and closer to the dog and the centerline between dog and sheep. Soon your dog will circle the flock from your side in either direction, and bring them to you without you moving a foot. Remember, if your dog starts cutting in on the sheep, go back to the mid-point, run out and block him to force him wide with the cane pole, or throw the cane in his direction. Do not strike him, however. Most dogs will naturally circle wide, like a wolf stalking prey, because they instinctively do not want to alarm the sheep.

The ideal outrun is pear-shaped with the wide end nearest the sheep. The fetch should be as straight as possible. If the dog comes up on the sheep too fast, stop him with the down or stand, and then command "Walk on Up" and "Steady." Subsequently, he should bring the sheep to you at an easy walk without exciting them.

The beginning outrun combined with a fetch. The handler stands midway to force the dog wide if necessary. After the dog reaches 12 o'clock, tell him to stay, then walk on up as you back up.

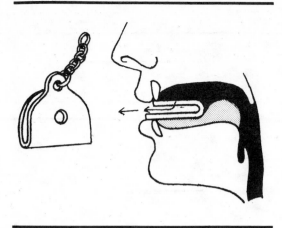

The shepherd's whistle. To play it, hold it between your lips with the hole "up" and open side facing out. Sound is produced by air entering the hole. Your mouth acts as an echo chamber.

Whistle Commands

After your dog has fully learned "go-bye," "way to me," "walk on up," "down," "stand," and "steady," he is ready to learn whistle commands. I use *ta-weet-ta-weet* for "walk on up," *wee-oo* for "down," *tweet* for "stand," *ta-ta* for "steady," *bob-white* for "go-bye" and *cheer-ee-oo* for "way to me." Practice with the shepherd's whistle before you try these out on the dog. A shepherd's whistle costs only a dollar or two, and is played by holding it between your lips and blowing into it from the folded over side. It takes practice, but once you get the hang of it, you can almost play a tune.

To teach your dog whistle commands simply give the voice command followed instantly by the whistle command. After a few days the dog will respond to the whistle commands alone. If the dog makes any mistakes, correct in the same way as before with voice commands. Go back to voice-whistle command if the dog seems confused.

Once the dog obeys the whistle commands without error, he is ready to work in a larger field. Whistle commands carry well at a distance, so they are particularly helpful here. Start with the sheep fairly close, and have your dog trail the cord at first. If he has good control, allow him to work the sheep at increasing distances until he performs outruns and fetches the full length of the field. Also have him continue to wear the sheep after you as you walk around the field. If at any time the dog gets out of control, go back to the small field and use the same corrections as before (such as running to force him out wide). Do not rush his training. It takes time and practice. Some dogs learn faster than others and no two dogs are the same.

Driving

Now that your dog is working well on outruns, fetches and wearing, he is ready to learn to drive. Whistle commands are not necessary, and some farmers never use them.

Driving is not natural to the Border Collie. It is performed in almost the same way as the fetch, except that the dog moves the animals away from you in a straight line instead of to you. Driving is required in sheep and cattle dog trials in combination with outruns and fetching. It is also used in everyday work on farms and ranches. The advantage of the Border Collie is that he can be sent to the distant pastures without his master accompanying him, and bring the flock or herd back, then be used to drive, load or unload the animals as the master wills. A dog who can only drive livestock must work with his master nearby, although some stockmen prefer this.

At first, do all drive training in the small field. Limit the amount of driving to avoid confusing the dog. It is easiest to start with the sheep against the fenceline. Work the dog on the ten foot cord. When the sheep begin wandering down the fenceline, your dog will want to circle them and stop them. Don't let him. Instead hold the cord in your hand, and command "Walk on Up" as you walk toward the sheep. Since the dog already knows the command from wearing and fetching, he will probably walk straight toward the sheep. This is ideal. If he does not, and tries to circle, gently guide him with the cord straight toward the flock. If he moves too quickly, command "Stand" and then "Steady." After about twenty yards, praise him, let go of the cord, and give a flanking command. Afterward let him wear the sheep around the field, and perhaps practice some outruns.

When he is obedient and doesn't try to circle on the "walk on up" command, let go of the cord and try working him loose. If he does circle

Teach driving along a fenceline. If the dog tries to head the sheep off, block him with your body and cane and tell him to "down" or "stand" (Photo: J.E.L.)

the sheep, don't punish him, just start over. You can remove the cord once you feel the dog understands the exercise and you trust him to obey you. Some very spirited young dogs must have the cord left on for a long time as a reminder of authority. With this type of dog, gradually shorten the cord until it is a few inches long.

Once your dog understands driving and does not try to circle, he is ready to start flanking on your side of the sheep. This enables you to direct the dog to either side and turn the sheep. To begin training, put the dog back on the ten foot cord. Tell him to "Go-Bye" or "Way to Me" and then immediately order him "Down" before he goes more than a few feet. Praise him and send him in the other direction. Then tell him "Walk on Up" and let him drive the sheep a few yards. When he has practiced this for a short time, send him around the flock and let him bring them back to you. Repeat these partial flanks and short drives until your dog is reliable. A well-trained Border Collie can combine driving with partial flanks to the left and right. Naturally, this takes practice, but eventually your dog will be trained to drive the sheep in any direction you wish. As the dog gains confidence, you will not have to walk along with him, but can trail behind. Eventually, you will be able to stand without moving and let him both drive the sheep away and bring them in to you. The Border Collie and Kelpie are both known for their ability to work livestock at great distances from their handlers. This independence stems from the heading wolf's instinct to work separately from the pack. While most herding breeds are dependent on their masters and like to work at close range, some breeds even work better in pairs or small groups. The Border Collie, however, works best alone, but fully trained individuals can be worked together by an experienced handler, providing each dog understands its own unique commands and whistles.

Turning and cross drives can be taught once the dog understands straight drives and partial flanking. To accomplish a cross-drive have the dog drive the sheep out and then direct him to go part way around the sheep and down. On the command to "walk on up" he should approach the sheep straight on from his new position to the side, causing them to move away from and laterally across the field.

When your dog fully understands the drive and cross-drive, combine these techniques with the outruns, fetches, and wearing in the larger field. Start with short distances and gradually increase the size of the field. Also work your newly-trained dog in different fields so he will learn to work reliably in any location.

Penning and Obstacles

Now that you and your dog have mastered driving, start teaching him to pen and take sheep through obstacles. It is very important to have a dog who quickly obeys all your commands. Timing and placement of the dog are extremely important to success. Livestock do not like to go into tight areas and will try their best to avoid going through gates or into a small pen. Sheep separated from their flock in a trial situation are extremely flighty, and sometimes very aggressive. Their primary instinct and desire is to rejoin their flock because there is safety in numbers. Their secondary instinct is to keep out of tight areas where they could be trapped. (Contrary to some spectator's opinion, it is much easier to work a dog on a large mob.)

To train your dog to pen, use gentle sheep until the dog understands what is expected. Assist him by first opening the gate. After he has brought the sheep up to you, give him his flanking command, which will give the sheep no choice but to enter the pen. At this stage, you may

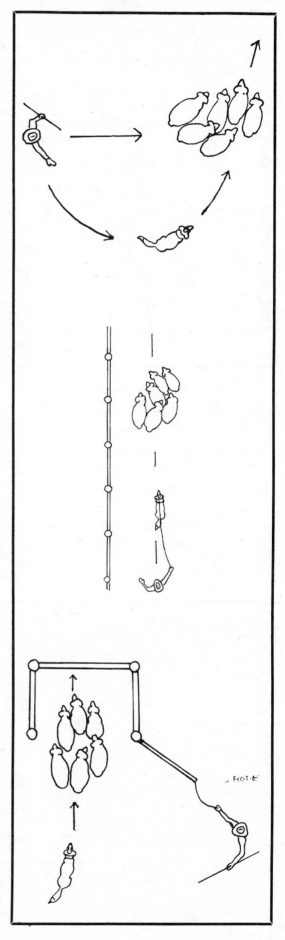

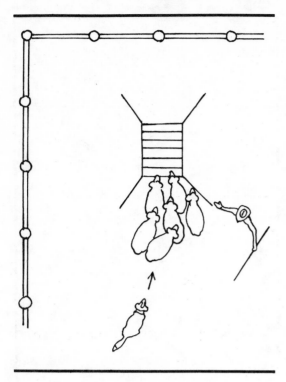

The bridge is manipulated by using flanking commands to position the sheep in such a way that crossing is easier than trying to escape.

help the dog. In sheepdog trial work, however, you are not allowed to help.

Panel and bridge obstacles are manipulated by using flanking commands in the same way as penning. The sheep respond by heading toward the obstacles, just as they do the pen. In a trial, you will not be allowed to leave the handler's post or circle (an area of ten feet) except during penning, but assisting the dog during training is perfectly permissible and necessary at first. To aid the dog, stand by the obstacle on the side the sheep seem most likely to try and break free. Use flanking commands to position the dog to force the sheep through the opening to the obstacle.

Shedding

Shedding is useful for separating animals from the flock or herd for medical treatment or any number of purposes. It is also used in all major sheepdog trials. Before you try shedding, the dog must know "come" and "stand." A dog standing on its feet is able to move more rapidly to keep the separated individuals from dashing back with the rest of the flock.

Position yourself and the sheep next to the fence. Stand with your back next to the fence, the sheep in front of you, and the dog on the opposite side. When the sheep calm down, use your cane to make a gap in the sheep, and tell your dog to "Come" through the gap. When he is between the two groups, have him "Stand," then "Walk on Up" to one group, driving them to the side.

Once they are separated, tell the dog "That Will Do" and praise him. Do not practice too often, since you do not want him cutting sheep out of the flock in his everyday work. Do not call the dog to you unless the gap is big enough for the dog to come through, or he will go around the flock instead. Also, be sure he is near enough to the gap to come through instead of going around. Once the dog understands shedding, you can ask him to cut out one or two sheep. Later, practice in the open away from the fence. In time you will be able to call him in at any point to separate any animals you may need.

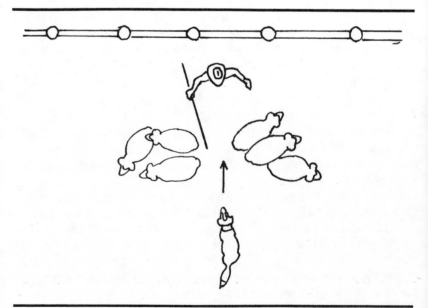

Shedding. Position yourself next to a fence with the dog holding the sheep to you. Make a gap with your cane and call the dog in to you through the gap. If you have ever abused your dog with the cane he will be afraid to come into the gap.

Imported Sadghyl Shadow in Pepperland and his four month old daughter, Imported Pepperland Phanta, blue merle Border Collies owned by Leslie B. Samuels of San Angelo, Texas.

Keeping your dog free of parasites, both internal and external, and vaccinating him regularly is essential. Parasites stunt the growth of both the body and brain by draining nutrients from the dog. Parasites such as roundworms clog the intestines of a young puppy and devour much of the nutrition from the food he eats. The pup may grow up to be small and stunted or may weaken and die. Hookworms suck the blood, producing anemia, weakness, and a toxin that affects the brain. Both roundworms and hookworm larvae can migrate from the mother into her puppies. At one stage of development, the larvae migrate through the lungs and are then coughed up and swallowed. These parasites damage the tissue of the lungs and can ruin a dog's stamina. Luckily, dogs develop a partial immunity to worms as time goes on, but some damage may already have been done.

Distemper, hepatitis, leptospirosis, parvovirus, and rabies are all deadly diseases that puppies must receive vaccinations and intermittent boosters for. Several of these diseases, such as rabies, are contagious to humans as well and could become serious health hazards if all dogs are not vaccinated.

As soon as you buy your puppy, have your veterinarian examine and start the pup on a parasite control and vaccination program. Many people assume the dog is protected for life once the shots are given. This is *not* true. Additional boosters are necessary at *regular intervals*. Today most veterinarians advise using a vaccine for distemper, hepatitis, leptospirosis, parainfluenza, and parvovirus. This vaccine is given initially at about eight weeks, with a second booster at twelve weeks, and a third booster at sixteen weeks. *Annual* boosters are required thereafter. Rabies shots are usually given at four to six months of age, with a booster at one year, and—depending on the brand of the vaccine and the state laws—a booster every one or two years. Regular vaccinations are the best insurance against disease and its ravages.

A healthy dog has a glossy coat, bright eyes, and an alert, happy outlook on life. His normal body temperature is around 101° to 102.2° F. Unless a dog has been running or working, his temperature should not exceed 103° F. If it does, you should check with a veterinarian because a heightened temperature may indicate a problem. Vice versa, a temperature below 100° F. may signal shock or an impending whelping; again, this should be checked by a veterinarian. Lameness points to an injury to legs or feet. A harsh or dull coat, lethargic behavior, lack of appetite and coughing are other signs of poor health.

Aust. Ch. Werlak Beau Jade, owned by Bill and Lynn Harrison of Morphettvale, South Australia.

Border Collies are also prone to several inherited defects, including progressive retinal atrophy, congenital deafness, and hip dysplasia (See Chapter on Genetics.)

INFECTIOUS DISEASES

Distemper

In the past distemper was the number one killer of dogs. It is contracted and spread through the feces, urine, and saliva and most commonly strikes during the winter months with a four- to seven-day incubation period. Because distemper is a virus, antibiotics are ineffective except as an aid to prevent secondary infections.

The virus attacks the central nervous system and even if the dog survives, brain damage may result. During the beginning stage of the disease the dog may seem a bit sleepy or out of sorts. Next, his eyes become watery, a minor cough develops, and he may have a slight temperature and decreased appetite. After another week more severe symptoms set in; the eyes and nose become runny, his temperature rises appreciably and he begins rapid breathing and coughing severely. The dog may lose all interest in food and therefore lose weight. His coat may appear dry and harsh.

After three to six weeks, twitching, "gum-chewing" fits, foaming at the mouth and convulsions appear. These symptoms are due to damage to the central nervous system and may be permanent if the dog survives. Anti-convulsant drugs are available to control these reactions, but there is no real cure.

Occasionally, distemper manifests itself by a hardening of the pads of the feet, followed by coughing, nasal discharge and runny eyes. The severity of the illness varies; about 50% affected show little illness, others mild, and some become severe or fatal.

To avoid the heartbreak and expense of distemper, have your dog vaccinated as a puppy and give regular boosters throughout his life.

Hepatitis

Hepatitis is a disease of the liver which is often fatal to dogs. The symptoms are similar to distemper. They include weight loss, depression, decreased appetite, vomiting, bloody diarrhea, runny eyes and nose, and high temperature.

In the acute form of the disease, the onset is very sudden. The dog's temperature may reach 106° F. Capillaries all over the body may hemorrhage from the lack of clotting agent produced by the liver. The pupils turn grey and the whites of the eyes a yellowish color. Acute cases must be treated under the close supervision of a veterinarian.

Leptospirosis

Leptospirosis is caused by a spirochete organism commonly spread by the urine of rodents such as rats and squirrels, as well as other dogs. In its milder form, leptospirosis affects only the kidneys, while in more severe cases both the kidneys and liver may be involved. The early symptoms are marked stiffness of the hind legs, a hunched up appearance, appetite loss, extreme thirst, vomiting, and diarrhea. Jaundice to the whites of the eyes indicates liver involvement. Antibiotics are successful in treating the infection if it is caught early enough, but permanent kidney failure sometimes results. All farm dogs should be vaccinated, with boosters as often as every six months in some high risk areas.

Parvovirus

Parvovirus is a relatively new disease particularly dangerous to puppies. The first cases were reported in 1978 following the Collie Club of America Specialty Show. This virus is apparently a mutated form of feline distemper and is deadly to dogs. The virus is spread through the feces of infected dogs, and is readily transmitted to the feet and hair of dogs and humans.

The first signs of parvovirus are severe diarrhea and vomiting; the feces are grey or often blood-streaked. A high fever, loss of appetite, and depression may be evident. Most deaths occur from twenty-four to seventy-two hours after the onset of symptoms. Infected young puppies sometimes die quickly without evidence of the usual symptoms. The few pups that do survive may have permanent damage.

Treatment includes replacing lost body fluids and electrolytes and controlling the diarrhea and vomiting.

As a preventive, puppies should be vaccinated at about eight weeks of age, and again at approximately eleven and fourteen weeks, followed by annual boosters. More frequent boosters may be recommended for show or breeding animals.

Parainfluenza

This virus is suspected to be the cause of the "kennel cough," or shipping fever common to show and trial dogs. The name kennel cough originated because once any dog in a kennel develops the disease, all the others soon do—often in a week or less. The virus is airborne and very contagious. It is more annoying than serious, but can effect the performance of a working or show dog. As a preventative, have your dog vaccinated as a pup and also given boosters each year before the start of the show or trial season.

Rabies

Rabies is a virus that attacks the central nervous system and is generally transmitted through the saliva of rabid animals. Airborne infections have been reported in experiments. The animals most commonly responsible for transmitting rabies to dogs and humans are rats, squirrels, skunks, foxes, bats, and rabbits. The average incubation period for the virus is three to six weeks from the time of exposure, but can be several months.

Rabies occurs in two forms, dumb and furious. In dumb rabies, the dog's jaw becomes paralyzed and drops. The dog cannot swallow his saliva, causing him to drool or froth at the mouth and behave as if something is stuck in his throat. However, the infected dog's temperament remains friendly throughout his torture. Eventually, he goes into a coma and dies.

The furious form of rabies is another story. The dog turns into a vicious maniac due to the infection in his brain and instead of barking he will howl like a wolf. Some dogs with this form of rabies even attack and mutilate their own bodies in their frenzy.

Rabies is always fatal. Most states require rabies vaccinations due to the potential public health hazards.

INTERNAL PARASITES

Most dogs have worms at some time in their life, usually as puppies. Worm eggs may be transmitted to the puppies through the dam's

This Border Collie appears to be enjoying himself as he clears the broad jump. To perform at peak ability, a dog must be free of parasites and disease. (P.A.K. photo)

Caora Con's Silver Mist, a black and white "mottled" Border Collie bitch of excellent type owned by Edgar Gould. Note the roan effect of the spotting. (Photo: J.E.L.)

bloodstream even before birth. They can also be transmitted by fleas and other insects, by contaminated food or water, and by contact with dog feces.

There are several different types of worms: roundworms, tapeworms, hookworms, whipworms, and heartworms. Most common are roundworms or hookworms, and puppies must be wormed by the breeder (usually at three and five weeks of age), and later by the new owner. Your veterinarian should examine a stool sample for the microscopic eggs and prescribe the correct medication. Worm eggs may not show up in the first test, so puppies should be checked again two to four weeks after treatment to insure that no worms are present.

Sometimes a dog will appear to be worm-free on one fecal exam and later check positive. The reason is that worms only lay eggs for one part of their life cycle.

Roundworms

Roundworms are the most common worm. Most puppies contract roundworms at some point. Though common, the parasites can cause death or stunt the growth of puppies that are not wormed. Larvae migrate to the muscles, connective tissues, kidneys, and other tissues of the pregnant bitch, and are passed on to the puppies before birth. About a week after the puppies are born the larvae reach the small intestine where they mature. Within three weeks they start producing eggs, which are passed out in the feces, which in turn the bitch eats to keep the nest clean. The eggs then hatch inside the bitch and larvae penetrate the intestinal wall and enter the blood stream where they migrate to the liver, lungs, and other tissues. Those that enter the lungs are coughed up and swallowed and develop into mature adult worms. The eggs of these worms are then passed in feces. Thus the cycle spreads and repeats itself. The migration of the larvae can cause permanent damage to the dog's lungs making him unable to run long distances. Symptoms may include a dull coat, coughing, diarrhea, and a "pot" belly.

Treatment for roundworms should include worming both the bitch and puppies three to four weeks after whelping, with a follow-up two weeks later. Adult dogs should be checked annually and wormed as needed. Piperazine is the drug of choice, and may be obtained at any livestock or pet supply outlet.

Hookworms

Hookworms are small in size (under one inch) but can cause serious damage. They attach themselves to the wall of the dog's intestine, where they suck blood. A dog with hookworms becomes anemic, with pale mucous membranes. If not eradicated, these worms cause stunted growth or death and in adult dogs, fatigue, lack of stamina, a poor coat, and diarrhea. Stools are often bloody or tarry black.

Most infestations are the result of sniffing the larvae from an infected dog's feces. The larvae stick to the dog's nose and are licked off and swallowed. The larvae are also capable of penetrating the skin or the feet. The larvae migrate through the tissues of the dog, eventually reaching the intestines, where they develop into adult worms. In pregnant bitches, the larvae can migrate to the unborn puppies and cause infestations in the puppies. A severe infestation can result in convulsions due to the build-up of toxins produced by the worms. Once infected, many dogs become carriers via cysts in the skin. New outbreaks can occur periodically even though all dogs tested clear in the interim.

Hookworm is a much greater problem in the South where the winters are not cold enough to kill the larvae. Treatment for hookworms requires host-specific medication and should be under a veterinarian's supervision. Telmintic and Dichlorvos are safe and effective if administered carefully per instructions.

Whipworms

The whipworm is common in the Southeast and other warm areas of the United States. They are not common in puppies. The adult worm is about two inches long and inhabits the large intestine. The eggs are passed in the feces, becoming infective in two to four weeks. Once the eggs are ingested, the adult worms will mature in the large intestine in about ten weeks, where they can live for over a year.

Symptoms include a dull coat, loss of weight, diarrhea, and anemia in some cases. See your veterinarian for diagnosis and treatment since whipworm medications can be very harsh and must be given in the proper dosage.

Tapeworms

Of all worms, tapeworms cause the least damage; symptoms include a dull coat and the dog scooting on his rear end. Often rice-like segments (containing eggs) can be found around the dog's anus or in his stools.

Tapeworms are transmitted via fleas, lice, and small rodents such as rabbits and squirrels, which act as intermediate hosts for these worms.

The worms live in the small intestine, where the scolex (head) fastens itself to the intestinal wall. The body of the worm, which may grow to several feet in length, is segmented. These segments, about one quarter inch long, break off and are passed in the feces. To successfully treat the problem, the scolex must be killed. Effective medication is *only available from a veterinarian*.

Heartworms

Heartworms, transmitted by mosquitos, affects thousands of dogs every year. When an infected mosquito bites a dog, it injects a fluid which contains microfilaria, which grow into worms that live in the dog's heart.

Heartworm is a problem nationally, whereas in years past it was primarily a problem in the Southeast. Recently the disease has been reaching almost epidemic proportions, especially in moist, swampy areas where mosquitos breed.

A head study of Robert the Bruce, a typical tri-color male Border Collie. (PAK Photo)

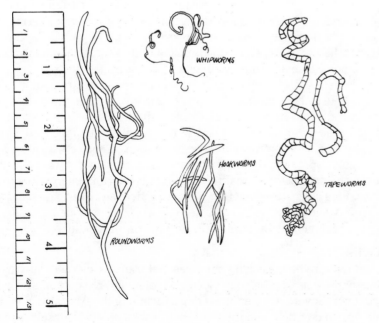

The symptoms of heartworm include shortness of breath, exhaustion, and later, a cough. Death is usually due to a worm breaking loose and causing an embolism. Treatment is dangerous and expensive.

Heartworms grow up to ten inches long and can clog the chamber of the dog's heart causing impairment, and eventually heart failure. If a dog gets heartworms and is not treated, he will die within a year or two after contracting the disease.

The *prevention* of heartworm is relatively inexpensive. First, a blood test is given every spring before the start of mosquito season to ensure that the dog is free of infestations. If healthy, your dog is prescribed daily medication (in either liquid or pill form) to be taken for a month prior to and for the duration of the mosquito season.

Coccidiosis

Coccidiosis is caused by a one-celled protozoan that can be fatal to young puppies, but is not dangerous to adult dogs. The disease is spread by direct contact with an infected dog's feces or by flies. Symptoms include fever, loss of appetite, weakness, persistent watery, bloody diarrhea, runny eyes, and weight loss. Coccidiosis usually lasts about three weeks, but can last much longer in puppies. Prevention inclues strict sanitation and a good, nutritious diet. Treatment must be under the supervision of a veterinarian.

Canine Strongyloids

The canine strongyloid worm (threadworm) is only about an inch long, but despite it's small size can be very serious. Often, this worm can kill an entire litter. Symptoms include bloody diarrhea, decreased appetite, weight loss, shallow and rapid breathing, and runny eyes. Later, pneumonia develops, usually killing the puppy. The symptoms of this ailment are similar to distemper, except that no fever develops. Infected dogs should be handled with care to avoid infecting humans and should be immediately taken to a veterinarian for treatment.

EXTERNAL PARASITES

Fleas

Two species of fleas commonly infest dogs: the brown dog flea and the black cat flea. Infestations predominate during the summer months, yet can occur all year in house dogs. The flea can act as an intermediate host for both tapeworms and heartworms. Many Border Collies are severely allergic to flea bites, and break out into what is commonly called "summer eczema" from the bites of even a single flea!

Female fleas lay eggs on the dog, in rugs, furniture, and crevices in the house. The eggs hatch in two to ten days, and go through several larval and pupal stages until they reach adulthood in about three weeks. The larvae can also lie dormant in the pupal stages for up to a year.

Fleas can be controlled by strict sanitation combined with a program of regular spraying, dipping, or powdering. During the warm months, it is often necessary to treat the dog and his quarters every week to ten days. Flea collars tend *not* to be very effective, and even cause a severe rash in some dogs. Do not use flea collars or insecticide strips if your dog is receiving daily doses of a heartworm preventative.

Ticks

Ticks are bloodsucking parasites that transmit diseases such as canine babesiasis, a protozoan blood infection, and rocky mountain spotted fever. Several species infest dogs, including the American dog tick, the brown dog tick, and the wood tick. Ticks imbed themselves in the skin around the dog's head, neck, chest and shoulders and engorge with blood.

Ticks can be removed by drenching them with rubbing alcohol or turpentine and then pulling them out carefully with tweezers. If the ticks are not doused with alcohol, their head may break off inside the skin and cause an infection. Applying alcohol also helps kill any germs that may have entered the hole where the tick's head was imbeded. Avoid getting alcohol in your dog's ears and eyes.

Prevention is the same as for fleas.

Lice

Two types of lice, the biting louse and the sucking louse, can infest dogs. Neither are very common. Lice are usually found on the head, neck, chest, and shoulders and may cause anemia in advanced cases. If infested with the biting variety, the dog will scratch and lose his hair.

Treatment for lice involves shaving the coat and using delousing powders or dips. Seek the advice of your veterinarian.

Ear Mites

Ear mites are small insects that live in the ear canal and suck blood. They create large amounts of waxy excrement that clog the ear and impede the dog's hearing as well as causing severe itching and discomfort. Symptoms include head-shaking and excessive ear scratching. To get rid of these mites, pour clean mineral oil or an ear mite medication down the dog's ear canal until it is brim-full. Squish this around by massaging the outside of the ear. Repeat this procedure every several days for two weeks. The dog will shake the solution out of his ears, so wear old clothes and administer outside. When the treatment is completed, give the dog a bath.

Mange Mites

There are two types of mange, both caused by tiny mites. The first is called sarcoptic mange, or scabies, and can be contracted by humans. Sarcoptic mange causes extreme itching, thickening, and reddening of the skin around the legs and face accompanied by a foul smell. This infection is diagnosed through a microscopic examination of skin scrapings and can be treated by dipping the dog once a week for three consecutive weeks in a solution active against the mites.

Demodectic mange has a high incidence in puppies. Patches of hair loss typically appear on the dog's face, ears, head, and forelegs, but may also spread over the entire body. It is far less itchy and ugly than sarcoptic mange, but is more difficult to cure. Treatment must be done under veterinary supervision.

COMMON AILMENTS

Diarrhea

Diarrhea may be a symptom of one of the diseases discussed earlier in this chapter. If you suspect one of these problems or if blood is present in the stool, contact your veterinarian immediately. Diarrhea can also result from overeating, change of food or water, or stress. Give your dog one or two tablespoons of *Kaopectate®* three times a day. If he still does not recover, or if the diarrhea is severe, take him to your vet.

Constipation

This can be caused by a lack of vegetable matter or fat in the diet. Give the dog a small amount of milk or cooked greens, fat, or other fi-

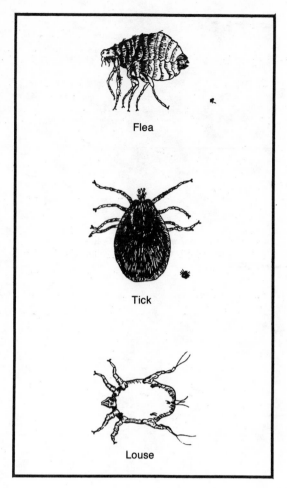

Flea

Tick

Louse

Sadghyl Gael, a red merle Border Collie bitch owned by Mrs. Edward Hart of Scotland. (Photo: Leslie B. Samuels)

brous foods. For a more stubborn case, a tablespoon of mineral oil should soften the dog's stools. When your home remedies fail to work, take your dog to a veterinarian.

Colds and Coughs

A dog with either a cold or cough should be treated the same as his human counterpart—plenty of warmth, rest, and doses of cough medicine. However, a dog exhibiting cold-like symptoms may be suffering from a more serious ailment such as distemper, hepatitis, leptospirosis, heartworms, or roundworms. Therefore, if his cold does not respond quickly to treatment, or the dog appears weak and shows other symptoms, see your veterinarian.

Eczema and Dermatitis

Moist dermatitis appears as a round, damp, pink spot that the dog licks continually. It can be caused by an allergy, infected wound, insect bite, or nervous self-mutilation. To treat, cut away the hair, wash and dry the infected spot and apply an antibiotic ointment. Since moist dermatitis can spread rapidly, you may want to seek professional help.

Dry eczema usually occurs around the tail and back and is characterized by a dry coat, hair loss, and dry, scaly skin. It is frequently caused by a lack of fat in the diet or by a heavy parasitic infestation. Again, consult your veterinarian.

Tumors

Tumors are abnormal growths that can be either benign or malignant. Older dogs frequently develop benign wart-like growths on the muzzle around the eyes or on the body. Whole male dogs are prone to tumors of the testicles and prostate glands while whole bitches are prone to tumors of the mammary glands.

If your dog develops an abnormal growth, consult your veterinarian so he or she can perform a biopsy to determine whether the growth is cancerous. Cancerous tumors are treated with radiation therapy or surgery.

Kidney Problems

Kidney problems are especially common in older dogs. Symptoms include weight loss, increased thirst, vomiting, frequent urination, stiff hindquarters, poor appetite, and lethargy. High protein diets in older dogs are a contributing factor in kidney failure. As previously stated, any dog over the age of six years should have his protein intake decreased by one-third to one-half. Many dog food manufacturers are now producing special low-protein rations for older dogs.

Epilepsy

Epilepsy is a brain disorder which causes periodic seizures or fits. It can be inherited or caused by a brain tumor, encephalitis, wound or blow to the head caused by an accident. Seizures usually can be controlled by the use of anti-convulsant drugs.

Heart Problems

Heart failure can be due to old age, heartworm, or congenital defects. Signs of heart failure are shortness of breath, coughing, irregular heartbeats, and a bluish tongue and gums following exertion. The bluish color signals a lack of oxygen in the blood. Many heart conditions can be controlled by oral medications prescribed by a veterinarian or by surgery. If you suspect your dog is suffering from a heart problem, consult your veterinarian.

Collie Eye Anomaly

A few cases of Collie eye anomaly have been reported in an increasing number of Border Collies. The disease is currently rampant among Collies and occurs in several other breeds as well, but conscientious breeders are trying to stamp out Collie eye anomaly by having their breeding stock pre-examined for signs of the disease.

Collie eye anomaly occurs in varying degrees, from mild symptoms to complete blindness. The concern for this problem arises because dogs affected with a mild defect (which can be observed only by an ophthalmologist) can theoretically produce blind pups. This disease, is inherited as a recessive trait.

Congenital Deafness

Congenital deafness is an inherited defect that commonly strikes predominately white Border Collies. The genes causing deafness are usually associated with doubling on the genes for the merle coat (blue or red) color. The double merle is almost pure white—the lips, nose, eyes, eyelids and pads are almost colorless. There may be a patch of merle color on the body. Some dogs are born without eyes. This type of white is not the same as the white caused by the white factor gene in blacks, reds, and tricolors.

Deaf dogs should never be bred but can be trained to respond to hand signals.

Progressive Retinal Atrophy

Two types of Progressive Retinal Atrophy strike the Border Collie: Progressive Retinal Atrophy (PRA), and Central Progressive Retinal Atrophy (CPRA). Both are inherited diseases and dogs with either PRA or CPRA should not be bred. Symptoms are similar for both but the mode of inheritance is different. CPRA is most common in Border Collies today. The disease unfortunately does not usually show up until the dog is around two years old. The first symptom is night blindness. This condition progresses for around eight years when the dog generally becomes totally blind. Dogs used for breeding should be checked by a certified veterinary opthamologist after they are two years old. This examination requires a veterinarian who has special training and equipment.

Hip Dysplasia

Hip Dysplasia is the most common cause of lameness in adult dogs weighing thirty or more pounds, and is becoming a problem among Border Collies in the United States. A recessive, polygenetic disease, it occurs more widely in some bloodlines than in others, and could severely hinder the working ability of our breed if breeders do not become aware of and test for the disability.

Hip dysplasia is the malformation of either, or both, the ball-shaped head of the femur (thigh bone) or the acetabulum (socket or cup). When the socket is not deep enough or is improperly formed, or when the ball does not fit into the socket as it should, the head of the femur will slip, causing pressure, pain, and/or restricted rear movement.

Some dogs with X-ray evidence of severe dysplasia go through life with no signs of lameness unless severely stressed by long periods of running and jumping. Others exhibit symptoms of lameness, a bunny-hopping run, swaying gait, or difficulty in getting up as early as eight months of age. Dogs with a broad pelvis, well-cupped acetabulum, tight ligaments and good muscle mass to size of bone ratio are less likely to develop the disease. Environmental factors also can cause or exacerbate the disease. These include "overnutrition" which results in

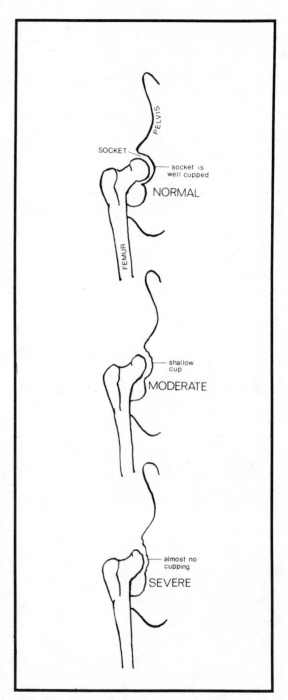

Hip Dysplasia is caused by a malformation of either, or both, the ball-shaped head of the femur (thigh bone) or the acetabulum (socket or cup). It is the most common cause of lameness in adult dog's weighing thirty or more pounds.

accelerated growth rates, lack of exercise, accidents or jumping before bone growth is complete.

Breeding stock and/or the parents of breeding animals should be X-rayed to determine if they are clear of the disease.

An organization called the Orthopedic Foundation for Animals (OFA) was established to certify dogs of any breed for freedom from hip dysplasia. To qualify, the dog must be two years of age or older. X-rays taken according to OFA specification are mailed by your veterinarian to the OFA, University of Missouri, Columbia, MO 65201. Here a panel of experts will examine the X-rays and assign a certification number to all unaffected animals. Hips are rated on a scale of one to seven. (For more information, write directely to OFA.)

Breeding only certified dogs will greatly reduce the odds of producing affected puppies; however it is possible for normal, certified parents to produce affected offspring due to the polygenetic nature of inheritance and the effect of environmental conditions.

Osteochondritis Desicans (OCD)

Osteochondritis Desicans (OCD) is becoming widespread in the Border Collie today. It is a degenerative disease of the joints which causes lameness. It usually occurs between six and twelve months of age when the pup's growth is most rapid. Males are more susceptible than females due to their faster growth rate. Although large and medium breeds tend to be most commonly affected, it also is common in several small breeds. The shoulder joint is most commonly affected, but it has also been observed in the elbow, stifle, and hock.

The exact cause is unknown, but it is often associated with "over-nutrition" which promotes accelerated growth rates, and jumping or strenuous exercise while the bones are still growing. Since the disease tends to run in families, a genetic basis for the disease is likely, and affected dogs should not be bred. Treatment consists of rest and restricted exercise, and is successful in milder cases. More severe cases require surgical removal of cartilaginous flaps or joint mice, or both. Surgery done before arthritic changes occur is usually successful.

A tri-color (black, white, and tan) Border Collie, Caora Con's Robert the Bruce, owned by Caora Con Kennels. (Photo: Janet E. Larson)

First Aid 10

VITAL SIGNS

To determine (and treat an illness) accurately, a dog's vital signs must be taken. First, find out if the dog is breathing by holding a thread or mirror in front of his nose. The slightest amount of air will move the thread or fog the mirror. His normal respiration rate should be about 12 to 14 breaths per minute.

You can feel a dog's pulse rate by placing your fingers on the inside of his thigh and pressing lightly. If this fails, check his heartbeat by placing your fingers on the left side of the rib cage. A normal pulse rate is 80 to 100 beats per minute.

To check a dog's temperature, rub vaseline on the bulb of a rectal thermometer and gently insert it about two inches into the dog's rectum. Keep the thermometer in for about two minutes. The normal temperature is 101.0^0 F to 102.5^0 F. A temperature below 100^0 F can indicate shock, while a temperature over 103^0 F signifies a fever.

A dog's tongue and mucus membranes are normally a healthy pink color. If they are white or very pale, it may indicate blood loss or internal injury. A bluish tongue and gums characterizes oxygen deprivation and heart failure and dark red, inflamed gums point to an internal infection, such as peritonitis.

The pupils of a dog's eyes should be checked with a flashlight to see if they are equal in size and reactive to light. They should constrict to small points when the light is shined into them. Dilated pupils that do not react to light can mean the dog has brain damage or a convulsion.

EMERGENCIES

Following are the signs and symptoms of the most critical emergencies. When these symptoms are present the dog should be rushed to a veterinarian immediately.

Shock is a serious emergency which is found in cases of severe trauma resulting from poor blood circulation. The symptoms of shock are fast and shallow breathing, rapid pulse, lowered body temperature, weakness and confusion. If not treated quickly it is irreversible and often fatal. Maintaining body heat is critical, as is the treatment of whatever is causing the shock (i.e., blood loss, infection, burn, fracture). Keep the dog quiet and reassure him constantly.

Respiratory failure can be caused by drowning, electric shock, and choking. Artificial respiration can be given by placing your hands on each side of the chest and pressing down with your upper hand and then releasing, so that air is expelled and inhaled. Mouth-to-mouth resuscitation can be given by holding the dog's mouth shut and placing

Pendulum's Image greets the receptionist at the veterinary hospital. Your dog should be on good terms with the veterinarian and staff.

your mouth over his nose after taking a deep breath. Exhale into the dog's nose, and repeat until the dog is breathing on his own.

Drowning　Before you start artificial respiration, press gently on the dog's stomach to expel the swallowed water. Then immediately administer artificial respiration as described above, and try to keep the dog from swallowing water or vomiting.

Electric Shock　Do *not* touch the dog until you disconnect the electrical source. Then administer artificial respiration if necessary, and treat for shock.

Airway Obstruction　If a foreign body is lodged in the air passages, try removing it with your fingers. A modified Heimlich maneuver may also be used by placing your fists under the rib case and jerking upward three times. If this is not successful, commence with artificial respiration on the way to the veterinarian.

Bleeding　A tourniquet should be used only as a last resort. Instead, use a pressure bandage made of folded cloth with gauze padding facing the wound. Direct the pressure with your hand and press as hard as possible, or wrap and tie the bandage in place. If the bandage is to be left on for any length of time, wrap the entire limb, including the toes, to prevent edema (excessive swelling).

Cardiac Arrest　Place the dog on his side, and start pressing down on the chest behind the shoulders every few seconds. Administer mouth to muzzle resuscitation. Due to the shape of the dog's chest, heart massage, as given to humans, is impossible.

Snake Bite or Insect Sting Anaphylaxis　Keep the dog very quiet and apply cold packs to the bite or sting site. Next, apply a one-inch wide constriction band between the bite and the dog's heart. If you have antihistamine pills or an adrenalin syringe on hand, administer the medication using a child's dosage.

Poison　Poisons can be inhaled, swallowed, injected, or transmitted through the skin. First, determine and quickly remove the poisoning source. Second, if the poison is ingested, find out if it is corrosive (i.e., acid, strong lye, gasoline) or non-corrosive (i.e., plants, drugs, foods). Non-corrosive poisons may be ejected by induced vomiting. A solution of one part hydrogen peroxide to ten parts water or the same solution of soap (*not* detergent) to water will impel vomiting. *Do not induce vomiting, however, if the dog has swallowed a corrosive poison* because ejection of the caustic solution will burn the esophagus and larynx. Instead, dilute the toxin and contact your veterinarian immediately.

If a veterinarian is unavailable the following table lists first-aid home remedies:

Poison	Emergency Treatments
Acids and Alkalis, - (Corrosives and Organic Solvents), Gasoline, etc.	Dilute with water but do not induce vomiting
Arsenic	Epsom salts
Cooking chocolate	Phenobarbital
DDT	Hydrogen peroxide and water
Food poisoning	Hydrogen peroxide and water
Laurel leaves	Dextrose or corn syrup
Lead	Epsom salts
Mercury	Eggs and milk
Thallium (insect poison)	Table salt in water
Strychnine	Sedatives, Phenobarbital, Nembutal

Always take the dog to a veterinarian as soon as possible in cases of chemical poisoning, and take the article containing the toxin.

Heat Stroke   Never leave your dog in a parked automobile. The temperature can go over one hundred degrees in a relatively short time, even with the windows open. Thousands of dogs are literally "baked" each year. Also, at home, always allow your dog access to a shady area and a dish of fresh water. If, in spite of these precautions, your dog does develop heat stroke, immediate action can save his life. Quickly immerse the stricken dog up to his neck in very cold water. If a tub isn't available, hose or dump cold water over him. High temperatures can cause brain damage, so lowering the dog's temperature quickly is critical.

Eye Injuries   If your dog has a foreign body in his eye, flush it out with lukewarm water and apply ophthalmic ointment containing an antibiotic. When the dog's eye has been scratched or injured more severely, take him to the veterinarian.

Broken Bones   For a broken leg, fashion a splint to keep the limb immobile. If you suspect the ribs, pelvis, or back is broken, keep the dog from moving until a veterinarian can arrive. If this is not possible, slide a stiff board under the dog without jarring him and then carefully transport him to the veterinarian.

Burns   Pour cool water over the burn; do not use greasy ointments. Cover with a sterile gauze pad. Unless the burn is minor, consult your veterinarian.

Bites and Cuts   Minor bites and cuts can be disinfected with hydrogen peroxide and treated with an antibiotic salve.

Porcupine Quills   Tie the dog or hold him down while you pull out the quills with pliers. If any of the quills are too deeply imbedded, call your veterinarian.

Insect stings   If your dog is stung, try to find the stinger and remove it with tweezers. Apply a bicarbonate of soda paste and watch the dog carefully for possible reaction; insect sting anaphylaxis (see section above under emergencies).

Bloat   Bloat is caused by excess stomach gas. In severe cases, gastric torsion (twisting of the stomach) can result, cutting off the blood supply to the stomach tissues. Unless prompt surgery is performed, this is usually fatal.

To relieve gastritis, give your dog anti-flatulent (gas) medication or a shot of whiskey to break up the pressure. Dogs prone to gas and bloat should be fed a low cereal diet, since gas is aggravated by grain fermentation in the stomach. They should also be fed smaller quantities three times a day instead of one large meal, and should be watered *before* they eat, not after.

Convulsions   Convulsions or "fits" may indicate the dog has a serious problem such as distemper, hookworms, poisoning, dietary deficiency, or epilepsy. The cause of the convulsions must be diagnosed by a veterinarian to be treated properly.

Vomiting   Vomiting is a symptom of many illnesses. It can be the sign of a disease such as distemper, worms, intestinal blockage, or simply eating grass. Bitches will also vomit solid food for their puppies to eat. If vomiting persists, consult your veterinarian.

High Temperature from Fever   For a temperature above 106⁰ F. immerse the dog in cold water with his head above the water level. Consult your veterinarian immediately.

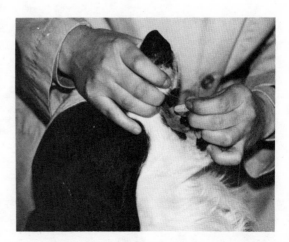

To give your dog a pill, have him sit on leash. Press his lips against his teeth to force his jaws open, then pop the pill onto the back of his tongue. Shut his mouth and stroke him under the chin to make him swallow. (Photo by Stephen Johnson)

ADMINISTERING MEDICATION

Though getting a dog to accept medication takes some "persuasion" by the owner, it need not be difficult. With a few simple steps, and plenty of patience and praise, administering medication should be easy.

When giving your dog a pill, have him leashed and sitting. Press his lips against his teeth to force the jaws open. (Your fingers are safe since he will not risk biting his own lips.) Next, place the pill at the back of his tongue near the throat and quickly clasp his mouth shut. To relax the dog's muscles and ease swallowing, gently stroke under his chin. Afterward, commend and praise your dog for a supreme performance.

To give liquid medicine, again make the dog sit. Tilt his head back to a 45 degree angle and pull his lower lip out to form a pocket. Pour the liquid into the pocket using a spoon, eye dropper, or small vial. Stroke under his chin to encourage swallowing.

Powdered medicine should be mixed with water and given as a liquid. If powdered medicine is given dry, the dog will choke on it.

Giving medicine in the dog's food rarely works. Dogs have super-sensitive noses, and they thus avoid the medicine by either picking around the area that contains it or not eating the food at all.

Why do puppies have to grow up? These two eight week old Border Collie babies are owned by Susan Laymance of Wenatchee, Washington.

Breeding Better Border Collies 11

Having owned and enjoyed a Border Collie, you may think that the next logical step is to breed him or her. Just sixty-three days after breeding your female you will have six to ten cute puppies, plus extra money when you sell them.

True, having a litter of puppies around can be a wonderful experience, but the glamour may quickly diminish. First, raising puppies can be a tiring, demanding job as they require plenty of time and attention, not to mention feed, veterinary bills, and advertising expense. Second, the fact that both parents are registered Border Collies does not insure that the pups will have the quality you want, or that they will be born with herding instinct. And finally, to get the same prices for your pups as do established breeders, you must first build up a reputation by exhibiting successfully in trials and shows. You also need satisfied customers to pass on the good word.

In addition, a breeder in the true sense of the word feels a responsibility and a need to preserve the traits and qualities that make the Border Collie unique, and to try to improve upon his or her dogs with each succeeding generation. In other words, breeding purebred dogs is not as simple as it may appear, and should not be entered into lightly or without dedication to the breed. There are millions of unwanted puppies being put to death in the pounds and humane societies of this country. A Border Collie without herding instinct or other important characteristics of the breed is a prime prospect to become one of these misfits.

Do breeders become rich selling puppies? Well, unless your bitch is a top working or show dog, no one will pay top price for your puppies. First, you must consider the stud fee for a good male. The stud fee is usually the same as the current price for a top quality puppy. Afterward, the cost of worming all the puppies at three and six weeks of age and the price of temporary shots take another chunk of your profits. Then you must advertise. A classified advertisement in a national dog publication will cost a fair amount. Local newspapers are also an excellent source, which in turn increases your outlay even more. All total, the breeder spends an amount equal to the price of three or four puppies just on their care and advertising. Since he is advertising them as "registered," he must spend more money to register the litter. Incidently, it is against most Registries' rules to charge extra for the registration of purebred dogs. If you do, the buyer can turn you in to the registry, and the registry will suspend your future registration privileges.

In addition to this, you must consider the cost of caring for your female even before her pups are born. A kennel run may cost several

Sadghyl Kizzy of Pepperland (left) owned by Leslie B. Samuels, and Mister Chips (right) owned by Mr. and Mrs. David Roy. (Photo: Leslie B. Samuels)

"Munro," owned by Susan Laymance.

hundred dollars. Over 400 hours of training is needed for your dog to obtain her working certificate. A professional trainer, if needed, may cost several hundred dollars. After she is trained, entering her in sheep-dog or obedience trials or dog shows will cost another several hundred dollars. All total, breeders often barely break even in the dog business! Then you must consider those puppies that don't sell. Perhaps they are mismarked or have shy personalities. Disease or injury may claim others. Do you have the courage to put down defective puppies if homes cannot be found?

If you do have the dedication, time, and money to become a breeder, start by learning all you can about the breed. Be able to recognize faults. Learn all you can about inheritance. Recognize the strengths and weaknesses of good Border Collies of the past and of current bloodlines and types. In essence, be able to know a quality dog or bitch when you see one.

An understanding of genetics is also important, and we will try to explain some of the basics and how they affect your breeding program.

GENES AND CHROMOSOMES

All living things contain cells, and all cells have a nucleus containing chromosomes. A dog has 39 pairs of chromosomes. Both the egg and the sperm from the female and male are cells with only 39 single chromosomes. Subsequently, when the egg and sperm unite, there are again 39 *pairs* of chromosomes, and new life begins. The reason the sex cells (egg and sperm) only contain 39 *single* chromosomes is that the cell that produces them undergoes meiosis. During meiosis, the pairs split apart, and one chromosome from each pair randomly goes to the opposite side of the cell. The cell then divides, and the chromosome in each new cell replicates. This process is repeated again until four new cells are formed which only have 39 individual chromosomes. Since the process is random, there will never be two sex cells with exactly the same genes. This explains why hidden recessive faults crop up, and how desired traits are brought out and purified through selective breeding.

Each chromosome is made up of hundreds of genes at certain positions that determine specific traits. When the chromosomes pair off, they impulsively pair up with another chromosome containing genes for the same traits. Pairs of genes containing identical traits are called *alleles*. If the genes are identical; for example, both possess the same color trait,

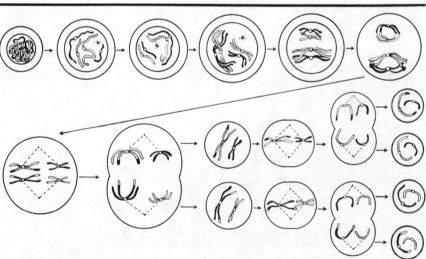

A simplified diagram of meiosis, sex cell production, using two marked pairs of chromosomes. The final result is four sex cells (egg or sperms) with a randomly selected chromosome from each of the original chromosome pairs.

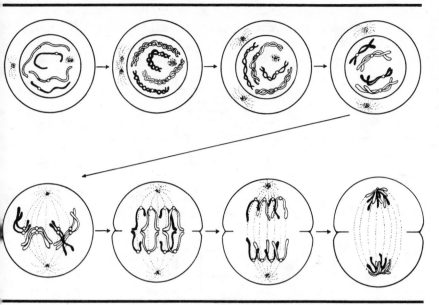

Mitosis is the process whereby cells reproduce themselves identically. This process is different from sex cell production.

they are said to be homozygous. However, if one gene is for black and white color and the other for red and white, the pair is said to be *heterozygous*, meaning different. This can occur because genes are either *dominant* or *recessive*. The dominant gene is always expressed, even when a heterozygous recessive gene is present. Recessive genes are only expressed when homozygous recessive genes are present for that trait.

A dog's genotype is his total genetic makeup containing both dominant and recessive genes. Alternately, phenotype refers to the dog's appearance, or those genes that are expressed (seen visually). Determination of a dog's genotype can only be guessed at by studying his pedigree and offspring. The presence of certain traits can sometimes be established by test breeding (i.e., known carriers of a defect to a dog suspected to be a carrier).

A dominant gene will hide or mask the recessive gene for the same trait. For instance, if a dog has both the dominant gene for black coat and the recessive gene for red coat color, the dog will be black. Some traits are determined by a single gene pair (simple dominant-recessive) while others are determined by a series of gene pairs (polygenic). Polygenic traits are very difficult to predict since thousands, even millions, of gene combinations are possible.

Coat length is an example of simple dominant-recessive inheritance. Rough or long coat, although more popular in Border Collies, is recessive to the smooth or short coat. To produce rough-coated offspring both parents must carry homozygous genes for rough coat and be rough-coated themselves. Two smooth-coated dogs that carry the recessive for rough coat will produce rough-coated puppies about one-fourth of the time. A smooth-coated dog with no recessive genes for rough coat mated with a rough-coated dog will produce only smooth-coated offspring, but all the offspring will carry the rough-coated gene.

This explains why many smooth-coated breeds such as the Australian Cattle Dog and the Kelpie that have Border Collie ancestry sometimes produce rough-coated offspring.

In charting genetic characteristics, letters are often used to indicate the gene for a particular trait, such as "S" for smooth coat. Since this gene is dominant, the letter is capitalized. The recessive rough coat would be represented by "r." Thus, the homozygous smooth coated dog would be "SS;" the homozygous rough-coated dog "rr;" and the heterozygous smooth-coated dog carrying a recessive for rough coat would

Jim, a son of "Old Hemp."

Tullaview Masterpiece, an eight month old dog owned by John and Joyce Sullivan of Australia.

be "Sr." The various combinations possible in the offspring of a particular mating where the genotype is known can thus be charted as follows:

	S	r
S	SS	Sr
S	SS	Sr

As you can see, all the offspring would have smooth coats, but half of them would carry the recessive for rough coats.

Let's take another example, this time breeding two smooth-coated dogs that each carry the recessive for rough coat:

	S	r
S	SS	Sr
r	Sr	rr

In this instance, one-fourth of the pups will be homozygous smooth coats; one-half of them would be heterozygous smooth coats; and one-fourth would be rough-coated.

Inheritance becomes much more complex when dealing with polygenic traits. Since these traits are governed by several interacting pairs of genes, the possible combinations and variations may be in the millions. For example, assume that there are four pairs of genes that determine hip dysplasia, a polygenic recessive trait. In this case, capital letters will represent the genes for normal hips, while small letters will represent the genes for malformed, defective hips.

When a normal-hipped dog, homozygous for normal hips (AABBCCDD) is mated to a dog with severe dysplasia (aabbccdd) the resulting litter will consist of apparently normal-hipped dogs each of whom carry the recessive genes for dysplasia (AaBbCcDd). When two of these carriers are later bred together, you will get offspring varying from crippled to normal and all degrees in between. Some of the possible combinations are:

AABBCCDD
AaBBCCDd
AaBbCcDd
AabbCcDd
AabbCcdd
Aabbccdd
aabbccdd

There are many other combinations possible and this determines the severity of the deformity, from mild to severe.

One of the difficulties in breeding dogs is that many traits are polygenic. Additionally, dominant traits may be expressed in varying degrees, known as *incomplete dominance*.

Test breedings and careful records kept over many generations can help determine how particular traits are inherited and whether they are dominant or recessive. Because of the variety of factors involved and the possibility for mutations, deviation from this pattern may occur. To the best of my knowledge and the experience of other breeders, the inheritance of the following traits have been documented in the Border Collie.

Robert the Bruce (tri-color) and Black Bison (right) are linebred to Gilchrist Spot #24981. Their sire, Jason-UD is a double grandson of Spot. Bhan-Tara-C.D.X., their dam, is a granddaughter and great-granddaughter of Spot. Line breeding causes uniformity in both mental and physical traits. Close breeding can also bring out hidden genetic defects, so must be done with care. (Stephen Johnson photo)

Chart of Dominant and Recessive Characteristics in the Border Collie.

A blue merle Border Collie, Imported Sadghyl Shadow in Pepperland, owned by Leslie B. Samuels. The merle color is due to a dilution gene that causes faded patches in black or red coated dogs.

TRAIT	DOMINANT	RECESSIVE	NOTES
HERDING ABILITY	Strong eye	Lack of eye	Polygenic, complex trait. Variable degrees of "eye" occur. The more homozygous recessive gene pairs present, the weaker the eye.
	Gathering instinct	Lack of instinct	Polygenic. Same as above.
	Shyness	Good temperament	Polygenic. Also influenced by environment.
COLOR AND MARKINGS	Black & white	Red & white	Merling due to dilution gene. Tan markings by an interacting gene for this pattern.
	Solid color	White markings	
	Mottled or roan in white markings	Unspotted markings	
	Black nose pigment	Brown pigment	Pink spots and butterfly noses are linked to excessive white on body and solid white markings.
	Dark brown eye	Light eyes	Yellow eyes linked to red coat. Blue eyes recessive, polygenic. Also linked to merling factor.
COAT	Smooth coat	Rough coat	
	Wavy coat	Straight coat	
	Coarse, hard texture	Soft, silky texture	
EYES	Round	Almond	
	Large	Small	
EARS	Drop	Prick	Polygenic trait.
	Large	Small	
SIZE	Large	Small	Polygenic trait creates wide variety of sizes. Also affected by environment.
TAIL	Low carriage	Gay tail	
HEAD	Wide skull	Narrow skull	
	Short, blunt muzzle	Long, lean muzzle	
LEGS	Correct	Cowhocks and crooked fronts	Polygenic. Many bones and muscles involved.

Caora Con's Black Bison, CDX, SchH3, WC showing "the eye of control" while working sheep. Working ability is very important when selecting breeding stock.

PRACTICAL APPLICATIONS OF GENETICS

Once we understand how the genes work and how characteristics are inherited, we can begin to put our knowledge to work in planned breedings. We can use this knowledge to understand where a trait comes from, to determine the percentage ratio we have of obtaining a particular trait in a mating where the genotype of the parents is known, and we can use it to plan breedings by either concentrating or diversifying the gene pool through our selection.

Inbreeding

By inbreeding, both good and bad traits are intensified. If the animals chosen possess highly desirable traits, inbreeding will strengthen and preserve these traits. Unfortunately, many dogs that appear to be almost perfect carry recessive genes that are undesirable, even lethal when concentrated. Genes for most hereditary defects are recessive and often polygenic. Concentrating the gene pool creates a higher risk that such defects will occur. Nonetheless, inbreeding can be very useful in developing a strain of good quality dogs.

Inbreeding may also decrease the size, fertility, and vigor of the dogs and increase the number of still births and deformed puppies. Consequently, unless you have truly outstanding dogs to use, don't try an inbreeding program.

Linebreeding

Linebreeding is a compromise on inbreeding. It is the mating of two related dogs within a certain family line who share a common ancestor such as a grandsire or granddam. Linebreeding is the safest way to preserve the genes of a great dog because, unlike inbreeding, a large quantity of unrelated outside genes are present to dilute undesirable and hidden recessive traits. For example, if a great dog possesses potentially harmful genes he should either not be linebred at all, or only with dogs who are strong on his weakest trait. It is also possible to linebreed to more than one individual to produce a superior combination of genes from the two types.

Outcrossing

Outcrossing is the mating of two dogs who are free of any common ancestors in the first five or six generations. Since all Border Collies trace back to a single sire, Old Hemp, it is impossible to outcross in the true sense of the word. Outcrossing (within the breed) results in greater heterozygosity and greater vigor in the descendants.

New Zealand Ch. Thunder boy of Clan-Abby, owned by Peter and Judy Vos. An excellent type, top winning, black and white Border Collie. (Photo: Starlite Studios, New Zealand)

THE BREEDING PROGRAM

To be successful, all breeding programs must have goals. Below are guidelines to follow to create a strain of Border Collies with distinctive characteristics.

1. Decide what mental and physical characteristics are absolutely essential, and which traits are intolerable. Traits to look for should include working ability, temperament, athletic ability, size, color, coat, fertility, and general vigor.

2. Score individuals based on your selected virtues and faults, and have a cut-off total score for all breeding stock retained. Cull unsuitable stock rigorously. As one trait becomes fixed start plac-

ing more emphasis on other traits that were previously less important until you reach your final aim.

3. Linebreed or inbreed to individuals who have proven through performance and progeny tests that they will improve your strain.

4. Outcross if necessary to bring in desired characteristics missing from your strain, but be careful in your selection of individuals, and continue to cull rigorously.

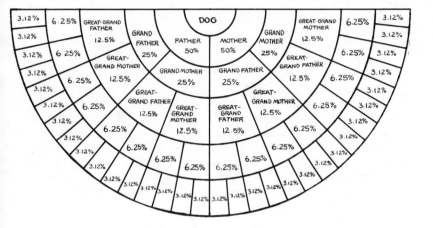

The influence of various ancestors on your dog depends on the frequency each ancestor appears in the pedigree and how many generations back they appear.

The modern Border Collie has reached its present superiority as a herding dog in the last 150 years as a result of selective breeding for sheepdog trial performance. James Ried, founder of the International Sheepdog Society, designed the International Trials course and Qualifying Trials courses to test every aspect of a sheepdog's work on the vast moor and mountain farms of Scotland, Northern England, and Wales. A farm dog had to be able to gather hundreds of wild sheep, often out of sight and hearing of his master, drive them to market, separate animals for veterinary care, pen and drive through gates or over bridges. During the qualifying trials, small numbers of sheep are used because they are more difficult to control and panicky away from the safety of the flock. The Driving Championships at the National and International level use flocks of 50 (or more.) sheep. Any dog capable of completing all the tasks in the allotted time had to be an outstanding dog, in intelligence, herding ability, speed and stamina. These trials have not only improved the working Collie, but the level of sheep husbandry around the world. Selective breeding, using the Trial Field as the testing ground for performance, has made the Border Collie the most used sheepdog in the world today.

The heritability of the group of instincts known as "herding ability" is broken up into gathering ability, balance, eye, barking, gripping, speed, stamina, courage and trainability. Rapid progress has been made by concentrating on these traits. If other traits such as ear shape, eye and coat color, and body size had been selected for at the same time, rapid progress would not have been made in the more important traits of herding ability. This is one of the scientific reasons that working dog breeders do not want the Border Collie to become a show dog.

Arthur Allen's famous Imported Rock, the first North American Supreme Champion. Six years undefeated Champion at all Official Trials sponsored by the North American Sheepdog Society in the United States and Canada. (Photo from "Border Collies in America" by Arthur N. Allen.)

O.T.Ch. HobNob's Optimistic, a red and white Border Collie owned by Janice DeMello (P.A.K. Photo).

GENETIC DEFECTS IN BORDER COLLIES

In recent years there has been an alarming increase in genetic defects in the Border Collie. This increase is most likely due to inbreeding and linebreeding to certain popular sires. The extensive use of these dogs has made it virtually impossible to find a line that is free of defects. According to veterinarians, the only way to eliminate hip dysplasia and eye defects in the breed is to check every animal used for breeding.

John Herries McCulloch, author of two important books, *SHEEP-DOGS AND THEIR MASTERS* and *BORDER COLLIE STUDIES,* made a remarkable prophecy during the early days of the breed. In 1938 he wrote the following statement about concentration of blood in the Border Collie:

"When quality has been confined to a large family, as it has been in the case of the modern Border Collie, the tendency is to keep on concentrating the desired blood. This is particularly so when conformation and performance are rated by important annual trial competitions. The man who owns a clever bitch is generally anxious to put her to a notable trial performer. The immediate results may be very good...In the long run however, weaknesses are sure to develop as a result of the increasing purity of blood and the gradual shift toward linebreeding and inbreeding...Fresh infusions of vigor, bone and intelligence are usually achieved by judicious out-crossing, and the truly great breeder will always know when to seek the strength of an outcross."

Some of the genetic defects appearing include:

Central Progressive Retinal Atrophy (C.P.R.A.) - Causes retinal degeneration and defective vision, even blindness. This disease is due to a dominant gene, with incomplete penetrance. It is a major problem in Border Collies today.

Lens Luxation - A malposition of the lens of the eye. Mode of inheritance is currently unknown. Research is being done. This problem affects a fair number of Border Collies.

Collie Eye Anomally (C.E.A.) - A recessive trait which includes retinal abnormalities, retinal detachment and intra-ocular bleeding. Cases have been found in Border Collies but it is more prevalent in other breeds.

Progressive Retinal Atrophy (PRA) - A recessive trait which causes retinal cell atrophy and reduction of blood vessel size in the eye. Common among hunting dog breeds but an increasing number of cases are showing up in Border Collies.

Hip Dysplasia (H.D.) - A developmental deformity of the hip joint. Causes lameness and premature arthritis in the hind legs. A recessive, polygenetic disease. An alarming number of cases are being found in the Border Collie.

Congenital Deafness - A recessive sex-linked trait usually found in double bred merles and predominatly white Border Collies. Found in a number of other breeds.

Epilepsy - A brain disorder which causes seizures and fits. Can be inherited or caused by encephalitis, brain tumors or a blow to the head. The exact mode of inheritance is unknown. Research is currently underway. Affects a number of breeds.

The Brood Bitch
And Stud Dog 12

The author with Caora Con Bhan-Righ, a black and white mottled female, bred by Arthur N. Allen of McLeansboro, Illinois. (Photo: Col. W. A. Johnston.)

SELECTION OF THE BROOD BITCH

The novice should try to start his new breeding program with a good quality linebred bitch. This leaves less chance for an error to occur in the selection of a mate since the linebred bitch is more likely to stamp her offspring with her positive traits. Before purchasing your bitch, visit several kennels and talk to breeders. Watch the bitch or her parents working livestock, and have her conformation and working style evaluated by an outside authority. She should also have a complete physical and reproductive tract examination and be tested for canine brucellosis, a disease that causes abortions and whelping disorders.

If you are purchasing a bitch puppy, make sure the parents are quality working dogs—preferably with working certificates, good conformation, and well-adjusted, stable temperaments. If you dislike the parents, chances are these same characteristics may be passed on to the puppy.

When the pup is fully grown and before breeding, have the following tests and steps taken:

1. X-ray for hip dysplasia and obtain an O.F.A. number.

2. Have an eye examination done by a board certified Veterinary Ophthalmologist to determine any hereditary eye defects.

3. Blood test for canine brucellosis (canine infectious abortion).

4. Evaluate for working ability and conformation.

5. Seek advice on the selection of a compatible stud that will offset your bitch's faults, both in working ability and conformation.

Once you have decided to breed your bitch and have selected a stud, start getting her into top condition. She should be free of internal and external parasites and in medium weight. Her muscular condition should be brought to optimum by regular exercise or work. Many people incorrectly assume a bitch should be fat before mating and kept heavy throughout pregnancy. This is not advisable. An overweight bitch will not conceive as readily and may have difficulty giving birth.

Booster vaccinations for rabies, parvovirus, distemper and other contagious diseases should be given *before* the bitch comes in season, and definitely before she is bred. A high level of immunity in the bitch insures that the puppies will get a high level of antibodies in the colostrum (first milk) to protect them until they can be vaccinated. However, most veterinarians do not recommend giving booster vaccinations to a pregnant bitch due to increased risk of abortion.

THE BITCH'S HEAT

Most bitches come into heat every six to ten months at regular intervals during any time of year, not just in spring as many people believe. The first heat occurs between six and twenty-four months of age. The first sign of the bitch's heat may be when males start following her, clicking their jaws and sniffing at her urine. She will also start to lick herself and urinate more frequently. If you think she is coming into heat, examine her vulva (reproductive and urinary opening) to see if it looks puffed up and swollen. When her heat starts, she will bleed for about eleven days (although some bitches don't bleed) after which the discharge tapers off or turns to a straw color. The average time to mate your bitch is between the ninth and fourteenth day after bleeding began.

Since Border Collies are naturally clean, you may never know your female is in heat unless you are very observant. This may also cause you to miscalculate the actual day her heat started.

If you are unsure of when your bitch came into heat, watch to see if she will stand and arch her tail to one side when you scratch her back near her tail. This means she is ready to be mated. Another method is to have a veterinarian do vaginal smears to determine the time of ovulation. Changes in the epithelial cells shed from the lining of the vagina show changes that coincide with hormonal changes during the heat cycle. By reading the smears every two days from about the sixth day of heat, the veterinarian can pinpoint the optimum day to breed.

Throughout the bitch's heat she should be kept away from all male dogs except the selected stud. She should also be placed in a secure kennel with a cement floor and wire roof. Male dogs have been known to tunnel underneath or even scale fences ten feet high to gain access to a bitch in heat. I even heard of a bitch that jumped through a glass window to get to a stray male.

Unless you are mating her with your own male, ship or take your bitch to the stud about her eighth or ninth day of heat so she can become accustomed to her new surroundings prior to breeding. You should expect to leave her for about a day or two so that she can be tested and bred as soon as she will accept the male.

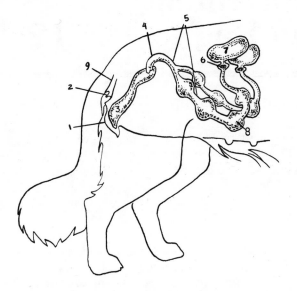

Reproductive System of the Bitch

1. Vulva
2. Anus
3. Vagina
4. Cervix
5. Uterus
6. Ovary
7. Kidney
8. Developing embryo
9. Rectum

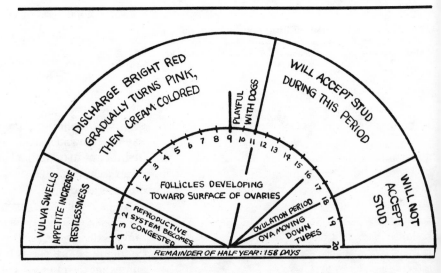

SELECTION AND TRAINING OF THE STUD DOG

Selecting a potential stud dog involves the same procedures as the brood bitch. Like the bitch, the prospective stud dog should have his reproductive tract examined for completeness. He should have two normal testicles fully descended into the scrotum. Monorchids (dogs with one testicle) are fertile, but they pass on their genes for retaining testicles to their sons, and their daughters become carriers of this trait. A cryptorchid has both testicles retained and is sterile, since sperm cannot survive any length of time at body temperature. The testicles are carried outside the body of the normal male so the sperm is kept cool. Also, the male's semen should be examined for fertility (sperm count) and he should be checked to see that he is free of canine brucellosis.

Once you have selected your future stud dog, be careful how you introduce him to breeding. The average male reaches puberty between eight and fourteen months of age. Dogs, like people, have different personalities. The young stud dog's first service should be on an older, experienced brood bitch who will not bite or frighten him. You should also have an experienced breeder on hand to help in case of problems.

Some stud dogs are naturally adept. A skillful stud sees the bitch, mounts immediately, and if the bitch is ready, enters her easily. You are very lucky if you have such a stud dog. However, you must be careful and keep the stud dog restrained on a leash if the bitch is nervous or uncooperative, since an anxious male will only upset her more.

The average dog may take a while before his instincts develop. Many dogs like to "court" the bitch before they mate by playing, nuzzling, and licking her ears and hind quarters. This type of dog can be turned off forever if his first service is to a nasty, uncooperative bitch, or his owner is impatient with him.

The fussy male is a problem. He may run away and ignore the bitch if his attempts to mount are unsuccessful. His ardor is easily quenched by just about anything, from attempts to assist him in mounting, to the bitch trying to play with him. Once tied, a fussy male struggles and panics in his attempts to escape, potentially hurting both himself and the bitch. This type needs very careful handling, and should only be allowed to serve calm, experienced bitches until he gains confidence, if ever.

The lethargic dullard is the worst type of stud dog. He has absolutely no interest in sex, though he may improve with age. Sometimes it is necessary to stimulate the dog manually and guide him by hand into the bitch, so that he gets the idea of what he is supposed to do. Hands should be clean, and friction applied very carefully.

THE MATING

If the mating is with an outside bitch, keep her on a leash at all times when she is not in a secured area. She should be handled quietly to prevent exciting her, and should be given a clean, comfortable kennel with a warm bed, food, and water. If she is still nervous, give her one-half of a sedative tablet and leave her alone for several hours until she settles in. Most importantly, treat the outside bitch with the same respect you would your own.

The maiden bitch must also be given special consideration. She may become very frightened in her new surroundings or around strangers. If the stud dog is rough, she may become terrified and snap at him. The bitch who is calm and relaxed will be no problem, but the nervous bitch should be given a sedative, soothed, and gently muzzled, after which

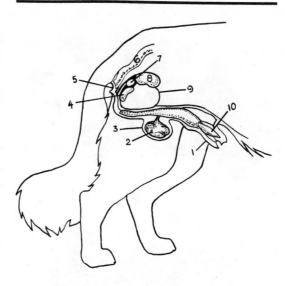

Reproductive System of the Stud Dog

1. Sheath	4. Pelvis	7. Prostate
2. Testicle	5. Anus	8. Bladder
3. Scrotum	6. Rectum	9. Vas deferens
		10. Penis

(Top) The stud dog penetrates the bitch. (Bottom) The "tie" is caused by a swelling at the base of the male's penis and a muscular constriction at the vagina opening.

A "mottled" Border Collie bitch with excellent head and ear set. (PAK Photo)

the stud dog is quietly re-introduced on a leash. The muzzle can be made out of 1½ inch wide gauze bandages, looped around her muzzle, tied under her chin and behind her ears.

Before the actual mating, trim the hair around the bitches vulva and wash it with warm mild soap on sterile cotton. Rinse and dry the area. Wrap and tape her tail in gauze bandage to keep the feathering from interfering with the stud dog, and lubricate her vulva with vaseline. The stud dog should also be clean and be washed gently with warm water and mild soap.

The most popular style of mating dogs is natural mating. The two dogs are brought together on leash, allowed to flirt, and then when the bitch is ready which you can tell by whether or not she arches and holds her tail aside, the stud dog mounts and penetrates. Once a tie has occured, turn the stud dog slowly by placing his front feet on the ground with him facing in the same direction as the bitch, and then lift the far hindleg over the bitch's back so he and the bitch are standing rear to rear. It may be necessary to hold the two together and calm them with soothing words to prevent them from pulling and hurting themselves.

The tie is caused by a swelling of the base of the male's penis, and a muscle constriction at the vaginal opening. This is nature's way of ensuring that sperm do not escape the female. Unlike other male mammals, dogs cannot eject semen in a quick squirt because they lack the "cowper's glands" present in other mammals. Therefore, a good tie is considered the sign of a successful breeding, although a successful mating can take place without one. The average tie lasts fifteen minutes, yet some dogs remain tied for as long as an hour.

Another popular mating technique is the hitching post or assisted method. The bitch's leash is secured to a wall or post, or she is held securely by an assistant. Make a chute of 1- by 8-inch boards to keep her from turning around and snapping at the stud dog, which will free your hands while you assist the stud dog to mount. Because a slippery floor can be dangerous, supply a rubber mat or wall to wall carpeting to give the dogs firm footing.

Once the bitch is mated, she *must* be kept away from all other males until she is out of heat. During her fertile period many unfertilized eggs can be fertilized by a different male. As a result, several pups could be purebreds and one or two could be obvious cross-breeds. Once this has happened and you are not really sure the ones that look purebred are not crossbred, you cannot safely sell these pups with papers. Even if the pups do look pure, they may grow up and turn into obvious mixtures and ruin your reputation as a breeder.

STUD FEES AND RECORDS

Unless a dog is a proven trial winner or show champion, a stud dog owner cannot expect to receive top dollar for his dog's services. Most stud dog owners ask the going rate for a puppy, or sometimes for the pick of the litter. If the stud dog is a top proven sire, his fees may be considerably higher. Most stud dog agreements provide a free return service if the breeding doesn't take.

Certain stud dog owners only allow their dog to service a bitch they have first approved because even a top sire bred to an inferior bitch can produce faulty puppies. Once these inferior puppies are seen by other people, the stud dog may be blamed and his reputation ruined. On the other hand, if the dog only services top bitches he will most likely produce top offspring, which in turn is a boon for the owner.

The stud dog owner should always fill out a "Stud Service Certificate" (advertised in most dog magazines), which states the fee, the bitch's name and number, the stud dog's name and number, address of the owner and the date of the mating. Once completed, the form must be signed by both the stud dog's and bitch's owner, and witnessed. Both owners then receive a copy of the certificate.

CANINE BRUCELLOSIS

Canine brucellosis was rare until a few years ago. Now it is reaching almost epidemic proportions, and can put a dog breeder out of business. The disease is caused by a bacteria, brucella abortus, or brucella canis. It occurs most often in dogs exposed to infected livestock and can be contracted by sniffing or eating aborted calves, pups, blood, urine, milk, or semen and vaginal secretion from infected dogs. Immunization and treatment of this disease so far have been unsuccessful, although veterinarians and scientists are continuing research. Once the disease is contracted, the animal will always be a carrier.

Infected bitches either abort entire litters during the third trimester of pregnancy, or the pups will be stillborn. Prolonged vaginal discharge occurs after the abortion, and the bitch will repeatedly abort during successive pregnancies. Male dogs frequently develop epididymitis, periorchitis and prostatitis.

Canine brucellosis is diagnosed by having a veterinarian examine the vaginal secretions of the bitch, semen of the male dog, aborted pups, blood, urine, or bitch's milk. Animals who are infected should be destroyed or isolated from other dogs and neutered.

O.T. Ch. Dreamalot Ben has been shown in 351 AKC shows. He is one of few dogs in any breed to show in over 300 AKC shows. "BEN" is owned by Karl and Sheryle Nussbaum of Floyds Knobs, Indiana.

Two ten day old Border Collie puppies. The dog on the right will be mottled, but the spotting will not appear until the pup is several weeks old. Mottling is a dominant trait. (Photo: J.E.L.)

Whelping 13

A proud mother nursing her puppies. (Photo: J.E.L.)

During the first four weeks after breeding, care for your bitch as usual. Sufficient exercise will help keep her muscles toned, and she will not need additional feed—but do feed a high quality ration.

Between the twenty-eighth and thirty-fifth day after breeding, your veterinarian may be able to palpate the whelps. By the sixth week you will notice obvious fullness in the loin area or girth if the bitch is pregnant. At this point, limit her activities and, if she is a working dog, she should not be worked after this point.

During the last trimester of her pregnancy, increase the bitch's rations and add a good vitamin/mineral supplement.

The gestation period in dogs is sixty-three days. If your bitch has not whelped by the sixty-fifth day, call your veterinarian. From sixty to sixty-four days can be considered normal. Maiden bitches whelping their first litter often whelp as early as the sixty-first day.

Many breeders believe that Border Collies should whelp normally in conditions as close to natural as possible and therefore leave the bitch to find her own spot outside in a barn or cave or under the porch. By nature bitches will tunnel to cool, dark, isolated spots to have their litter. The only problem is, this so-called natural method of whelping, where the bitch is left out in a shed unattended is the major cause of whelping complications and deaths for both the bitch or her puppies. There is no excuse for this, and it is cruel to the bitch and the pups. Often, one or more puppies will die unnecessarily when they could be saved with very little effort. This does not, however, imply that you should hover over the bitch and interfere with the birth of each puppy. Many bitches resent this, and will try to hold back their puppies, which in itself causes problems. The best bet is to be there, but keep out of the way unless needed.

A better alternative is to set up a whelping box several weeks in advance in a quiet place away from the hustle and bustle. It is important that you introduce the bitch to it several weeks in advance or she will select a secluded place on her own. To accommodate the bitch and her pups, the box should be four feet square and about one foot high. Place it in a draft free area and line it with newspaper. You might consider placing a guard rail about four inches from the floor around the inside to prevent any puppies from being accidently crushed.

Keep the bitch clean and trim the hair on her abdomen and around the vulva a week before the pups are due. Clean her teats with mineral oil about the fifty-eighth day.

Beside the whelping box, place a supply of newspapers, a pair of scissors that have been boiled, several clean towels, tincture of iodine, a baby scale to weigh each puppy, and paper and pencil.

ATTENTING TO THE WHELPING

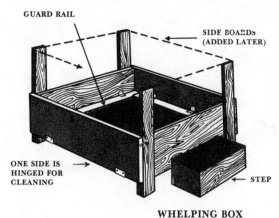

GUARD RAIL

SIDE BOARDS
(ADDED LATER)

ONE SIDE IS
HINGED FOR
CLEANING

STEP

WHELPING BOX

You can tell when your dog is ready to deliver by taking her temperature every morning and evening, near the whelping date, and observing her behavior. When her temperature drops to around 99⁰ F. she will whelp within the next 24 hours. At this time she will probably nest, digging up her bedding or newspapers. When the time is near, make sure the newspapers in her whelping box are fresh and clean. Also, leave the bitch alone for the 24 hours preceding delivery to prevent her from becoming nervous and agitated.

Immediately before she starts whelping, she will probably quiet down and stretch out full length. She will begin panting, breathing heavily, and may even cry out. She may also look anxiously at her rear, refuse all food, and vomit. Her vulva will be swollen and flaccid, and producing a clear discharge. Some bitches press their rears against the sides of the whelping box while heaving or straining to expel a puppy.

The time the bitch actually starts straining should be noted as the beginning of hard labor. The bitch normally whelps within one and a half hours after the onset of hard labor. The puppy emerges encased in a membranous sack, followed by the placenta, which is a greenish-black mass. The bitch normally eats the placenta— which is nutritionally rich and has a natural laxative effect. She will also eat the membranous sack and sever the umbilical cord with her teeth. She will energetically lick the pup and rough it around with her nose to stimulate his heart and lungs. Finally, she will nuzzle the pup toward a nipple. The bitch will then settle down until another puppy is born, one-half hour to three hours later, repeating the entire process.

If the bitch is slow in removing the membranes, pull the sack off yourself to save the puppy from oxygen deprivation damage. If the bitch does not immediately start licking and ignores the pup, rub him dry with a clean towel and rough him up a bit. The cord should be squeezed flat about two inches from the body to stop the blood circulation and then be torn or cut on the side away from the puppy with sterile scissors. Dip the end of this remaining umbilical cord in iodine solution.

It is a good idea to record the weight, sex, color and exact markings, coat type, etc., as soon as each puppy is born. Also make a note of whether or not the birth of the puppy was followed by a placenta, or if any of

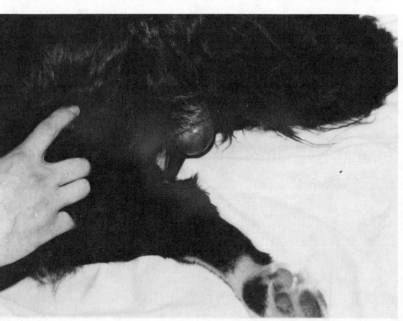

A Border Collie bitch giving birth to a puppy. (Photo:
J.E.L.)

88

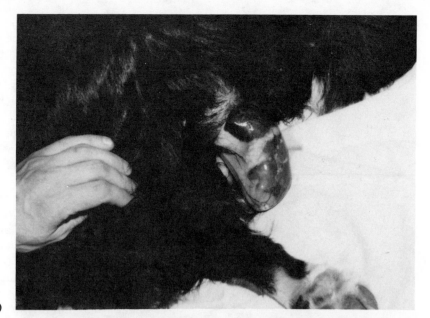

Birth Sequence- #2 (Photo: J.E.L.)

Note the sack has been opened so the puppy can breath. (J.E.L. Photo)

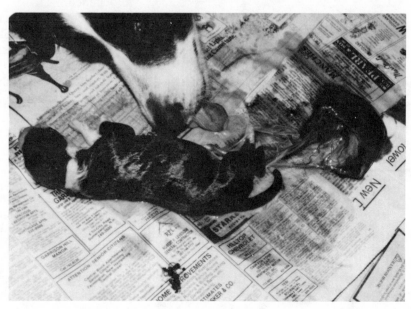

The mother dog is cleaning her puppy, then she will sever the umbilical cord and eat the afterbirth, which is rich in iron and nutrients and has a natural laxative effect. (J.E.L. Photo)

the placenta seemed to tear off inside the bitch. If you think a placenta or puppy may have been retained, the bitch should receive a shot of oxytocin within 24 hours after whelping to ensure that they are expelled.

If the bitch does not deliver a puppy within three hours of the onset of actual labor, you can expect trouble and should call your veterinarian. The same is true if the bitch continues to strain three hours after the birth of the last puppy. Someone should always be present throughout the whelping in case of complications.

Whelping Problems

If a water sack appears and bursts, but no puppy follows within two hours, especially if the bitch continues to strain, call your veterinarian. This could be indicative of severe problems.

Breech births are fairly common and not too difficult if dealt with properly. If you see hind feet (pad upward) and a tail being presented instead of a head, and the puppy is not expelled easily, you may have to help. To do this, stand the bitch and gently press upward on her abdomen with one hand while you stretch the vulva apart with the other hand. Next, either you or an assistant should hold both of the puppy's hind feet with sterile cotton and gently work the puppy out, pulling *down* toward the bitch's abdomen. Never pull straight out. If only one hind foot is sticking out, hold it, and insert a finger lubricated with vaseline into the vagina to find the other foot. Then gently work it out, grasp it with cotton, and being careful not to release the other foot, draw the puppy out cautiously. A breech puppy not born in a reasonable period will drown by inhaling fluids, so you should quickly remove the membrane and clear out the mucus in the nose and mouth. Rub the puppy briskly with a towel to stimulate breathing. If necessary, breath gently into the nose, or hold the pup head downward between your palms and swing him to clear out the air passages.

Other complications include sideways or upside-down presentations. Two or three puppies presented at once can become tangled, often requiring a caesarean section. This may be the problem if a bitch strains for three hours with no result.

When the front legs are tucked back against the chest, instead of alongside the nose, the pup will have trouble passing through the birth canal. To compensate, the legs must either be drawn forward into proper position, or the pup must be eased out. Veterinary assistance should be obtained.

If a placenta is retained, but is still attached to the cord, you can carefully work it out like you would a puppy. Do not jerk or yank it, or a piece might tear off. Instead, put a steady downward pressure on the placenta and work it out slowly. Or, simply clamp the cord with a hemostat so it cannot slip back into the birth canal and wait for the placenta to be expelled with the next contractions.

POST-WHELPING PROBLEMS

Mastitis

Mastitis is infection of the mammary glands. The infected teat will be hard and hot to the touch, and will often be very painful. The treatment is frequent milking out by hand or applying moist heat. In severe cases the milk can poison the puppies. Veterinary treatment is advised.

Milk Fever

Milk fever, or eclampsia, is a metabolic disorder where calcium is not mobilized fast enough to keep up with the milk production. This

Above: Breach births are fairly common. You will see the hind feet (pads upward) and a tail being presented instead of a head.

Below: A normal presentation. The head and front feet are presented first.

deficiency causes the blood calcium rate to drop below normal, creating stiffness, high fever, muscle spasms, and leading to paralysis, coma, and possibly death. An immediate injection of calcium gluconate will restore blood calcium levels.

Ironically, this disease can be brought about by giving calcium supplements to the pregnant bitch. This suppresses bodily production of calcium and makes her artificially dependent on outside sources.

Poor Milk Supply

This can be due to an inadequate diet for lactation. (See the section on feeding the lactating female.) If a proper diet does not encourage greater milk production, you may end up hand feeding the puppies.

Metritis

Metritis is an infection of the uterus acquired during whelping or the bitch's heat. Retained placentas, membranes, dead fetuses, or blood where bacteria can thrive are common causes. The symptoms include depression, high fever, vomiting, diarrhea, and a uterine discharge. A bitch with chronic metritis may appear sick off and on for months, and may fail to conceive at subsequent matings. Treatment should always be under the supervision of a veterinarian.

Pyometra

Pyometra occurs most frequently in older bitches and is similar to metritis. If left untreated it may cause death. The signs of this disease are depression, excessive thirst, frequent urination, vomiting, distended abdomen, lack of appetite, and sometimes a vaginal discharge. The most common treatment is to spay the bitch.

FEEDING THE LACTATING BITCH

Too many bitches are overfed during pregnancy and underfed during lactation. This is due to the erroneous idea that fetuses cause a greater nutritional drain on the bitch than do nursing puppies. The reverse is true, since the greatest growth in the puppy takes place after birth. Modern dairy cows are fed special diets during lactation to increase their milk supply—the same should be done for the lactating bitch. She should be given all she can eat to amply supply enough food energy to produce milk. Do not worry about the female gaining weight during this time, as this is not a problem.

A mother Border Collie and her litter of six week old pups. (Photo: J.E.L.)

Raw eggs should *never* be given to the bitch. Raw eggs contain a chemical which prevents the dog from absorbing several important vitamins into the blood stream. Cooking nutrilizes the chemical, however, and makes the egg a safe and nutritious food. In addition, milk should not be given to adult dogs because they no longer produce the enzymes necessary to digest it. As a result, milk can cause diarrhea and digestive upset.

After weaning the pups, dry the bitch up by cutting off all her food for 48 hours. After this period feed half her normal (non-lactating) ration with no supplements for a few days, gradually increasing them to normal. Do not supplement with any fat, calcium, or cod liver oil until she is completely dried up since these items, especially fat, encourage milk production. The bitch should also be exercised moderately.

Orphaned puppies should be fed six times a day. Weak or small pups may also be given supplementary feedings.

The Puppies 14

CARE OF THE NEWBORN

Newborn puppies should be kept in a warm area at a temperature of about 75° F. The floor of the whelping box should have wall to wall carpet or a rug to give the bitch and puppies firm footing. Shredded newspaper makes an ideal nesting material. Spread the newspaper abundantly over the carpet, and change it frequently.

Check the puppies' umbilical cords every day to make sure they do not develop an infection. Their toenails should be trimmed every week so that they do not scratch the bitch while nursing. Remove only the pointed tips. If the pups are born with hind dew claws, remove them with sterile scissors, when the pups are two days old and paint the spots with iodine. The scissors should be boiled for twenty minutes to ensure sterility.

It is a good idea to weigh the puppies every week and keep records of their mental and physical progress. Between one to three weeks of age, note which pups are more vigorous, which win the fight for the teat, and which ones are consistently outside the pile. Give these weaker pups supplemental feeding from a baby bottle using an artificial bitch's milk such as *Esbilac®* or *Vetlac®*. All the puppies should be handled gently for a few minutes each day; when doing so, note those who become the most disturbed and cry.

Because they have little resistance, puppies die rapidly if they contract disease. Sudden diet or temperature changes can often be the cause. A normal, healthy puppy has pink mucus membranes, elastic skin, a heart rate of about 200 beats per minutes and respiration rate of 20 to 30 breaths per minute. His body temperature is 100° F.

Sick puppies cry a lot, their skin wrinkles, loses springiness, and they feel cool and clammy. For this reason puppies should be observed and handled every day, and weighed weekly to note their health and progress. When a puppy dies, take him to the veterinarian immediately to determine the cause of death. By doing so, you could save the lives of the rest of the litter. Internal parasites are the major cause of death in young puppies. Chilling, which can lead to pneumonia, is another major killer. Viral infections such as parvovirus and distemper and bacterial infections are also potentially fatal for puppies.

ORPHANED PUPPIES

If a bitch dies or rejects one of the puppies, it can be kept alive by hand feeding. Chilled pups can be warmed in a box placed in an open oven at 100° F (the dog's body temperature). Keep the door open for

A tri-color Border Collie puppy. The pink spots on the nose will probably disappear by eight to twelve weeks of age. (PAK Photo)

A typical young Border Collie puppy. This pup will be "mottled" as an adult.

Another typical young puppy. This puppy will not be mottled.

Start feeding solid foods when the puppies are about 3 weeks old. A scientifically balanced puppy chow is best.

ventilation. Use a small bottle with a soft nipple to feed the orphan(s). Boil the bottle for three minutes before each feeding to ensure that it is sterile. The orphan should be fed warm water with 2 tablespoons of Karo syrup per cup the first day since his digestive tract is too immature to handle the milk substitutes. At two days old he can be fed *Esbilac®* or *Vetlac®*.

Orphaned puppies should be fed six times in each 24 hour period. The glucose may give a weak pup enough strength to suck. Colostrum (first day's milk) from the bitch is preferable because it provides the puppies with a temporary immunity to diseases, and it is easier to digest. Hold the bitch down, if necessary, to let the pups drink.

If the pup remains weak and cannot drink from a bottle, you will have to tube feed him. To do this, you will need a sterile catheter tube (size 21) and a 10 cc syringe. It is best to have your veterinarian show you how to tube feed your puppy. The tube is inserted gently into his mouth and slowly eased into his stomach; if the pup gags, the tube may have entered his lungs. Boil both the tube and syringe for at least three minutes both before and after use to kill germs.. As soon as possible, switch the puppy over to a sterilized bottle.

After each feeding it is essential to gently massage the puppy's stomach, anus, and vulva or penis to stimulate defecation and urination. At this age puppies cannot control their own movements and are completely dependent, so you must take the place of the mother. Keep the puppy in temperatures of 85° to 90° F for the first week. If necessary, use a heating pad under some blankets in a box or an incubator. After the first week, gradually drop the temperature to about 80° F. If the pups have not received colostrum, they should be given their first vaccination earlier than normal. Your veterinarian can advise.

WORMING

More puppies die every year of worm infestations than die of distemper. Worms cause anemia, convulsions, vitamin deficiencies, mental impairment, and stunted growth. (For more information on the various species of worms, see chapter 9.) When your pups are three or four weeks of age, take a random fecal sample to your veterinarian for microscopic examination. If worms are present, the puppies should be wormed at this time. About six to seven weeks of age, the pups should have another random fecal sample taken and if this sample shows worm eggs, the treatment should be repeated.

IMMUNIZATION

At seven to eight weeks of age, and before they go to a new home, all puppies should be given their first vaccination to protect them against distemper, hepatitis, leptospirosis, parvovirus, and parainfluenza. The buyers should be advised that a booster will be needed in three weeks. The rabies vaccination can be given between four and six months of age.

HEALTH CERTIFICATES AND PAPERS

Every buyer should be given a health certificate signed by your veterinarian indicating the dates of wormings, the first vaccination, and stating that the puppy is healthy. Certificates are not required by law for in-state sales, but are required for interstate transport and are highly advised in all cases. The certificate both protects you from lawsuits in case the puppy becomes ill and is insurance for the buyer.

94

You should also provide the new owners with a complete pedigree, date of birth, the names of the sire and dam, the registration numbers of the sire and dam, the registry name and address, and your name, address, and phone number. Supply a feeding schedule, and recommend that they see their veterinarian about a health program. As a nice gesture you may also give them a day's supply of dog food or training manuals and instructions with their pups.

If the puppy is a purebred and eligible for registration, register him with the rest of the litter and mail the papers to the purchaser. If for some reason you feel the puppy is of inferior quality and should not be bred, you can have the buyer sign a statement that papers are being withheld and that they agree to having their pet spayed or neutered.

SELLING BORDER COLLIE PUPPIES

Border Collies are not a well-known breed, and are therefore harder to sell than more popular breeds. Many Border Collie puppies are sold at sheepdog trials where the public is exposed to the breed working. Since they are not physically impressive, most Border Collie sales are based on their intelligence and trainability, which is why owners of top trial dogs have no trouble selling puppies.

Advertising is also a great aid to selling puppies. The best place is in the classified ad section of your local or regional paper. Other good places are in dog magazines such as *Dog Sports* or *Dog World*. Be careful not to make exaggerated claims about your dogs which can make other breeders and wary purchasers skeptical. Try to make your kennel advertisements honest, orderly, and well-presented. If you use a photograph, be sure it is a quality photograph, since nothing can turn prospective purchasers off as easily as a blurry picture or a dog that looks like a speck in the corner of a landscape. If necessary, have a professional photographer take telephoto pictures of your dog working or a close-up portrait. Always clean and groom the dog thoroughly before having his picture taken. Many breeders sign annual contracts for advertising their kennels in order to obtain reduced rates in the various periodicals.

A classified advertisement in a newspaper may be worded like this: "Border Collie puppies; registered, shots and wormed, health certificate. Home raised, mother on premises; (price, and phone number)." The earlier you advertise, the better. Start advertising as soon as the puppies are born or even before to insure they are all sold by eight weeks of age.

If you are unable to sell your pups by eight weeks, their chances of being properly socialized and absorbed into family life are reduced and you lose money on feeding and veterinary bills. The longer you keep the puppies, the less profit you make.

FEEDING

When the puppies are about three weeks of age, start them on solid food. A scientifically balanced puppy chow is the best. Soak the food well until it is soft, and mash it up or mix with a milk replacer to make it more palatable. It should be fed in a low dish or a feeding tray. As the pups get older, start feeding them more often and as much as they will eat.

At five to six weeks of age, replace the milk substitute with a vitamin/mineral supplement and cod liver oil. The mother can now be allowed to leave her pups for several hours at a time and weaning can begin. Slowly increase the amount of time the bitch is away until the pups are completely weaned. They should be fed three to four times a day. At eight weeks of age, they should be completely weaned and the bitch dried up.

EARLY HOUSE BREAKING

It is possible to start housebreaking the pups at four or five weeks of age. They will no longer be confined to their box, and will probably have free run of some room or shed. At first, cover the whole floor with paper. If you sprinkle commercial housebreaking scent in a corner of the room (not the corner they usually sleep in), you will soon find they usually go in this corner. You can then gradually reduce the paper in the room until you have only a four-foot square area covered. Be sure to roll up soiled papers before they track excrement around the room. By the time the puppies are six weeks old, they should be fully paper trained.

EVALUATING TEMPERAMENT IN PUPPIES

Dog temperament tests were originally formulated by psychologists and geneticists doing research at the Jackson Memorial Lab in Bar Harbor, Maine. These researchers were trying to determine which puppies in a litter would later be suitable for training as guide dogs for the blind, possessing the traits to think independently and take great responsibility. Before these tests were used, guide dog schools had a 90 percent failure rate. Now the *success* rate is over 90 percent. It was found that temperament traits are inherited, and already exhibited when pups are only a few weeks old. These traits remain constant throughout a dog's life, unless the animal is isolated during the critical socialization period (seven to 16 weeks of age), or is abused by his owner.

Guide dog schools also employed these tests to select superior individuals to use for training and breeding future guide dogs. Because the quality of dog bred outside was so low, the schools had to resort to breeding almost all their own. These temperament tests were later modified by the military for the *Army Superdog* breeding program with excellent results and are now commonly used to select prospective schutzhund or police dog puppies.

The tests outlined below are designed to help the Border Collie breeder select puppies that will grow up to be superior working dogs. The ideal working dog is self-confident, stable, well-adjusted, and has enough courage to face a stubborn sheep or to work cattle. A superior working dog will not run and hide under the bed during a thunderstorm or when the hunting season starts.

The tests are divided into two parts: *Part I* is for puppies from birth to five weeks of age, and *Part II* is for older puppies, from about five weeks to 10 weeks of age. Record the results of these tests for future reference.

A Border Collie and his young son. (PAK Photo)

TEMPERAMENT TEST
PART I — BIRTH TO FIVE WEEKS

(Note: Tests 1 and 2 are group tests; tests 3 through 5 are individual tests.)

1. Which pups are more vigorous and competitive while nursing (desirable), and which pups seem to consistently lose the fight for the most productive teats and seem to be outside the pile (undesirable)?

2. Which puppies are quiet and content (desirable) and which cry more, especially when the mother leaves the nest (undesirable)?

3. Which puppies (one to five weeks) cry the soonest and act most disturbed when placed on a cold surface (undesirable)?

4. Which puppies (three to five weeks) calm down soonest and are least disturbed when pinched between the foretoes, and petted gently (desirable)?
Which puppies remain excessively distressed or snap (fear biter) at the tester (undesirable)?

5. Which puppies (one to five weeks) are quiet and content when handled (desirable) and which cry and squirm excessively (undesirable)?

PART II — SIX TO TEN WEEKS OLD

(Note: All these tests are performed individually.)

1. *Trainability:* Observe the pup's reactions to being walked on a leash, having his rear end pressed into a sitting position, and coming to the handler when the handler kneels and claps his hands, saying "Here Puppy."
   a. Pup follows readily, sits, then bounces up immediately; comes promptly (ideal response).
   b. Pup follows, sits, and comes with some resistance, no fear (good response).
   c. Pup resists strongly (borderline).
   d. Pup is timid, does not want to move after being placed in sit position (failure).

2. *Confidence Test:* Observe pup's reaction to being in a new area with strange people walking around.
   a. Confident and friendly; readily investigates new areas and people (ideal response).
   b. Walks close to handler for security, but tail wagging (good).
   c. Reluctant to follow handler, tail low, draws back from strangers (borderline).
   d. Terrified, tail tucked, crouches, piddles, or defecates from fear (failure).

3. *Negotiation — Moving Object Test:* Observe pup's reaction to stairs, an auto passing on a nearby road, and to a cart or wheelbarrow pushed within five feet of the pup and handler.
   a. Negotiates stairs with little trouble, alert to auto and cart, but calms down quickly (good).
   b. Negotiates stairs with some difficulty, startled by auto and cart, but calms down quickly (good).
   c. Negotiates stairs with difficulty (frightened), fearful of auto and cart (borderline).
   d. Cannot negotiate stairs (terrified of them), terrified of auto and cart (failure).

4. *Umbrella Test:* An umbrella is snapped open five feet from dog and handler, then placed on the ground.
   a. Pup is alert, then investigates umbrella (ideal).
   b. Pup is startled, then investigates umbrella (good).
   c. Pup is frightened, then investigates umbrella (borderline).
   d. Pup is terrified, crouches, piddles, defecates or growls (failure).

5. *Handling Test:* A stranger picks up pup and pets him.
   a. Pup enjoys being petted, but struggles against being held ("harder" personality) (ideal).
   b. Pup enjoys being petted, and submits to being held ("softer" personality) (good).
   c. Pup rigid and fearful, but calms down (borderline).
   d. Pup piddles, growls, or snaps at the stranger out of fear (failure).

6. *Hardness Test:* How does the pup react to having the web between his front toes pinched?
   a. Pup immediately forgives handler; bounces around, active (ideal).
   b. Pup acts subdued and quiet after pinch — forgives handler (good).
   c. Pup cries excessively and crouches submissively to handler (borderline).
   d. Pup snaps at handler (fear biter or neurotic) (failure).

7. *Fetch Test:* Throw a rag or ball for pup. Call him. (It was found that pups who failed this test failed to take responsibility or think independently, and were unsuitable for guide dog work.)
   a. Pup chases rag and brings it back (ideal).
   b. Pup chases rag and brings it partway back, or picks it up (good).
   c. Pup chases rag and sniffs it (borderline).
   d. Pup does not chase rag (failure).

A six-week-old puppy at Caora Con Kennels showing herding instinct. Six to eight weeks is a good time to temperament test puppies and check for herding potential. (Photo: J.E.L.)

8. *Sound Sensitivity Test:* Fire a blank pistol twice, about twenty feet from where pup is playing by himself or with another pup. Note his reactions. A sound-shy dog is automatically excluded from guide dog training, military, shutzhund, or police work. This is also undesirable in a stock dog working in area with thunderstorms, or a dog working with hunters.
   a. Pup alertly looks toward origin or noise, then returns to play (ideal).
   b. Pup startled by noise, then goes back to play (good).
   c. Pup startled and somewhat frightened by noise, goes back to play (borderline).
   d. Pup terrified by noise; crouches, tail tucked; perhaps hides in a corner (failure).
9. *Herding Instinct Test:* Release 3 ducks in front of a pup in an enclosed area.
   a. Pup circles, "eyes" and stalks. May pounce on ducks (ideal).
   b. Pup stalks and "eyes" ducks. Does not circle. (good).
   c. Pup circles ducks, but does not stalk or "eye" (good).
   d. Pup chases and pounces on ducks (fair).
   e. Pup ignores ducks (failure- retest later).

A pup that receives many A's is very desirable. Such a dog will make a good cattle dog, schutzhund dog, guide dog for the blind, or all-purpose dog.

A pup with B's and A's will probably make an excellent working dog, but may not be as good as the first type. A dog with C's and B's may make a fair working dog in the right hands, while a dog with D's is timid and unstable and is not suited for much except as a pet in the proper environment.

The dominant, aggressive, hard pups who lack fear and score well in all areas make the best training prospects for the experienced handler who wants a top notch, tough dog, with the courage to work beef cattle, do schutzhund, or guide the blind. The softer, placid, stable pups who score well make good working dogs on sheep, dairy cattle, for obedience, and guiding the blind. Some may do well at schutzhund. The quiet, friendly, timid, but not neurotic pup will make a suitable pet in a quiet environment, or as an obedience dog. The very timid, snappish, or hysterical puppy may turn into a neurotic fear biter, especially if teased.

When placing a pup with a prospective buyer, try to find out the buyer's level of experience and ability as a trainer, and the purpose of the dog (sheep, cattle, obedience, schutzhund, pet), and the type of environment the dog will live in (noisy — lots of active children, quiet, or in between), and match the puppies to the people. The cutest puppy may be the worst one for the purposes, spelling disaster.

The research team at the Jackson Lab also found that puppies who were raised with little physical human contact during the critical socialization period between seven and fourteen weeks of age tended to be untrainable and never developed full attachments to humans when they were adults. This was part of the reason for the high failure rate at the guide dog schools. Now all guide dog puppies are raised by 4-H Club members in a home situation until they are a year old, instead of being raised in a kennel. Puppies raised in kennels should receive a minimum of five minutes of individual handling a day until they are sold. Puppies older than eight weeks need more handling and attention or they will develop kennel shyness. Many breeders also raise their puppies in their home prior to sale.

EVALUATING THE CONFORMATION OF PUPPIES

Do not expect any puppies in a litter to be exceptional if both parents are mediocre in type. Study the parents carefully for weak points such as cowhocks, fiddle front, poor ear carriage, or poor movement. If the

Caora Con's Black Bison, SchH 3, CDX, TD, WC at age 9 weeks. Sire: Cooperlane's Jason, UD; Dam: Caora Con's Bhan-Tara, CDX.

parents have a particular fault, look especially closely at the puppies to see if they, too, possess that fault.

You can tell what type of coat the pup will have (rough, smooth, curly, or straight), whether the whites of the eyes will be prominent (excessive haw is undesirable), whether the eye will be large and bulging like a toy spaniel (undesirable), or moderate in size and set in somewhat obliquely. Also undesirable are small, beady, or sunken eyes. All pups are born with bluish eyes that turn dark later on, unless wall-eyes run in the line.

The legs should be sturdy and straight, and the body symmetrical and blocky. All young puppies carry their tails up, so you can't tell much about tail carriage. The head should be blocky, with a blunt, square muzzle. A puppy with a fine, snipy nose will mature into a pointy-nosed adult, rather than having the correct, blunt, well-rounded muzzle. The puppy's teeth should meet in a scissors bite. A *slightly* overshot bite may correct itself as the pup gets older. An overshot bite of more than an eighth of an inch will probably remain incorrect.

The ears should tip well forward, but not hang slack and flat. An ear that barely tips at this age will be pricked as an adult, although ear carriage can be altered artificially with weights or props.

The size of the pup does not matter unless the line is noted for undersize or oversize, but do beware of dwarf puppies. They are a genetic mutation and often have health problems. A true dwarf has a refined head, light bone structure, and often small, beady eyes. Normal puppies of the same age are sturdy and blocky in build.

The coat should be dense and furry, and straight to slightly wavy. An excessively curly "Poodle-type" coat may straighten out with age, but in an adult, excessive curliness is undesirable.

The pup should carry himself with an air or style that catches the eye. Check the male puppies for two testicles. Most puppies have two testicles at eight weeks of age, although in some lines the testicles are slow to descend. They are generally down at three months, although rarely as late as five months. If the pup does not have two testicles and you plan to breed him, don't take the chance that they will descend, particularly if cryptorchids or monorchids run in the line.

Color is a personal preference, although rich coloring is desirable. A washed-out red or tri-color isn't pleasing to the eye, yet a rich red or tri-color with tan markings is very attractive. White markings are also preferable, such as four white paws, white tail tip, chest, neck ring or patch, and blaze up the face.

Correct nutrition and adequate exercise are necessary to develop the puppy to his full potential. Daily exercise can strengthen tendons and muscles and increase the depth and spring of ribs to make room for a healthy, athletic heart and lungs. Adequate nutrition is required for correct tooth and bone formation, muscle development, and coat.

From the top: Caora Con's Black Bison, SchH 3, CDX, TD, WC at six months, nine months, and twelve months of age. (Photo: J.E.L.)

TRAINING THE EARS

Ideal ear carriage is very hard to obtain, since it is not a homozygous condition and cannot breed true as do drop or prick ears. Many early working collies had heavy drooping ears, and others had totally pricked ears. Neither of these types are desirable in the show ring.

High ears can be corrected by not allowing them to remain pricked for even a day. The tips should be rubbed with *antiphlogistine* salve or pine tar, then dipped in powder or soil to add extra weight and absorb the stickiness.

Low ears can be propped up using moleskin ear braces tied over the top of the head with yarn. The ears should first be cleaned with alcohol so the moleskin will stick. The moleskin braces may have to be reinforced with matchsticks fastened down with adhesive tape. Bend and glue or weight the tips to make them break forward.

Ear braces and weights should be put on around three months of age, and reapplied periodically until the dog has completely finished teething and the cartilage of the ear is set. You must be on the lookout for infection. If the ears get hot and red, remove the props or weights, since infected ears left untreated may have to be amputated. If the ears have not attained the correct position by about eight months of age, they probably never will.

Pulfer's "Dell" at Blue Hill, Maine Sheepdog Trial. (Photo: Carole L. Presberg)

The sheepdog trial is the true test of a Border Collie's breeding. Dr. Johannes Caius' remark in 1576 that "with little labour and no toyle or moving of his feete, he may rule and guide his flocke, according to his own desire," is certainly true, even after four hundred years. The sheep are tense and frightened in strange surroundings, and their antics are often wild and unpredictable. Subsequently, the dogs are also tense and nervous in strange surroundings. Their ability to cope and think under stress is tested to the limit at a trial. Only a well bred, sound dog can withstand the exacting pace, make the sweeping outrun, quick turns of flanking, driving through obstacles and penning, while remaining in control of his charges at all time. Any dog who wins such an event in a field of tough competition could certainly handle almost any situation in real life on a farm or ranch, and most do, every day.

A sheepdog trial is a crowd pleaser, provided the caliber of dog and trainer is high. Unfortunately, many local trials turn off people who could use a well-trained Border Collie because the dogs are poorly bred or improperly trained and handled. The difference between a novice and a professional dog handler is that the professional, utilizing his skill, can make a mediocre dog look better than a good dog trained by a novice. Among professionals, the training skills and knowledge are usually equalized, so the man with the best dog generally wins.

The sight of a champion Border Collie silently racing into a semi-circle to crouch behind a flock of skittish Highland Sheep a half mile away is thrilling. On a barely audible whistle the dog rises to his feet and stares fixedly at the stubborn animals until they turn and trot away in the direction desired by the dog. A lightning dash keeps any stragglers with the bunch. Halfway down the field, a shrill whistle pierces the air and the dog turns the sheep and drives them over a wooden bridge.

The handler whistles again, and the dog drives the sheep through a set of panels located two hundred yards away, requiring the sheep to turn at a ninety-degree angle. One sheep decides to make a dash for its freedom but, without command, the dog heads off the ewe and brings her back to the flock. The dog's ever-present stare and crouching, snake-like stalking keep the sheep obedient.

Hearing another whistle, the dog drives the sheep through one set of flags and then another in a slalom course as difficult as any on the ski slope. Meanwhile, the sheep look for any opportunity to bolt and dash away to freedom. At the end of the course, all five sheep must be penned in a cramped six-foot-square pen. This takes several commands from the shepherd, but the dog, once he knows what is expected, works almost entirely on his own, deciding his own moves in an attempt to

A Border Collie driving a flock of sheep at a sheepdog trial. (Photo: J.E.L.)

A Border Collie using the power of "eye" to force his sheep through the panels at the University of Connecticut sheepdog trial held in May. (PAK Photo)

pen the claustrophobic sheep. They are finally penned, and the dog crouches at the gateway, staring fixedly into their eyes to keep them intimidated. The crowd roars in appreciation, and the handler tells the dog "That will do, good dog." The dog leaves the sheep pen and returns to his handler to be rewarded for a job well done.

Scenes similar to these are duplicated in all the major sheep raising countries, where the use of trained Border Collies is a necessity for managing flocks economically.

U.S. TRIALS

Informal trials are organized throughout the country by local herding clubs. Official trials are run under the rules of the United States Sheepdog Trial Association, the North American Sheepdog Society, and the American International Border Collie Registry.

The United States Sheepdog Trial Association is separate from the two registries. It's purpose is to choose dogs to represent the United States in the World Championship Sheepdog Trial held every two years. Several top dogs are selected from each of six districts in the United States.

The North American Sheepdog Society (NASDS) holds three classes of trials. Class III trials are local and held under NASDA rules. Class II trials are limited in number (about six each year) and are Championship trials. The single Class I trial, called the North American Supreme Championship Trial, rotates around the country each year. Only the top dogs nationally compete. All NASDS licensed trials are held in a field at least 250 yards long by 150 yards wide. The gather must be no less than 150 yards, and the two drives 75 yards long through gates that have a 21-foot opening. These gates must be at least 25 yards from any fence. The shedding ring, marked on the ground, is not less than 20 yards in diameter. The pen must be at least 6 by 6 feet and no more than 8 by 8 feet square.

The dog will be assigned no less than three nor more than five sheep. The time limit is 12 minutes. The course is scored as follows:

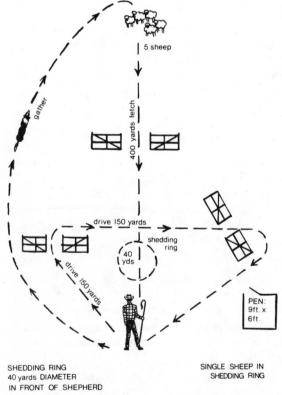

SHEDDING RING
40 yards DIAMETER
IN FRONT OF SHEPHERD

SINGLE SHEEP IN
SHEDDING RING

1. Gather (outrun 10, lift 5, fetch 10 points)......25 points
2. Driving (7½ points for each drive and gate)....15 points
3. Shedding (separating 2 unmarked sheep from the flock)..................................... 5 points
4. Penning.................................15 points
5. Single Sheep (separating one sheep from the flock). 5 points

MAXIMUM TOTAL SCORE   65 points

Trials held by the American-International Border Collie Registry are held under the same general rules as NASDS trials, although the number of points allotted to each section differs. Additional obstacles such as bridges and slews are also permitted, as are blind-gathers (out of sight of the dog).

102

NORTH AMERICAN SUPREME CHAMPIONS
FROM 1954 TO 1983

1954   *Imported Rock #7222 (166)* - Arthur N. Allen, McLeansboro, Ill.

1955   *Ben #4250* - Willard Potts, Lometa, Texas

1956   *Imported Nan #9065 (199)* - Arthur N. Allen, McLeansboro, Ill.

1957   *Imported Nan #9065 (199)* - Arthur N. Allen, McLeansboro, Ill.

1958   *Imported Roy #8399 (270)* - Arthur N. Allen, McLeansboro, Ill.

1959   *Imported Roy #8399 (270)* - Arthur N. Allen, McLeansboro, Ill.

1960   *Imported Roy #8399 (270)* - Arthur N. Allen, McLeansboro, Ill.

1961   *Imported Roy #8399 (270)* - Arthur N. Allen, McLeansboro, Ill.

1962   *Imported Roy #8399 (270)* - Arthur N. Allen, McLeansboro, Ill.

1963   *Imported Roy II #18009 (371)* - Arthur N. Allen, McLeansboro, Ill.

1964   *Imported Roy II #18009 (371)* - Arthur N. Allen, McLeansboro, Ill.

1965   *Imported Roy II #18009 (371)* - Arthur N. Allen, McLeansboro, Ill.

1966   *Imported Moss #35813 (417)* - Arthur N. Allen, McLeansboro, Ill.

1967   *Imported Moss #35813 (417)* - Arthur N. Allen, McLeansboro, Ill.

1968   *Imported Moss #35813 (417)* - Arthur N. Allen, McLeansboro, Ill.

1969   *Imported Moss #35813 (417)* - Arthur N. Allen, McLeansboro, Ill.

1970   *Imported Fleet #50891 (560)* - Arthur N. Allen, McLeansboro, Ill.

1971   *Imported Fleet #50891 (560)* - Arthur N. Allen, McLeansboro, Ill.

1972   *Imported Fleet #50891 (560)* - Arthur N. Allen, McLeansboro, Ill.

1973   *Imported Fleet #50891 (560)* - Arthur N. Allen, McLeansboro, Ill.

1974   *Imported Bill #65470 (600)* - Arthur N. Allen, McLeansboro, Ill.

1975   *Imported Bill #65470 (600)* - Arthur N. Allen, McLeansboro, Ill.

1976   *Imported Bill #65470 (600)* - Arthur N. Allen, McLeansboro, Ill.

1977   *Imported Craig #80254 (826)* - Jack Knox, Montello, WI

1978   *Imported Craig #80254 (826)* - Jack Knox, Montello, WI

1979   *Imported Cap #96168 (833)* - Arthur N. Allen, McLeansboro, Ill.

1980   *Imported Mac #69113 (722)* - Inez Schroeder, Wilcox, Ar

1981   No Trial

1982   No Trial

1983   *Imported Bill #102167 (1036)* - Lena Bailey, Wilcox Ar.

Aust. Ch. Tullaview Temptress faces up to an aggressive ewe with a lamb at her side. A show dog can also be a good working dog!

HERDING TRIAL CHAMPIONSHIP (H.T.Ch.)

Guidelines and regulations are currently being drawn up by the Border Collie Club of America (BCCA) and the United States Border Collie Handler's Assoc. (USBCHA) in cooperation with the ABCA, AIBC and NASDS. Championship points will be awarded only to dogs winning first or second place at an open sheepdog trial following the guidelines for herding trials by the International Sheepdog Society and North American Sheepdog Society contained in this chapter. Trials put on that do not follow these guidelines do not count. Trial results are published in BORDER COLLIE NEWS.

The dog approaches the sheep carefully to avoid startling them. (Photo: D. Reinke)

SCALE OF POINTS

NUMBER COMPETING	POINTS FOR FIRST PLACE	POINTS FOR SECOND PLACE
6-10	2	0
11-15	4	1
16-20	6	2
21-25	10	3
26-30	14	4
31-35	18	5
36-40	22	7
41-45	26	9
46-50	30	11
51 +	34	13

REQUIREMENTS:

1. Shall have won 100 points in Open Class Competition; and
2. Shall have won three first places provided there are at least 6 dogs in competition; and
3. Shall have won these first places under three different judges. H.T.Ch. CERTIFICATE: The H.T.Ch. Certificate will be issued for each dog, and will permit the use of the letters H.T.Ch. preceeding the name of each dog.

For more information contact the BCCA or USBCHA listed in the Appendix

NORTH AMERICAN SHEEP DOG SOCIETY COURSE OUTLINE AND RULES OF CONDUCT OF OFFICIAL SHEEP DOG TRIALS

Heading off an attempt to break for freedom. Owner, Les Bruhn. (Photo: Reinke)

The purpose of holding Sheep Dog Trials is to measure the intelligence, talent, and ability of Sheep Dogs at the work for which they are bred. Trials serve also, as a guide to breeding and training and to encourage the development of highly capable dogs for the better handling of sheep and other livestock. Indirectly, trials furnish a spectacular display of animal intelligence which is entertaining and instructive. Finally, trials tend to promote, through a mingling of people from city and country, a common understanding of each other's problems.

Class I. NORTH AMERICAN SUPREME CHAMPIONSHIP SHEEP DOG TRIALS

Class II. CHAMPION SHEEP DOG TRIALS
(Sponsored by or financed by a Sponsoring Agency or Society with Approval of the North American Sheep Dog Society.)

Class III. OFFICIAL COOPERATIVE CHAMPIONSHIP SHEEP DOG TRIALS
(These trials to be conducted jointly by the Society and a local sponsoring organization or agency on a cooperative basis.)

Sheep Dog Trials conducted on any basis other than under one of the three classifications above are UNRECOGNIZED by this Society covering Cooperative Trials.

OPEN TRIAL
COURSE OUTLINE

1.   The Trials Course for all official Sheep Dog Trials shall be the Official Course Outline as defined and adopted by the North American Sheep Dog Society, together, with governing rules as presented herewith.

2.   The Trials Course shall be set up on land area which permits all work to be conducted in full view of contestants, officials, and patrons, UNLESS a blind-gather-course (sheep out of sight at start) shall be designated when the trials are announced.

3.   The minimum field area for holding official outdoor trials must be at least 250 yards long and 150 yards wide to permit use of a minimum distance, in each phase of work hereafter defined, and with sufficient "overage" to allow for good dog work and unhampered sheep and dog movement. Minimum distance for each phase of work shall be as follows:

(a) Gather - not less than 150 yards from center of Shedding Ring to point of pick-up.

(b) Drive - not less than 75 yards on diagonal from center of Shedding Ring to Gate No. 1 on the left: and not less than 75 yards in the Drive Across from Gate No. 1 to Gate No. 2 on the right; both gates to be set with a 12 foot opening.

(c) Shedding Ring - not less than 20 yards in diameter.

(d) Pen - shall be 6' x 6', or 8' x 8' or any square dimension between these two - and shall be set not less than 10 yards outside of the above working field.

(e) overage - no fixed obstacle or point on the course shall be closer than 25 yards to any limiting fence.

4.   Special Courses may be approved from time to time by the Society to meet certain need, but any records of dog performance thereon shall be designated "Special Course Records," with the standing of such records to be determined by the Executive Board.

WORK REQUIRED AND SCORE ALLOWED

1.   Dogs entered in official trials will be required to perform four phases of work: GATHERING, SHEDDING, DRIVING, and PENNING; with such additional work as may be specified in any particular trial or for retesting any particular dog in any trial as rules or rulings under circumstance may require. The full testing of each dog in each phase of work is the objective.

2.   Each dog will be assigned not less than three (3), usually five (5) sheep for the course work.

3.   Time allowed each dog will be 12 minutes, unless change decided on by Judges.

4.   Each dog will be scored individually in each phase of work according to the following Score of Points.

(a) Gathering 25 points - divided into "Out-run," 10 points; "lift," 5 points and "Fetch," 10 points.

(b) Driving, 15 points (7½ points on each drive).

(c) Shedding, 5 points.

(d) Penning, 15 points.

(e) Single Sheep, 5 points.
      Total - 65 points.

GATHERING

THE OUTRUN: In starting each run, the contestant and his dog shall take position at any point in the back of Shedding Ring - this same position to be the "fixed" position for all work during the GATHER and DRIVE. With the sheep in place, and upon signal from the Course Director, the run for each dog begins. On the out-run the dog may be directed to go either "right" or "left," and each dog shall carry along on this given line until beyond the sheep. Cross-

Arthur N. Allen with three of his champions, Imported Bill, Imported Fleet, and Imported Spot. (Photo: J.E.L.)

A Border Collie driving sheep over a bridge at the Skowhegan, Maine sheepdog trial. (photo: J.E.L.)

over or disposition to cross-over shall cause deduction of points according to the Judge's decision. The dog shall go "wide" and "beyond" the sheep before circling in so as to come upon the sheep from the "far side" in preparation for the LIFT; the dog's "come-on to sheep" should be cautious and well balanced on the flock.

THE LIFT: The introduction of dog to sheep should be cautious and calmly done without fright of sheep. The LIFT should be cautious, the sheep not unduly startled, held quietly and firmly, and moved off steadily with the dog in full control.

THE FETCH: The fetch should be on a straight or near straight line from point of contact and lift to the handler; swerving, zig-zagging, wide and hard flanking, or other deviation from the near-straight line to involve loss of points according to the Judge's decision under the circumstances - the nature of the work, and the condition and handling of the sheep to be the foremost consideration. The fetch ends when the sheep are around or behind handler.

DRIVING

From the handler's position in the back of the Shedding Ring, the dog is required to drive the sheep away on a diagonal to the left, toward and through "gate No. 1;" thence horizontally across the field to and through "gate No. 2" on the right side of the course. If either gate is not negotiated on first try, no re-try will be allowed. Failure to negotiate either gate will involve a loss of points or not, according to the decision of the Judges under each circumstance - the nature of the work, and the condition of the sheep being the foremost consideration. The drive ends when the sheep are through or past gate No. 2. The contestant shall proceed to the Shedding Ring, with the dog required to bring the sheep up for Shedding.

Top and Bottom: Nursery Sheepdog trial at Essich, Invernesshire, Scotland. (Photos: Carole L. Presberg)

SHEDDING

The dog will be required to shed two unmarked Sheep within the Shedding Ring 20 yards in diameter. Dog must be in full control of sheep and his work shall be deliberate and decisive otherwise, the Shed will not be deemed satisfactory. Shedding includes dog's work bringing sheep from end of drive to shedding ring.

PENNING

The pen, set not less than 10 yards outside the gathering, Shedding, and driving field, shall be located for the best view of the work by patrons. The pen shall be anchored securely at three points but in such way that gate opening may be made either to the right or to the left, according to the contestant's decision. The opening corner of the pen shall be the one nearest to the hurdle number 2 on the driving field.

At the completion of the Shedding, the contestant shall proceed to open the gate of the pen, either to the right or to the left, so that it continues in a straight line the side of the pen to which it is fastened, and this opening shall not be changed until the sheep are confined. When the gate is opened, the contestant shall grasp the end of a rope 6 feet long, tied to the open end of the gate, and shall confine his movements to the limit fixed by this rope.

Each dog shall work its assigned sheep into the pen unassisted in any way by the handler, other than directions given by spoken, whistled, or otherwise imparted command. Contestants who may by choice carry a cane or shepherd's crook (whips and lashes being barred) shall not employ same for blocking or hindering sheep, nor shall canes or crooks be used in a manner to indicate that the dog requires intimidation for control. A dog that works too loosely or too tight to maintain control shall lose points.

Work at pen shall involve such awarding or loss of points as the Judges may decide, with the restriction that any dog that fails to pen all assigned sheep cannot be awarded for the effort to pen more than two-thirds of the total points allowed for penning.

SINGLE SHEEP

Competitors will proceed to shedding ring leaving the Dog to bring the lot from pen to ring Shedding off one unmarked sheep within the ring and thereafter, worn (in or outside of the ring) to the Judges satisfaction. Competitors are forbidden to assist the dog by driving off the single any distance or to press it on the dog. His work shall be deliberate and decisive.

STYLE

Separate points for style alone are not awarded; but allowance for good style is included in points allowed in each phase of work. The Judging Committee shall have regard for the fundamental consideration that every movement of sheep or results. Faulty style includes such mannerisms as excessive clapping, freezing to position, much bouncing around, dodging in and out, over-running, too wide or too sharp flanking, over-cautious waiting, belly-crawling and hiding, indifference, shyness, and similar. Good style distinguishes the dog that is alert, fast, concentrated, intelligent, forceful, earnest, straightforward, and altogether sedate.

COMMAND

Points for command, as with style, are included in the score allowed in each phase of work. Obedience to command is vital.

The handler who works his dog with the fewest commands, quietly given, gains preference over the handler who directs his dog with excessive or confusing commands, much noisy shouting, whistling, waving of arms, or otherwise causes unneccessary commotion, distraction, or disturbance. The Judges shall appraise the manner in which the dog accepts commands given and responds to them.

Here, in part, are the General Rules:

1. ORDER OF RUNNING: The order of running shall be determined either by the Trials Committee or by "drawing for position" by the contestants prior to the Trials. If the order is fixed by the Committee, each contestant shall be notified by the Secretary as soon as possible after the entries close. If the order is determined by drawings, the contestants shall draw for only one dog in turn, and if a contestant has more than one entry, the dog for which each drawing is to be made must be stated before each drawing is made.

2. COURSE USE: Contestants may appear on, or travel over any officially designated course before the trials have begun, but a contestant, under no circumstance shall take his dog or dogs over the course, or allow the dog access to the course under direction or otherwise, before the time the dog is called to appear for his run in the trials. Violation of this rule shall disqualify any entry known, or determined to have had this advantage.

3. UNSOUND SHEEP: It shall be the aim to provide each contestant with sound, healthy sheep. Should an unsoundness, such as blindness, short-wind, nervous collapse, or similar show after the sheep are "lifted" by the dog, the Judges may have the Course Director order the unsound sheep dropped from the group and the contestant directed to continue without loss of points, or given a re-run. Sheep which turn unruly or stubborn or unneccessarily wild or exhausted as a result of faulty work on the part of the dog, shall not be treated as "unsound" sheep.

4. OVERDRIVING: Exhausting sheep through much running and faulty work may, in extreme cases, disqualify, or the dog may continue with loss of points, according to the Judges' decision. The object is to handle sheep quietly, easily, confidently, having control and directing movement without injury of any sort.

5. GRIPPING or BITING: If a dog bites a sheep in a severe manner, the dog may be disqualified and removed, or the dog may continue according to the Judges' decision; but any biting or severe gripping shall involve a loss of points at the Judges' discretion. In the case of injury to a sheep, the contestants shall be held financially liable for any damage his dog may do, but not to exceed the value of the sheep injured.

Betty Levin's "Tyne" at New Boston, N.H. Sheepdog Trial. (Photo: Carole L. Presberg)

6. UNEARNED POINTS: In case where sheep follow the prescribed course in prescribed manner without the dog actually causing the sheep to so follow the course, a case of unearned points shall be declared. The contestant may accept a deduction of points for that sectional phase of work involved (with Judges announcing the deduction), or the contestant may be granted retrial in that phase of work where the deduction occurred - the points in the retrial to become a part of final score, with earlier points to be disregarded.

7. INCOMPETENT DOG: The Judging Committee may terminate the run of any dog judged "incompetent" of the work assigned.

8. UNFINISHED WORK: A dog which fails to complete the work in the time allowed, shall be allowed the points earned up to the expiration of the time-limit set.

9. COMPLETED COURSE: The course shall be declared completed when the dog has had an opportunity at all phases of the work. The highest scoring dog in all phases of the work will be declared the winner of the contest.

10. SHEEP LOST OR OFF COURSE: Sheep which break off the Course, or are otherwise lost from the group the dog is handling (after due opportunity to reunite the group by the dog) shall involve loss of points at the Judges' discretion and according to the circumstance, and if half or more of the assigned sheep are lost or off course, the run shall be terminated and the dog called in.

11. BREAKING OUT OF POSITION: Each contestant shall have regard for assigned position for each phase of work; and breaking out of or leaving position without instruction shall involve loss of points according to the Judge's decision.

12. DELAYED APPEARANCE: Any contestant who fails to enter the ring within five (5) minutes after being called shall forfeit his entry; or under acceptable excuse, shall run last in the contest.

13. HEALTH OF DOG: - FEMALE IN SEASON: Under no circumstances will a dog suffering infectious disease or a female dog "in season" be allowed on the trial grounds before or during a contest. "In-season" females, if so decided by officials before the trials, may run in one-day events AFTER all other dogs have finished their work and final scores determined; the admittance of entry to rest with the officials for the day or the event, and admittance of the dog to the grounds to follow after all other runs have been completed.

14. NON-CONTESTING DOGS: Non-Contesting Dogs of all descriptions and under any circumstance are barred from the trials grounds.

15. OUTSIDE INTERFERENCE: Any disturbing incident which interferes with each and every contestant having equal opportunity shall be ruled on by the Judging Committee and the Committee's decision shall be final.

GREAT BRITAIN SHEEPDOG TRIALS

Sheepdog trials in Great Britain are held under the rules of the International Sheepdog Society. Again, there are three types of trials. Local trials are held all over Great Britain. Qualifying or National Championship trials are held in Scotland, Wales, England, and Ireland each year. The top dogs at the qualifying trials in each country then go on to compete at the International Supreme Championship held every year.

In a Qualifying Trial, the dogs must gather the sheep at a distance of 400 yards. The driving is for a total of 200 yards, the shedding ring is 20 yards in diameter, and the pen is six feet square. The time limit is 15 minutes. Dogs are scored as follows:

Gathering (Outrun 5, Lift 5, Fetch 10) . . . . 20 points

Driving (2 gates) . . . . 10 points

Shedding (separate 2 unmarked sheep) . . . . 5 points

Penning . . . . 5 points

The International Supreme Championship Trial Course.

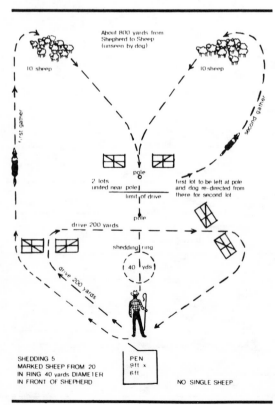

About 800 yards from Shepherd to Sheep (unseen by dog)

10 sheep

10 sheep

first gather

second gather

2 lots united near pole

limit of drive

first lot to be left at pole and dog re-directed from there for second lot

pole

pole

drive 200 yards

shedding ring

40 yds

drive 200 yards

SHEDDING 5
MARKED SHEEP FROM 20
IN RING 40 yards DIAMETER
IN FRONT OF SHEPHERD

PEN
9ft x
6ft

NO SINGLE SHEEP

Single Sheep (separate 1 marked sheep)........ 5 points

Style of Working.......................... 5 points

MAXIMUM TOTAL SCORE 50 points

The International Course is more difficult. It involves an 800 yard gather of 10 sheep concealed from sight, and brought through a central gate, then redirection to a second gather of 10 sheep also hidden from sight and brought through the central gate, and a triangular drive through a set of two gates and 200 yards apart, for a total drive of 400 yards (the drive ends at the second gate).

Gilchrist's Spot 24981, the Scottish National Champion of 1965 and 1966. (Photo from "A Lifetime with the Working Collie" by Arthur N. Allen.)

THE INTERNATIONAL SHEEP DOG SOCIETY
6 Pelham Road, Sherwood Rise, Nottingham, England

Notes For The Guidance Of Judges

INTRODUCTION

February, 1965

The object of a Trial Course is to test the ability of a dog to manage sheep properly under the differing circumstances which may be encountered in everyday work. Hence the various tests such as Gathering, Driving, Shedding, Singling and Penning are all tasks which may be necessary as the shepherd goes his daily round.

These notes are prepared for the guidance of all who act as Judges at Local, National or International Trials. They are not designed as hard and fast rules which must be strictly obeyed on all occasions, but they are the considered opinion of a number of well-known handlers and Judges.

The I.S.D.S. stands firmly for a common standard and this should and must be the constant aim of every Judge and every handler. In producing and issuing these notes the Society hopes that it will be able to guide Judges at Local Trials to adopt similar standards to those applicable to National and International Trials. It is, therefore, essential that we should have some sort of common standard on which to work and the aim of these notes is to achieve such a standard.

In suggesting the need for a "Guide on Judging" the Society starts with the problem facing the Committees of the many Local Trials in appointing suitable Judges. The number of experienced Judges available for these Trials is so restricted that many Trials depend upon accepting Judges with limited experience in this most important part of a Trial. The shortage of Judges is caused by the restricted number of experienced handlers who are prepared to share this work at, in most cases, a sacrifice of financial gain.

The Council of the Society is satisfied that the whole future of Sheepdog Trials in the country is dependent upon Judges of experience and integrity who are prepared to study and understand the Society's "Rules for Trials" and then apply them impartially. We cannot emphasize too much this simple fact — All the information to cover almost every possible set of circumstances is in the Rules for Trials.

With little guidance available on the principles of judging it is not surprising that many Judges are influenced by the reputation of the dog and/or the handler, and in consequence the use of the discretion afforded to Judges by the Society's Rules in difficult cases is often impossible to exercise because they have no basic principles to guide them.

It must be acknowledged that it is not always an easy task to decide the merits of a run AS A WHOLE and Judges should always have a good look at the score sheet after the run has been completed and should then decide whether or not they have been too severe or too lax in any one aspect after marking.

The following general observations on the various parts of a Trial Course give the considered opinion of the Society and should always be followed by Judges at any Trial organised by or affiliated to the I.S.D.S.

OUTRUN

The dog must be positioned nearby the handler and may be sent out on either side. He should not be too straight or too wide and in going out the dog should not require nor should he receive any commands.

The command by whistle is to be regarded as the same as a spoken command.

If a dog crosses the Course, a minimum of 50% of the total points for the Outrun is to be deducted and, in addition points must be deducted for commands.

The perfect outrun should be completed without any commands and Judges should deduct points for every command given and the loss of points will depend upon the Judge's views of the seriousness of the mistakes. The dog should not stop and should not cut in.

It is obviously more serious if a dog stops on his outrun than if he goes on after being re-directed, and Judges should mark accordingly.

A good Outrun should be in the shape of one side of a pear with the blunt end of the pear at the far end of the field near the sheep. The dog should finish far enough away from the sheep so as not to disturb them.

Where the Outrun ends will vary with the actual position of the sheep. If the sheep have left their appointed place at the post the Outrun should end at the point where the dog is facing them in order to bring the sheep in a direct line to the first obstacle. In effect, this means that if the sheep have left the post, the dog is to finish his Outrun facing the heads of the sheep. This might necessitate the dog stopping on the side of his Outrun if the sheep happened to be coming to meet him, and conversely could mean him going a long way past the post if the sheep were going away from the post in the same direction as he is running.

If the sheep remain at the post, the Outrun will end when the dog is behind them and in line with his master.

He must always finish facing them in order to be in a position to fetch them direct to the first obstacle.

LIFT

At the end of the Outrun, whether the dog has come to a full stop or merely slowed down, his approach should be smooth, cautious and steady and the main feature of the "Lift" is an ability to take control in a firm and quiet manner without disturbing the sheep.

He should not rush in and thus startle the sheep and he should not lie back and require numerous commands before getting his sheep on the move.

Judges will deduct points for excessive commands, slowness, etc., at this phase of the Trial. Apart from these observations Judges must use their personal knowledge of sheep and sheepdogs to decide whether a lift has disturbed the sheep unduly and must mark accordingly.

FETCH

The sheep should be brought at a steady pace and in a straight line from the place of lifting to the first obstacle, and thereafter in a straight line to the handler.

The dog should not hurry or over-flank his sheep (this means that he should not go too far on either side thereby turning his sheep across the course and giving a zig-zag movement).

He should require few, if any, commands, and where the sheep are inclined to stray from the true line the dog's ability is judged by his control to them and his immediate answer to all commands.

If the gates are missed or if the sheep are off-line, the penalty must reflect all the circumstances, and in particular the amount of fault attributable to the dog and/or the handler. Both can be the subject of penalties. If the sheep are docile and mistakes are made then the penalty should be more severe than where the sheep are awkward and thereby contribute to diversions which the dog is unable to avoid.

If a gate is missed there should be a minimum deduction of half a point per sheep but Judges must take into consideration all the relevant circumstances

Rob Roy, a top-winning trial dog in the New England area, owned by Maurice MacGregor.

Aust. Ch. Tullaview Temptress driving sheep with typical Border Collie style. Ewes with lambs at their side can be extremely aggressive, and it takes a good dog to handle them effectively. She is owned by Bill and Lynn Harrison of Australia.

contributing to the missing of the gate and adjust deductions accordingly.

The sheep should be passed behind the handler as close to the post as practical and the whole work should be done in a steady and smooth manner.

DRIVING

The "Drive" takes place in a triangular direction and can be run either from left to right or right to left according to the course and the decision of the Trials Committee.

The first leg of the triangle starts immediately the sheep have passed behind the handler and the sheep are required to go in a straight line for 150 yards (or 200 yards at the International) to the first set of gates.

Having got the sheep through the gates they should be turned immediately on to a direct line across the course to the second set of gates. When through these gates they should then be turned as neatly as possible on a straight line to the shedding ring.

It is important that the last leg of the triangle should be in a straight line to the shedding ring which is usually situated to make this also the most direct line. The dog should show obvious ability to drive steadily without excessive commands. Reasonable turns at the post and at both gates are expected.

Good handling in difficult situations will be taken into consideration by the Judge.

As in the "Fetch" the gates are guides to the alignment of the sheep.

Throughout the "Drive" the sheep should be kept moving gently—excessive bursts of speed and subsequent stopping is not desirable and should be penalised. If a gate is missed there should be a minimum deduction of half a point per sheep but Judges must take into consideration all the relevant circumstances contributing to the missing of a gate and adjust deductions accordingly. The handler must not leave the post until the sheep are actually in the shedding ring.

SHEDDING

Shedding necessitates negotiation of the sheep within the ring by the handler and dog to the best position for effecting the deliberate shed by the dog of two specified sheep. Having got the sheep suitably positioned the dog should come in and take off the required sheep and once having taken them off he must have them under control before the "Shed" can be deemed satisfactory. The important aspect here is to test the dog's ability to shed or separate the two unmarked sheep from the rest of the flock.

The dog must be in full control of the two shed sheep, otherwise the "Shed" will not be deemed satisfactory and should be penalized. The ideal "Shed" occurs when the dog comes towards the handler when commanded by him; e.g., cuts off the sheep which are to be shed and holds them away from the rest.

The "Shed" is complete when the dog has come in when commanded by the handler and is in control of his two sheep. It is not necessary for the dog to come right through to the handler.

On completion of the "Shed" the handler should bring his sheep together in a practical and workmanlike manner.

PENNING

There is no rule about bringing the two sheep to the remaining three or vice-versa. The "pen" will be 6 ft. x 9 ft. with a gate to which is secured a rope 6 ft. long. On completion of shedding, the handler must proceed to the "pen" leaving his dog to bring the sheep to the "pen." The handler is forbidden to assist the dog to drive the sheep to the pen. The handler will stand at the gate holding the rope and must not let go of the rope whilst the dog works the sheep into the pen. The handler will close the gate. After releasing the sheep the handler will close and fasten the gate and shall be penalized for failure to fasten the gate.

All these points must be marked and each failure to pen shall be the subject of a penalty deduction.

SINGLE

The handler will proceed to the shedding ring leaving the dog to bring the sheep from the pen to the ring.

Imported Spot owned by Carrol Shaffner (PAK Photo).

Alex McKinvin's "Kate" at Cummington, Mass. Sheepdog Trial. (Photo: Carole L. Presberg)

One of two marked sheep will be shed off within the ring and thereafter "worn" (inside or outside the ring) to the Judges' satisfaction. Handlers are forbidden to assist the dog in driving off or attempting to drive off the single any distance or by forcing it on the dog.

If the Judges are agreed that a dog has not been fairly tested owing to the disposition and action of the sheep they may order the handler to collect the sheep again and shed off and wear any other sheep. As with the "Shed" the dog and not the handler should come in and cut off the single sheep.

Far too many handlers are seen cutting off the sheep whilst the dog lies back acting as an almost uninterested spectator. This should be heavily penalised. The greatest help the handler can give his dog is by getting out of the way and allowing his dog room to prove his ability to take off and wear a single sheep. It is essential that the dog should be able to keep the "single" sheep away from the remainder and the Judges should not express their satisfaction until the dog has been thoroughly tested and they are satisfied that he has proved his ability to do this. Here again, the behaviour of the sheep should be considered by the Judges when deciding whether the "single" has been effectively completed or not.

To sum up:—

(1) Almost every possible set of circumstances is covered in the Society's Rules for Trials (copies can be obtained from the Secretary) and every Judge should know these Rules.

(2) Every Judge accepting an invitation to act at any of the Society's Trials will be held, by his acceptance, to have given an undertaking that he will judge strictly according to the Rules laid down by the Society and that he will not favour any dog, man or country.

SHEEP DOG TRIALS IN NEW ZEALAND AND AUSTRALIA

New Zealand has three types of trials: local, district, and open trials. Dogs are run on trials similar to those in Great Britain, except there is also a class for "Hunt-a-ways" (Barking dogs—usually Border Collie/Labrador crosses). In the Border Collie classes, two different events are held. Dogs are scored as follows:

FIRST EVENT
(time limit 8 or 10 minutes)

1. Heading (outrun)..........................44 points
2. Pull back (fetch)..........................44 points
3. Holding (in a marked ring)..................12 points
    MAXIMUM TOTAL SCORE   100 points

SECOND EVENT
(time limit 14 minutes)

1. Heading..................................36 points
2. Pull....................................36 points
3. Driving.................................20 points
4. Yarding (penning).........................8 points
    MAXIMUM TOTAL SCORE   100 points

In Australia, there are a wide variety of trial courses. The scoring at the Brisbane and Melbourne Royal Agricultural Shows is as follows:

1. Cast (Outrun)...........................12 points
2. Approach (Lift)......................... 5 points

Melbourne (Australia) Royal Agriculture Show Sheepdog Trial Course.

MELBOURNE SHOW GROUND trial course

112

3. Bringing (Fetch). . . . . 8 points
4. Command (Obedience). . . . . .20 points
5. Obstacles. . . . . .25 points
6. General Work (Style, Force and Control of Sheep). .30 points
MAXIMUM TOTAL SCORE   100 points

The scoring at the Sydney Royal Agricultural Show and Sheep Show is slightly different. The scale of points is given below:

1. Cast (Outrun). . . . . 8 points
2. Steadiness. . . . . .15 points
3. Command (Obedience). . . . . .20 points
4. Dog's Command of Sheep (Control). . . . . .10 points
5. Approach (Lift). . . . . 6 points
6. General Working. . . . . .20 points
7. Gate. . . . . 6 points
8. Bridge. . . . . 7 points
9. Yarding (Penning). . . . . 8 points
MAXIMUM TOTAL SCORE   100 points

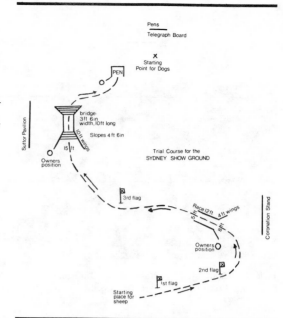

The Sydney (Australia) Royal Agriculture Show Sheepdog Trial Course.

WINNERS OF INTERNATIONAL SUPREME TRIALS
From 1906-1981

1906 *Don (11)* - Richard Sandilands, South Queensferry, Scotland

1907 *Moss (22)* - William Wallace, Otterburn, England

1908 *Kep (13)* - James Scott, Troney Hill, Ancrum, Scotland

1909 *Kep (13)* - James Scott, Troyen Hill, Ancrum, Scotland

1910 *Sweep (21)* - Adam Telfer, Fairnly, Cambo, England

1911 *Lad (17)* - Thomas Armstrong, Greenchesters, Otterburn, England

1912 *Sweep (21)* - Thomas Armstrong, Greenchester, Otterburn, England

1913 *Lad (19)* - T.P. Brown, Oxton, Berwickshire, Scotland

1914 *Don (17)* - Thomas Armstrong, Greenchester, Otterburn, England

1915-1918 Trials not held

1919 *Midge (152) Walter Telfer, Cambo, Morpett, England*

1920 *Hemp (307)* - S.E. Batty, Kiveton Hall, Sleffield, England

1921 *Haig (252)* - Adam Telfer, Fenwick, Stam Fordham, England

1922 *MEG (306)* - William Wallace, Otterburn, England

1923 *Spot (308)* - George P. Brown, Oxton,Berwickshire, Scotlant

1924 *Jaff (379)* - Thomas Roberts, Corwen, Wales

1925 *Spot (303)* - Mr. A. Millar, Highbowhill, Newmilns, Ayrshire, Scotland

1926 *Glen (698)* - Mr. Mark Hayton, Clifton, Otley, Yorkshire, England

1927 *Lad (305)* - Mr. J. B. Bagshaw, The Mantles, Blyth, Rotherham, England

1928 *Fly (824)* - Mr. James M. Wilson, Holmshaw, Moffat, Scotland

1929 *Corby (338)* - Mr. S. E. Batty, Letwell, Worksop, England

1930 *Craig (1048)* - Mr. James M. Wilson, Holmshaw, Moffat, Scotland

1931 *Jess (1007)* - Mr. John Thorp, Old House, Derwent, Sheffield, England

Jack Knox and "Jed" at Bond Head, Ontario, Sheepdog Trial. (Photo: Carole L. Presberg)

(Winners of International Supreme Trials - Continued)

1932   *Queen (533)* - Mr. W. B. Telfer, Fairnley, Cambo, Morpeth, England

1933   *Chip (672)* - Mr. George Whiting, Tir, Mawr, Aberdare, Wales

1934   *Roy (1665)* - Mr. James M. Wilson, Holmshaw, Moffat, Scotland

1935   *Jaff (2199)* - Mr. John Jones, Tany-y-gaer, Corwen, Wales

1936   *Roy (1665)* - Mr. James M. Wilson, Whitehope, Innerleithen, Scotland

1937   *Roy (1665)* - Mr. James M. Wilson, Whitehope, Innerleithen, Scotland

1938   *Jed I (1492)* - Mr. W. J. Wallace, Jr., East Otterburn, Otterburn, England

1939-1945 - Cancelled

1946   *Glen (3940)* - Mr. J. M. Wilson, Whitehope, Innerleithen, Scotland

1947   *Spot (3624)* - Mr. J. Gilchrist, Haddington, Scotland

1948   *Glen (3940)* - Mr. J. M. Wilson, Innerleithen, Scotland

1949   *Chip (4924)* - Mr. D. W. Daniel, Ystradgynlais, Wales

1950   *Mirk (4438)* - Mr. J. M. Wilson, Innerleithen, Scotland

1951   *Pat (4203)* - Mr. E. A. Priestley, Bamford, England

1952   *Chip (4924)* - Mr. D. W. Daniel, Ystradgynlais, Wales

1953   *Roy (7976)* - Mr. W. J. Evans, Magor, Wales

1954   *Mirk (5444)* - Mr. J. McDonald, Lauder, Berwicks, Scotland

1955   *Bill (9040)* - Mr. J. M. Wilson, Innerleithen, Scotland

1956   *Moss (6805)* - Mr. G. R. Redpath, Jedburgh, Scotland

1957   *Moss (11241)* - Mr. J. H. Holliday, Pateley Bridge, England

1958   *Tweed (9601)* - Mr. W. J. Evans, Tidenham, Glos, England

1959   *Ben (13879)* - Mr. Meirion Jones, Llandrillo, Wales

1960   *Ken (13306)* - Mr. E. L. Daniel, Ystradgynlais, Wales

1961   *Roy (15393)* - Mr. Alan Jones, Pontllyfni, Wales

1962   *Garry (17690)* - Mr. A. T. Lloyd, Builth Wells, Wales

1963   *Juno (17815)* - Mr. H. J. Worthington, Abergavenney, Wales

1964   *Craig (15445)* - Mr. L. R. Suter, Cross Keys, Wales

1965   *Wiston Cap (31154)* - Mr. J. Richardson, Peebles, Scotland

1966   *Ken (17166)* - Mr. Tim Longton, Quernmore, England

1967   *Gael (14463)* - Mr. T. T. McKnight, Canonbie, Scotland

1968   *Bosworth Coon (34186)* - Mr. Llyr Evans, Towcester, England

1969   *Bet (40428)* - Mr. H. Huddleston, Carnforth, England

1970   *Wiston Bill (36391)* - Mr. D. McTier, Peebles, Scotland

1971   *Glen (47241)* - Mr. J. Murray, Sanquhar, Scotland

1972   *Cap (50543)* - Mr. J. J. Templeton, Kilmarnock, Scotland

1973   *Gel (63023)* - Glyn Jones, Bodfari, Wales

1974   *Bill (51654)* - Gwyn Jones, Penmachmo, Wales

1975   *Zac (66166)* - Raymond McPherson, Hallbankgate, England

1976   *Shep (73360)* - Gwyn Jones - Penmachmog, Wales

1977   *Craig (59425)* - John R. Thomas - Llandovery, Wales

1978   *Mirk (67512)* - Robert Shennan, Turnberry, Scotland

1979   *Zac (66166)* - Raymond MacPherson, Hallbankgate, England

1980   *Jen (93965)* - Tom Watson, Lauder, Scotland

1981   *Bill (78263)* - Wyn Edwards, Ruthin, Wales

Obedience Trials 16

The Retrieve over the high jump, an Open level obedience exercise, combining retrieving and jumping. (Photo: J.E.L.)

Obedience trials are great fun. After watching my first trial, I decided my Border Collie could do whatever the other dogs could do! I was right. By the end of that summer I trained my four-year-old dog Pendulum through the novice exercises and entered him in his first show. To my delight, he won first place in the novice class and went on to highest scoring dog in trial (with a nearly perfect score).

AMERICAN TRIALS

There are six titles your dog can win in Obedience competition in the United States. Companion Dog (CD), Companion Dog Excellent (CDX), Utility Dog (UD), Tracking Dog (TD), Tracking Dog Excellent (TDX), and Obedience Trial Champion (OTCH). In order to compete, your dog must have an Indefinite Listing Privilege Number. He does not have to be registered to get an ILP, but must fit the breed Standard. In fact, many purebred, registered Border Collies are not given ILP numbers because they do not look anything like the Standard for the breed. The ILP is issued by a committee at the AKC on the basis of how the dog looks in a series of photographs.

NOVICE

In the Novice class, the dog competes for the Companion Dog (C.D.) Degree. To gain this title he must earn a qualifying score under three different judges at three different shows. A qualifying score must be at least one half the points available for each exercise, with an overall score of 170 or more out of a possible 200 points. In the Novice A division, the only dogs eligible are those handled by a person who has never won an Obedience title on any dog before. Conversely, the Novice B class is for persons who have shown a dog to an obedience title.

The following is a list and description of Novice Class:

1. Heel on leash............................40 points
2. Stand for examination (off leash).............30 points
3. Heel off leash............................40 points
4. Recall (come and finish off leash).............30 points
5. Long sit (1 minute—all dogs in ring & off leash)................................30 points
6. Long down (3 minutes—all dogs in ring & off leash)................................30 points

MAXIMUM TOTAL SCORE 200 points

OPEN

In the Open class dogs compete for their Companion Dog Excellent title. The scoring and requirements are the same for the C.D.X. as for the Companion Dog title, except that the exercises are different. Open A is for dogs who have their C.D. only and Open B is open to any dog with at least a C.D. title. Licensed obedience judges and professional trainers are not allowed to compete in the "A" division but are eligible for the "B" division. Below is a list of exercises and a short description of each:

1. Heel (off leash)...........................40 points
2. Drop on recall............................30 points
3. Retrieve on flat..........................20 points
4. Retrieve over high jump...................30 points
5. Broad jump...............................20 points
6. Long sit (3 minutes—handler out of sight).....30 points
7. Long down (5 minutes—handler out of sight)...30 points

MAXIMUM TOTAL SCORE   200 points

Most Border Collies enjoy the Open class far more than Novice. My first dog loved retrieving anything from frogs to birds, and took great pleasure in doing so. Whereas some dogs of non-hunting breeds retrieve only with great reluctance, not so with Border Collies. A quick dash out and dash back, skidding to a halt with eyes gleaming, and that takes care of the retrieve. One Border Collie loved jumping and retrieving so much that he once jumped over the high jump *six* times back and forth with the dumbbell in his mouth instead of just once as was required. In another instance, a Border Collie I owned could easily clear an eight-foot long, two-foot high broad jump, a seven-foot scale jump, and a four-foot fence.

The Bar jump with a glove. It is wise to mix up the routines in practice to prevent boredom. (Photo: J.E.L.)

UTILITY

In the Utility Class, the dog must again qualify with a score of 170 or above and pass each exercise before earning a "leg," or qualifying score. He must qualify under three different judges at three different shows and must already have his C.D.X. degree. The U.D. is difficult to obtain, as you can see. The exercises are listed below:

1. Signal exercise...........................40 points
2. Scent discrimination—leather article..........30 points
3. Scent discrimination—metal article...........30 points
4. Directed retrieve (of a glove)...............30 points
5. Directed jumping (bar & solid)..............40 points
6. Group stand for examination (3 minutes)......30 points

MAXIMUM SCORE   200 points

Utility, though difficult, is by far the most fun and exciting of all classes. The exercises used in this competition can easily be modified into practical or fun tricks. Often I have given demonstrations for small children at school, 4-H Club meetings, and other occasions. A modification of scent discrimination is a real hit. I have an assistant line up different colored blocks. Then I tell the dog to go find the green one or the blue one. This convinces the children the dog can tell colors, whereas it was really his scent discrimination at work.

Utility hand signals-the "sit." Donna Lee and Bradford show how its done.

TRACKING

To receive a tracking degree, the dogs compete at a tracking test (separate from a dog show) and are judged by two judges. Both judges must give the dog passing marks before he can obtain his Tracking Degree. The track is designed to test a dog's ability to track a person.

For further information on tracking rules and regulations, or addresses of clubs, write to AKC.

OBEDIENCE CHAMPIONSHIPS

The Obedience Trial Championship (OTCH) is a relatively recent addition to the AKC's list of awards, with the first championship points awarded in July, 1977. To become an Obedience Trial Champion, a dog must have a Utility degree and earn a total of 100 points by winning first or second in the Open B and Utility Classes at Obedience Trials. The dog must win three first places under three different judges with a first place in both the Open B and Utility classes. The number of points awarded are based on the number of dogs entered.

DOG WORLD AWARD

Dog World magazine awards a certificate to any dog earning any obedience title in his *first* three consecutive attempts with scores of 195 or above. Winning this award is a coveted honor. If your dog is eligible, send his scores, name, and date of the shows along with his registration number (or ILP), breeder's name, sire and dam, and your name and address to the magazine. If he qualifies, your dog will be enrolled in their file of great dogs of the past and present, and you will receive a certificate.

BRITISH TRIALS

In Great Britain there are three classes of Obedience trials: A, B, and C. Obedience *Certificates* are only awarded at test C trials to dogs who have won a first prize with no less than 190 points of a possible

Gussie-U.D.T. owned by Susan and Michelle Luebbert of California, hard at work on a track. Border Collies make excellent tracking dogs. (Photo: Courtesy of Susan & Michelle Luebbert)

The broad jump is easily cleared by Donnalee's Bradford - U.D. owned by Donna C. Lee of Swanton, Ohio. This is an Open class exercise.

Here Gussie has found the glove at the end of the track.

200. A dog becomes an *Obedience Champion* if he wins three Obedience *Certificates* under three different judges.

Titles of Companion Dog (C.D.), Utility Dog (U.D.), Working Dog (W.D.), Police Dog (P.D.), and Tracking Dog (T.D.) are earned by winning three first places at a Championship trial with at least seventy percent of the possible points for each exercise. To qualify for an added "X," meaning excellent, the dog must gain 80 percent of the possible points in each exercise.

At test A trials, no Obedience Champions or dogs who have previously won four first prizes may compete. In test B trials, no Obedience Champions or dogs who have won four first places in a test B or C trial may compete. At a test C show, the judging is much stricter. Only one command or signal may be used. All dogs may compete. The exercises are as follows:

COMPANION DOG (CD) STAKES

1. Heel on leash . . . . 5 points
2. Heel off leash . . . . 15 points
3. Sit (2 minutes—all dogs in ring, handler out of sight) . . . . 10 points
4. Recall (with sit in front and finish) . . . . 10 points
5. Send away, drop and recall . . . . 10 points
6. Down (10 minutes—handler out of sight) . . . . . . 10 points
7. (a) Scale jump—6 feet high . . . . 10 points
   (b) Clear jump—3 feet high . . . . 5 points
   (c) Long jump—9 feet long . . . . 5 points
8. Retrieve on flat . . . . 10 points
9. Elementary search (must find an article with handler's scent dropped in ring) . . . . 10 points

Total Score   100 points

UTILITY DOG (UD) STAKES

1. Heel off leash . . . . 5 points
2. Send away (20 yards), drop and recall . . . . 10 points
3. Retrieve on flat . . . . 5 points
4. Down (10 minutes—handler out of sight) . . . . . . 10 points
5. Steadiness to gunshot . . . . 5 points
6. (a) 6 foot scale (3); stand (2); and recall over scale jump (6 ft. high) . . . . 10 points
   (b) Clear jump—3 feet . . . . 5 points
   (c) Long jump—9 feet . . . . 5 points
7. Search (dog must find 4 stranger's articles in a 25 square yard area) . . . . 35 points
8. (a) Track (on leash—½ mile or more, ½ hour or older) . . . . 95 points
   (b) Indicate article at end of the track (belonging to track layer) . . . . 15 points

Maximum Total Score   200 points

WORKING DOG (WD) STAKES

1. Heel off leash . . . . 5 points
2. Send away (20 yards); stand; recall . . . . 10 points
3. Retrieve on flat . . . . 5 points
4. Down (10 minutes—handler out of sight) . . . . . . 10 points
5. Steadiness to gunshot . . . . 5 points
6. (a) 6 foot scale (3); stand (2); recall over jump (5) . . . . 10 points

   (b) Clear jump (3 feet)..................... 5 points
   (c) Long jump (9 feet).................... 5 points
7. Search (4 strange articles, 25 yard square area)..35 points
8. (a) Track (½ mile or longer, aged
      1½ hours or more)....................80 points
   (b) Recognition of 2 articles on track
      (belonging to track layer)...............30 points
             Maximum Total Score 200 points

Tara finds the correct scent article. This is a Utility class obedience exercise. (Phogo: J.E.L.)

TRACKING DOG (TD) STAKES

1. Heel off leash............................ 5 points
2. Down (10 minutes—handler out of sight).......10 points
3. Send away (50 yards), redirection (20 yards)....10 points
4. Speak and case speaking (on command)....... 5 points
5. Steadiness to gunshot.................... 5 points
6. (a) 6 foot scale (3); stand (2);
      recall after scale jump..................10 points
   (b) Clear jump—3 feet.................... 5 points
   (c) Long jump—9 feet.................... 5 points
7. Search (4 stranger's articles in a
    25 yards square area).....................35 points
8. Track (½ mile or longer, aged 3 hours
    or longer, crosstracks)...................100 points
9. Recognition of 3 articles (belonging
    to track layer)..........................30 points
             Maximum Total Score 220 points

POLICE DOG (PD) STAKES

1. Heel off leash........................... 5 points
2. Down (10 minutes—handler out of sight).......10 points
3. Send away (50 yards); redirection (20 yards)..10 points
4. Speak and cease speaking (on command)...... 5 points
5. Steadiness to gunshot..................... 5 points
6. (a) 6 feet scale jump (3); stand (2);
      recall over scale jump (5)...............10 points
   (b) Clear jump—3 feet.................... 5 points
   (c) Long jump—9 feet.................... 5 points
7. Search (4 articles in a
    25 square yard area).....................35 points
8. (a) Track (½ mile or longer, aged
      1½ or more hours)....................50 points
   (b) Recognition of two articles
      belonging to track layer................20 points
9. Quartering and "baying," and refusing
    food from "lost" person..................35 points
10. Test of courage against attack
    on and/or off leash.....................20 points
11. Search and escort of criminal (defend
    handler when attacked, and cease
    when commanded)......................50 points
12. (a) Recall from criminal running
      away (after attack command)...........20 points
   (b) Pursuit and detention of criminal
      (until handler arrives).................15 points
             Maximum Total Score 300 points

Utility hand signals-the "down," demonstrated by Donna Lee and her Border Collie Bradford.

Indiana Lady, a Border Collie owned by Barbara LeFevre, and Great Dane, Gin-Ed's Indian Chief. Lady has accumulated numerous obedience and Schutzhund titles, including: C.D.X., T.D., V.B. (street dog), A.D. (endurance), W.H. (watchdog), F.H. (advanced tracking), and SchH III, the highest Schutzhund title available. (Photo by Fred Lidam)

Schutzhund Trials 17

Schutzhund training originated in Europe over 80 years ago. It combines tracking, obedience, and protection work, and is the forerunner of modern obedience trials and tracking tests. Schutzhund was designed to test the dog's complete character: temperament, courage, protective instinct, toughness, alertness, freedom from fear, responsiveness, and eagerness to please. On the European Continent, registries for working and herding breeds require that both parents must pass either a Schutzhund, herding, police dog, or military dog trial before a litter or individual may be registered. It is no wonder that the European working dogs have strong working characteristics as well as good looks.

A Schutzhund dog is highly trained, well adjusted, friendly, and versatile. He is capable of high scores at obedience trials, of tracking a lost child, or of protecting his master or his master's property. He attacks only on command unless his master is actually attacked. Even then, the dog only tries to hold the attacker by the arm, and never "goes for the jugular" or tries to kill.

Training a Schutzhund is much different from training a conventional guard or attack dog, where the dog is trained to hate everyone, and is used for warehouse or plant security. The so-called "guard" dog is often abused to make him vicious and neurotic. Such dogs are really only fear biters (dogs who attack out of fear), and are often unreliable and try to escape.

Schutzhund training, on the other hand, is a long process, taking from six months to a year for each level. It utilizes only the dog's natural prey chasing, capturing, tracking, and pack-follower instincts. The protection aspect starts out as a fun game of "catch the burlap sack" and "tug-o-war," which most dogs love, and progresses to catching and holding the puppy sleeve, then the "hard" sleeve, and much later a hidden sleeve. Most dogs love to growl and act fierce when playing tug-o-war. This is encouraged. The barking exercise is taught by not letting the dog have the sack or sleeve until he gets excited enough to bark, and then immediately letting the dog have the sack or sleeve as a reward. From the dog's point of view, Schutzhund is just a game, although the results are impressive.

The Schutzhund dog is also trained in tracking and in obedience, equivalent to Companion Dog Excellent and Utility degrees. If you have a dog with a C.D.X. and T.D. degree, he is already two-thirds of the way to a Schutzhund I degree. Dogs must be at least fourteen months old to compete for Schutzhund I, sixteen months for a Schutzhund II, and eighteen months for a Schutzhund III degree. Other degrees are the A.D. (Endurance Test), and the F.H. (Advanced Tracking degree).

Caora Con's Black Bison, CDX, SchH3, WC barking at the blind after he found "the bad guy" at the Greater Northeastern Schutzhund Club trial.

The maximum total available points for each degree is 300 (100 for protection, 100 for tracking, and 100 for obedience). A dog must receive a score of at least 70 points in tracking and obedience, and at least 80 in protection in order to pass. A total of 0 to 109 points is Unsatisfactory (U), from 110 - 219 Insufficient (I or B), 220 to 239 Satisfactory (S or M), 240 to 269 Good (G), 270 to 285 is Very Good (SG/VG) and from 286 to 300 Excellent (V or E). In the case of a tie, the dog with the highest score on protection wins.

SCHUTZHUND I (SchH I) REQUIREMENTS (300 POINTS TOTAL)

Part A. Tracking: 450 yards of track, aged for at least 20 minutes. The dog has two turns and two articles, and the track is laid by the handler.
Total Score Possible: 100 points

Part B. Obedience

1. Heel on lead . . . . 15 points
2. Heel off lead (through crowd
   of people, with gunshots) . . . . 15 points
3. Sit in motion (from heel) . . . . 10 points
4. Drop and recall . . . . 10 points
5. Retrieve on flat (14 ounce dumbbell) . . . . 10 points
6. Retrieve over high jump (40 in.) . . . . 20 points
7. Sendaway and drop . . . . 10 points
8. Down with distraction (10 minutes, gunshots) 10 points
   Total Score Possible   100 points

Part C. Protection

1. Search, find, and bark (3 blinds) . . . . 10 points
2. Heeling, attack on handler (do attacks) . . . . . . 20 points
3. Release on command and guard suspect . . . . . 10 points
4. Courage test: pursuit and catch . . . . 35 points
5. Release and guarding suspect . . . . 15 points
6. Overall courage and hardness . . . . 10 points
   Total Score Possible   100 points

The retrieve over the eight foot scale jump. This is a Schutzhund/police dog agility exercise. (Photo: J.E.L.)

SCHUTZHUND II (SchH II) REQUIREMENTS (300 POINTS TOTAL)

Part A. Tracking: 750 yards of trail, aged for at least 30 minutes, two turns, two articles, laid by a stranger.

Total Score Possible: 100 points.

Part B. Obedience

1. Heel on lead . . . . 10 points
2. Sit in motion (from heel, in crowd of people) . 5 points
3. Heel off lead, (through crowd with gunshots) . 15 points
4. Drop and recall (through crowd of people) . . . 10 points
5. Retrieve over high jump (40 inch
   jump, 1.5 lb. dumbbell) . . . . 20 points
6. Retrieve on flat (2.2 pound dumbbell) . . . . 10 points

7. Retrieve over 6 ft. scaling wall............10 points
8. Sendaway and drop....................10 points
9. Down with distraction (10 minutes
   with gunshots)........................ 10 points
                Total Score Possible   100 points

Part C. Protection

1. Search and find (6 blinds)............... 5 points
2. Barking and guarding suspect at blind......10 points
3. Escape and capture of suspect............20 points
4. Release and guard suspect...............10 points
5. Transport of suspect by handler and dog.... 5 points
6. Defense of handler....................10 points
7. Courage: pursuit and capture of suspect.....15 points
8. Releasing and guarding suspect...........15 points
9. Overall courage and hardness.............10 points
                Total Score Possible   100 points

Caora Con Lochinvar - CDX clears the broad jump from a stand. The Seven foot broad jump is a Schutzhund III and police agility exercise. (Photo: Col. W.A. Johnston)

SCHUTZHUND III (SchH III) REQUIREMENTS (300 POINTS TOTAL)

Part A. Tracking: 1300 yards, aged for at least 60 minutes, four turns, three articles, laid by a stranger.

Total Score Possible: 100 points.

Part B. Obedience

1. Heel off leash (through crowd,
   with gunshots)........................ 10 points
2. Stand in motion (from heel,
   in crowd), with recall...................15 points
3. Retrieve on flat (4.4 pound dumbbell)....... 5 points
4. Retrieve over high jump
   (1.5 pound dumbbell)...................10 points
5. Retrieve over 6 foot scaling wall..........20 points
6. Sendaway and drop....................15 points
7. 7 foot broad jump with stand.............15 points
8. Down with distraction
   (10 minutes, with gunshots)..............10 points
                Total Score Possible   100 points

Border Collies make excellent tracking dogs, drug and bomb detection dogs and search and rescue dogs because they have such keen noses. (Photo: Col. W.A. Johnston)

Part C. Protection

1. Search and find (8 blinds)............... 5 points
2. Barking and guarding suspect at blind......10 points
3. Escape and capture of suspect............20 points
4. Release and guard suspect...............10 points
5. Transport of suspect by handler and dog.... 5 points
6. Defense of handler....................10 points
7. Courage: Heeling, then pursuit
   and capture of suspect..................20 points
8. Releasing and guarding suspect...........10 points
9. Overall courage and hardness.............10 points
                Total Score Possible   100 points

FAHRTENHUND (FH)
OR ADVANCED TRACKING DEGREE (ATD)

The track is at least 2,000 yards long, at least three hours old, crosses at least one road, one change of vegetation, with at least six turns, three cross-tracks and four articles. Total possible score: 100 points.

four articles: 28 points (7 points each)
correct tracking: 72 points

Deductions: 1-4 points off for faulty starts, circling on turns, carelessness, not working continuously. 1-8 points off for impetuous tracking and overshooting corner (except when due to prevailing winds) 10 points off for urinating and/or defecating on track.

Ratings:
     0 - 35 U (unsatisfactory)
    36 - 69 points I/B (insufficient)
    70 - 79 points S/M (satisfactory)
    80 - 89 points G (good)
    90 - 95 points SG/VG (very good)
    96 - 100 points V/E (excellent)

ENDURANCE TEST (AD OR ET)

The dog must run 12.5 miles in two hours, with a 10 minute rest halfway. The handler may run with the dog or ride a bicycle. After completing the test, the dogs may rest for 15 minutes, and then must be able to perform basic obedience and clear the 40 inch high jump in both directions.

For more information on Schutzhund, write:

The North American Schutzhund Association (NASA)
George Theriot; Business Administrator
7318 Brennans Drive
Dallas, Texas 75214

The United Schutzhund Clubs of America (USA)
Kay Koerner, Treasurer
1926 Hillman Avenue
Belmont, California 94002

Working Dogs of America (WDA)
Dr. Dietman Schellenberg
1164 Watt Road
Webster, New York 14580

DVG America (DVG)
Carole Patterson - Secretary
75343 South Gartner Road
Evergreen, CO 80439

The Window Jump. This is an advanced Police agility exercise. (Photo: J.E.L.)

The Breed Standard 18

WHAT IS A STANDARD?

A breed standard is the written description of the hypothetical perfect dog. It defines the characteristics that are the trademarks of the breed, what traits are desirable and undesirable, and why the breed is distinct from all others. The Standard describes what every breeder should strive to attain in his breeding program. Whereas some breeds are bred purely for their physical appearances and attributes, others are judged on how they perform. For instance, Border Collies have been bred to pedigree on a basis of their working style for over one hundred years, and have subsequently achieved a remarkably standardized level of working performance.

All breed standards are written by their respective breed clubs or associations. Breeders determine good and bad points and traits that make their breed unique. This procedure can often take months or years, since the breeders' opinions can vary greatly. Once the clubs reach a final decision about what the "perfect" dog of their breed is, the standard is written.

The breed standards define the ideal bone structure and gait of the dog, which is fairly universal in all working breeds since a dog with poor angulation, a weak back, weak hindquarters, or an unsound gait could not work or hunt as efficiently as a properly conformed dog. Other traits, such as ears, eyes, coat and color differ from breed to breed and are the areas of greatest disagreement when standards are being resolved. Often these points are largely a matter of what was popular at the time the standard was written.

The Standards for the Border Collie in the various countries where it is popular describe the ideal for the breed, while still allowing a variety of colors and either rough or smooth coats. This gives the individual some choice in what his dog will look like. Until recently, Border Collies throughout the world have been bred only for working ability; in fact, there is even a "working standard" specifying the desirable instincts and behavior patterns for a dog while working livestock. As in Conformation, there are specific traits such as "eye" (the intense stare), heading instinct (the desire to head off running animals), and an extreme desire to please. Without these traits, a dog cannot be considered a good specimen of the Border Collie breed. It is for this reason that the Border Collie Club of America also has a written standard of excellence for working ability.

Despite the fact that many breed standards have been around for nearly a hundred years, there has yet to be born the "perfect" dog. Every dog has some fault, either minor or major, that prevents it from being

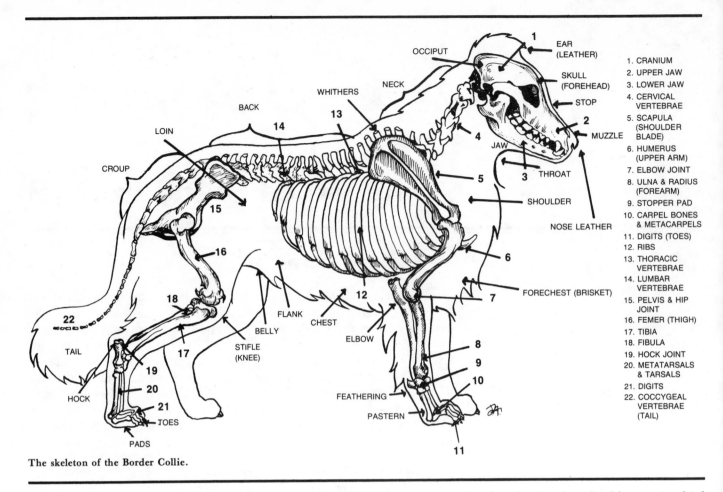

EAR (LEATHER)
OCCIPUT
SKULL (FOREHEAD)
STOP
WHITHERS
NECK
BACK
2
MUZZLE
LOIN
13
JAW
4
14
CROUP
5
3 THROAT
15
SHOULDER
16
NOSE LEATHER
6
22
18
FORECHEST (BRISKET)
7
TAIL
12
FLANK
BELLY
CHEST
17
STIFLE (KNEE)
ELBOW
8
19
9
20
10
HOCK
FEATHERING
21
PASTERN
TOES
PADS
11

1. CRANIUM
2. UPPER JAW
3. LOWER JAW
4. CERVICAL VERTEBRAE
5. SCAPULA (SHOULDER BLADE)
6. HUMERUS (UPPER ARM)
7. ELBOW JOINT
8. ULNA & RADIUS (FOREARM)
9. STOPPER PAD
10. CARPEL BONES & METACARPELS
11. DIGITS (TOES)
12. RIBS
13. THORACIC VERTEBRAE
14. LUMBAR VERTEBRAE
15. PELVIS & HIP JOINT
16. FEMER (THIGH)
17. TIBIA
18. FIBULA
19. HOCK JOINT
20. METATARSALS & TARSALS
21. DIGITS
22. COCCYGEAL VERTEBRAE (TAIL)

The skeleton of the Border Collie.

perfect. People must remember that the dog described in any standard does not really exist, but is just an ideal.

OFFICIAL STANDARD OF AMERICAN REGISTRIES

All three "official" Border Collie Registries in the United States, the NASDS, the AIBC, and the ABCA, are opposed to a written conformation standard. Their only standard is WORKING ABILITY.

Size: Large, Medium or Small
Coat: Rough, Medium or Smooth
Color: All colors accepted
Ears: Prick, Semi-prick or Drop

THE AMERICAN BORDER COLLIE STANDARD
Approved June 1980 by the Border Collie Club of America (Amended January 1985)

General Appearance   The general appearance of the Border Collie is that of a medium sized, alert, well-proportioned dog, with the strength, stamina, and agility to endure long periods of active duty in its designated task as a working stockdog. The double coat may be rough or smooth, and the coloring offers a wide variety of individuality in each specimen. Soundness of structure and movement, and freedom from exaggeration of coat and type are of utmost importance in a working breed such as the Border Collie. Dogs should be presented in their natural, untrimmed coats, and be in a hard, working condition, without excess finish.

Imported Toss, owned by Edgar Gould of Massachusetts. Prick ears are fairly common in the breed and can be traced back to the Viking Spitz ancestors brought over to the Brittish Isle by raiding Vikings. Drop ears trace to the Roman Herding dogs. (Photo: J.E.L.)

Characteristics   The Border Collie is necessarily extremely intelligent and very responsive to training for a wide variety of tasks. A well bred dog will instinctively circle wide around livestock with no training, will control it with its keen and intent gaze or "eye," seeming to hypnotize its charges, and is ready for instant action should they try to break away. The breed exhibits a remarkable dexterity in stopping, turning, and dropping, and possesses unusual speed and stamina for a dog of its size.

Head   Skull basically box-like in shape, broader between the ears, giving ample brain room, and narrowing slightly to the eyes. Muzzle moderately blunt, with length slightly less than or equal to the length of the skull. Stop moderate. Lips tight and clean. Nose is black, except in the case of red or red merle colored dogs, which have a matching brown nose.

Teeth   Strong, well-developed, meeting in a perfect, regular scissors bite, with upper teeth closely overlapping but touching the lower teeth, and set squarely in the jaw. Teeth broken by accident not to be penalized.

Eyes   Fairly large, oval shaped, and set well apart at an almost imperceptable slant. Color may be brown, blue, or amber. Preferred color is medium brown, except in the cases of blue or blue merle colored dogs, where one or both eyes may be blue, and red or red merle dogs, which may have amber eyes. The expression should be mild, yet keen, alert, and intelligent.

Ears   Should be of medium size, set well apart, tapering to a rounded tip, and sensitive in their use. Ear carriage varies from drop to prick, however, usually carried from one quarter to three quarters erect, with the upper portion of the ear breaking forward to protect the entrance of the ear canal from sleet, snow, and insects.

Neck   Of good length, strong and muscular, broadening into the shoulders, and carried level with the back in motion. When standing at attention, the head and neck is raised alertly.

Forequarters   The shoulders are long and well angulated, meeting the upper arm at a right angle, with the elbows close to and parallel with the body. The forelegs are well boned and straight when viewed from the front or side. Pasterns show a slight slope when viewed from the side.

Body   Body moderately long, ribs well sprung, tapering to a deep and moderately broad chest. Back strong and level in its topline, loins broad and deep with a slight muscular arch. In profile the croup slopes slightly to the set on the tail.

Hindquarters   The hindlegs are longer than the forelegs and set on wide. Thighs long, broad and well muscled, with well bent stifles, and strong, well let down hocks, showing no signs of weakness. Viewed from behind, the hindlegs should be parallel from the hocks to the ground.

Feet   Oval in shape, with well arched toes and pads tough enough for heavy field work. Nails short and strong. Feet and legs are judged by having the dog walk into a natural, unposed stance.

Tail   Long, reaching at least to the hock joint, set on low and carried low, in line with the curve of the hind legs, swirling upwards slightly at the tip. The tail may be raised in excitement but not carried over the back.

Coat   Double, with a dense, medium textured topcoat, and a short, soft undercoat, making weather-resisting protection. Rough coats are

Correct scissors bite

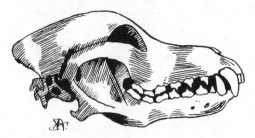

Overshot (buck) teeth

Undershot (bulldog) teeth

A head study of a Border Collie of the old-fashioned type. Note the broad, box-like skull for ample brain room, and the blunt, powerful jaws to fend off predators. The drop ears protect the ear canal from sleet, snow and insects. Todays fashion calls for higher ear carriage to give a more "alert" appearance (Photo: R.B. Harrison)

Imported Jill, a red and white "mottled," prick eared Border Collie bitch owned by Edgar Gould. (Photo: J.E.L.)

moderately long, may be wavy or slightly curly, with more abundant coat to form mane, breeching, brush, and feathering on the backs of the forelegs. Hair short on the face, fronts of the forelegs and from the hocks down. Smooth coated dogs have a short, dense, smooth topcoat over the entire body.

Colors   A variety of colors are permissable. Black and white most common, followed by tri-color (black, white, and tan, with black body retained). Other colors are blue and white (any shade of grey), blue merle and white (body color grey with broken patches of black), red and white (any shade of brown from light red or fawn to chocolate), red merle and white (body color light red or fawn with broken patches of chocolate), sable and white, or mottled (black or red with white markings that are speckled or spotted, causing a roan effect). Tan markings on the face and legs, as in the tri-color, are permissable in all of these colors. White markings common and desirable as: full or partial ring around the neck, tail tip, blaze up the face, forechest, and belly. Predominately white individuals do occur, but are undesirable, as sheep do not respect a white dog as much as they do a dark one, mistaking it for another sheep.

Size   Height varies from 17 to 26 inches at the withers, weight from 25 to 65 pounds, however, most dogs average 19 to 22 inches, bitches 18 to 21 inches. Average weight is 30 to 50 pounds. Size varies with type of work. No preference providing bone and musculature is that of a dog quick on its feet.

Movement   Action should be free, smooth, and tireless, with a minimum lift to the feet, conveying the impression of ability to move with great stealth. The action viewed from the front should be straight forward and true, the feet tracking comparatively close together at the ground, without weakness at shoulders, elbows, or pasterns. Viewed from behind the quarters thrust with strength and flexibility, with the hind legs straight, tracking comparatively close together at the ground. Any tendency toward stiltiness, cow or bow hocks in motion, or weakness at the shoulders or pasterns is a serious fault.

Faults   Exaggerated type, long-narrow head, tail carried above the back, excessively long and abundant coat, stilty or unsound movement, coarseness, over-refinement, predominately white color, shyness, lack of angulation, any deviation which would adversely affect the working ability of the dog.

Disqualifications   Bob-tail; any dog showing evidence of being cross-bred with any other breed; any dog which attacks or attempts to attack the judge, its handler, or another dog, albino coloring, overshot or undershot jaw, lameness, deafness, or blindness.

Note   Male animals should have two apparently normal testicles fully descended into the scrotum.

THE U.S. BORDER COLLIE CLUB DESCRIPTION

The *Border Collie* is a medium sized dog ranging in *weight from 25 to 65 pounds,* with the average between 30 and 50 pounds; and in height from *17 inches to 26 inches at the withers,* with the average between 18 and 21 inches. *Ears may be pricked, semi-pricked, tuliped or down,* and not necessarily matching. Eyes should be round and alert with dark brown the preferred color, although lighter, amber eyes are quite acceptable. Sometimes one or both eyes may be light blue. The tail is long, often fringed, and should be carried low with an upward swirl at the

Left: correct, sloped pastern and oval foot with well-arched toes. Center: splayed foot. Right: Flat foot.

tip. When working, the tail is a barometer of concentration, and low tail carriage, often between the hind legs, is strongly desired. In obedience or at play it can be carried up and sometimes curls over the back. Puppies often carry their tails up, usually until several months of age. *Coats may be rough—long and fluffy, sometimes straight and sometimes curly; or smooth—short and straight.* Most *Border Collies* are black and white, but there are also reds, chocolates, merles, black and tan, all black and tri-colors, with or without white markings. The traditional marking is black and white with a white ruff and chest, four white feet and legs, white tip on the tail and a white snip or blaze on the nose. There are, however, an infinite variety of markings, ranging from all black to all white with black ears, a white stripe going up a hip, a white spot on the back or a half white/half black face. To owners who want dogs for herding livestock such markings make no difference. To owners who want to show their dogs in obedience trials the more traditional markings are preferable and this should be borne in mind when selecting a puppy.

THE BRITISH KENNEL CLUB STANDARD

Amended Interim Standard for the Border Collie Arising from the Breed Standard's Sub-Committee 11th November 1980

Characteristics   Should be neither nervous nor aggressive, but keen, alert, responsive and intelligent.

General Appearance   The general appearance should be that of a well proportioned dog, the smooth outline showing quality, gracefulness and perfect balance, combined with sufficient substance to convey the impression that it is capable of endurance. Any tendency to coarseness or weediness is undesirable.

Head and Skull   Skull fairly broad, occiput not pronounced. Cheeks should not be full or rounded. The muzzle, tapering to the nose, should be moderately short and strong, and the skull and foreface should be approximately the same length. Nose black, except in the case of a brown or chocolate coloured dog when it may be brown. Nostrils well developed. Stop very distinct.

Eyes   The eyes should be set well apart, oval in shape, of moderate size and brown in colour, except in the case of merles, where one or both, or part of one or both, may be blue. The expression, mild, keen, alert and intelligent.

Ears   The ears should be of medium size and texture, set well apart. Carried erect or semi-erect and sensitive in their use.

Mouth   The teeth should be strong, with perfect regular and complete scissor bite, i.e. the upper teeth closely overlapping the lower teeth and set square to the jaws.

Neck   The neck should be of good length, strong and muscular, slightly arched and broadening.

Forequarters   Front legs parallel when viewed from front, pasterns sloping slightly when viewed from side. Bone should be strong but not heavy. Shoulders well laid back, elbows close to the shoulders.

Body   Athletic in appearance, ribs well sprung, chest deep and rather broad, loins deep, muscular, but not tucked up. Body slightly longer than height at shoulder.

Correct, straight forelegs and front.

Front faults. Left, fiddle front. Right, pidgeon toes or toeing in.

Spunky C.D. owned by Jean Ramsey. A smooth coated Border Collie.

Correct rear stance.

Rear faults. Left: cowhocks. Right: hocking out or bowed legs.

Hindquarters   The hindquarters should be broad and muscular, in profile sloping gracefully to the set on of the tail. Thighs should be long, deep and muscular with well turned stifles and strong hocks, well let down. From hock to ground the hind legs should be well boned and parallel when viewed from the rear.

Feet   Oval in shape, pads deep, strong and sound, toes well arched and close together. Nails short and strong.

Gait   Movement free, smooth and tireless, with the minimum of lift of feet, conveying the impression of the ability to move with great stealth and speed.

Tail   The tail should be moderately long, the bond reaching at least to the hock joint, set on low, well furnished and with an upward swirl towards the end, completing the graceful contour and balance of the dog. The tail may be raised in excitement but never carried over the back.

Coat   There are two varieties of coat, one moderately long, the other smooth. In both, the top coat should be weather resistant. In the moderately long coated variety, abundant coat forms a mane, breeching and brush. On face, ears, forelegs (except for feather) hindlegs from hock to ground, the hair should be short and smooth.

Colour   A variety is permissible, but white should never predominate.

Size   Ideal height: Dogs 53 cm (21''), bitches slightly less.

Faults   Any departure from the foregoing points should be considered a fault and the seriousness with which the fault should be regarded should be in exact proportion to its degree. NOTE: Male animals should have two apparently normal testicles fully descended into the scrotum.

AUSTRALIAN BORDER COLLIE STANDARD
Approved by the Australian National Kennel Club, January 1981

General Appearance   The general appearance is that of a well proportioned dog, the smooth outline showing quality, gracefulness and perfect balance, combined with sufficient substance to ensure that it is capable of enduring long periods of active duty in its intended task as a working sheep dog. Any tendency to coarseness or weediness is undesirable.

Characteristics   The Border Collie is highly intelligent, with an instinctive tendency to work and is readily responsive to training. Its keen, alert and eager expression add to its intelligent appearance, whilst its loyal and faithful nature demonstrates that it is at all times kindly disposed towards stock. Any aspect of structure or temperament foreign to a working dog is uncharacteristic.

Head   The skull is broad and flat between the ears, slightly narrowing to the eye, with a pronounced stop, cheeks deep but not prominent. The muzzle, tapering to the nose, is strong and the same length as the skull. The lips are tight and clean and the nose is large with open nostrils. The nose colour conforms to that of the body coat.

Teeth   The teeth should be sound, strong and evenly spaced, the lower incisors just behind but touching the upper, that is a scissor bite.

Eyes   The eyes are set wide apart, oval shaped of moderate size harmonising with the colour of the coat but darker colour preferred except in the case of chocolate where a lighter colour is permissable and in the case of Merles, where blue is permissable. The experssion is mild but keen, alert and intelligent.

Ears   The ears should be of medium size and texture, set well apart, carried semi-erect. They are sensitive in their use, and inside well furnished with hair.

Forequarters   The shoulders are long, and well angulated to the upper arm, neither in nor out at elbow. The forelegs are well boned, straight and parallel when viewed from the front. Pasterns show flexibility with a slight slope when viewed from the side.

Body   The body is moderately long with well sprung ribs tapering to a fairly deep and moderately broad chest. The loins are broad, deep, muscular and only slightly arched, flanks deep and not cut up.

Hindquarters   The hindquarters are broad and muscular, in profile sloping gracefully to the set on of tail. The thighs are long, broad, deep and muscular with well turned stifles and strong hocks, well let down, and when viewed from the rear are straight and parallel.

Feet   Oval in shape, pads deep, strong and sound, toes moderately arched and close together. Nails short and strong.

Tail   The tail is moderately long, set on low, well furnished and with an upward swirl towards the end, completing the graceful contour and balance of the dog. The tail may be raised in excitement, but not carried over the back.

Coat   Double coated, with a moderately long, dense, medium textured topcoat while the undercoat is short, soft and dense, making a weather resisting protection, with abundant coat to form mane, breeching and brush. On face, ear tips, forelegs (except for feather), hind legs from hock to ground, the hair is short and smooth.

Colour   Black and white, or black, white and tan, chocolate and white, blue and white, with the black, chocolate, or blue body colour being retained. Tan patches on the body are not desirable. Tan undercoat is not permissable. Blue Merles - clear silvery blue is desired, splashed and marbled with black.

Size   The height at the withers should be:
 Dogs.....48 to 53 centimeters (approx. 19-21 inches)
 Bitches..46 to 51 centimeters (approx. 18-20 inches)

Movement   The movement is free, smooth and tireless, with a minimum lift of the feet, conveying the impression of the ability to move with great stealth. The action, viewed from the front, should be straight forward and true, without weakness at shoulders, elbows or pasterns. Viewed from behind the quarters thrust with strength and flexibility with hocks not close nor too far apart. When trotting, the dog's feet tend to come closer together as speed increases, but when the dog comes to rest he should stand four square.

Faults   Any tendency to stiltiness or to cowhocks or bowhocks is a serious fault. Any departure from the foregoing points should be considered a fault. The seriousness with which the fault should be regarded is in exact proportion to its degree.

Faulty gay tail.

Correct tail set. Note low tail carriage.

131

Blue-C.D. a blue eyed, smooth coated Border Collie owned by Louis and Rena New of Vermont. Blue eyes are fairly common in the breed, especially in merles. (Photo: J.E.L.)

THE STANDARDS COMPARED AND JUDGING THE BORDER COLLIE

The British, Australian, and American Standards all call for a medium-sized dog around 21 inches tall and weighing approximately 45 pounds. The dog should also be well proportioned and pleasing to the eye. In the United States, type varies considerably, some having no resemblance to what most people consider a Border Collie to be.

The head of the Border Collie is very different from that of the Collie and Shetland Sheepdog. The skull is broad and boxlike in shape, with a slight dome at the top to give ample brain room. The stop (indentation between the eyes) is pronounced, although not as much as that of a Spaniel or Setter. The muzzle is full and blunt, and the jaws powerful. The lips do not sag like the Spaniels, but are tight and firmly held. In general, the head shape is similar to a field type Golden Retriever.

The eyes are large, set well apart, and expressive. In color they are lighter than most show breeds. The small black eye, so prized by show breeders, may denote a dull animal according to John Holmes, the well-known herding dog trainer. Eye color seems to be connected with coat color. Red and white, red and white mottled, and red merle dogs tend to have amber brown eyes, while black and white and tri-color dogs usually have medium coppery-brown eyes. Black and white mottled (blue roan) dogs, which are darkly pigmented all over the body, often have dark chocolate brown eyes, or, similar to blue and white and blue merle dogs, have one or both eyes blue in color. The blue-eyed gene can be traced back to the Scandanavian Viking Spitz dogs that are one of the ancestors of the modern Border Collie.

The gaze of the Border Collie is very intense and penetrating when the dog is alert and it is soft and gentle when the dog is at rest. An eye that is too dark and small cannot look as soft and fails to change in expression. Dog trainers find it next to impossible to try to guess a dog's feelings if he has expressionless eyes, which makes it difficult to know what type of training methods to use. For this reason, eyes are the most important feature when judging expression.

Many breed ring judges today are placing far too much importance on ear carriage. The way the ears are carried is a very minor characteristic when considering the working ability of the dog. Proper angulation of the bones in the forequarters and hindquarters, set of the tail, and the way the dog moves are of much greater importance than ears. Without a physically well-built and sound body, the dog is worthless as a worker, no matter how pretty his face. Ear carriage in the Border Collie tends to be much lower than that of the Collie and Sheltie because his ears are larger and heavier. They are also set much wider apart, since the proper skull is wide and box-like. The lower ear carriage of the Border Collie prevents sleet and snow from entering the ear canal and gives some protection against biting insects in the summer months. A lower ear is also less prominant, and therefore, less likely to get ripped or torn while fighting predators. The dominant low ear carriage comes directly from the major ancestor of the Border Collie, the Roman herding dog.

Unlike the Collie and Sheltie, ear carriage doesn't alter the Border Collie expression, as you can see by covering up your dog's ears and looking at his facial expression. It is not the ears but the correctly shaped head and large, expressive eyes that combine to make expression in the Border Collie.

Tail carriage in the Border Collie is very important. The preferred tail is set on and carried low, and for a good reason. A tail carried over the back ("gay" or "cocky" tail) has long been considered a serious fault by shepherds in Great Britain. According to John Holmes and fellow trainer and trial competitor Tim Longton, a gay tail indicates a dog lacks the necessary concentration for sheep or cattle work. Whereas the correct low set tail can be used as a rudder when the dog is darting and dodging (much like a fox uses his tail), a gay tail is ineffective as a rudder since it is above the dog's back line and any counter force exerted by swinging it would be weakened because it would be out of line with the dog's body. A gay, flapping tail also distracts the sheep's attention, making it impossible for the dog to stare down and control them with his hypnotic eye. A flopping tail could also be enough to make skittish sheep scatter.

In size, Border Collies vary from about 17 to 26 inches with most standing about 19 to 22 inches at the shoulder and weighing about 30 to 50 pounds. Size alone is not important if the dog is well proportioned and agile. It only becomes a problem if the dog is cloddy or too delicate and fragile. The overly large, cloddy, coarse-boned dog is too slow on his feet to herd sheep and tends to tire easily from moving his own bulk. Not all large dogs are at a disadvantage, however. A well proportioned, medium-boned large dog can often outwork the best smaller dog by performing a wider variety of tasks, but the general tendency is for big dogs to be cloddy and clumsily built. Tall dogs are sometimes very weedy and long-legged and a bit too light-boned to withstand hard work. An overly small dog may be too delicate to withstand the rigors of farm work, although they are better suited for the pet owner.

A rough Border Collie coat should be dense and full, with a soft, furry undercoat. The outer coat usually has a soft, medium texture, neither silky and fine spun nor coarse and wiry. The texture and length of the rough coat is quite similar to that of the Golden Retriever and, as in that breed, is water repellent. The soft, dense undercoat provides insulation and protection from predators, brambles and thick brush. The rough coat should never be as long and profuse as that of the Rough Collie nor as feathered as the coat of modern show Setters since these coats are impractical in the field and matt quickly.

The smooth-coated Border Collie has a dense, wooly undercoat, but the outer coat is short and flat over the entire body like the coat of a German Shepherd dog.

The Border Collie comes in a wide variety of colors. In all countries, black and white is by far the most common color, followed in order by tri-color, red and white, red merle, blue and white, blue merle, and mottled (which has roan or speckled white markings).

The red and white Border Collie varies in shades of brown—light red, fawn, dark chocolate and liver. The color is uniform throughout, and the dog may have distinct tan markings on the face and legs as in the tri-color. The nose leather is a matching shade of brown, as it is in liver Spaniels, red Siberian Huskies, red Dobermans, and other recessive brown breeds.

Mottled coloring in red or black and white dogs is restricted to where the typical white markings occur—stockings on the legs, patches on the chest, ring or patch on the neck, blaze up the face, and tail tip. The mottled color is a mixture of black or red with white hairs.

The blue and white Border Collie is a solid, uniform grey. The blue merle has black marbling (patches) on a grey coat, while the red merle has chocolate marbling on a light red coat.

White dogs do occur, but they should have dark markings on their heads. Predominantly white dogs, however, often carry genes for deafness and blindness and should never be bred to another white dog. Tradi-

At rest, the Border Collie's ears are usually laid back flat. Laying back the ears can also indicate submission to the handler or a dominant pack member. (PAK photo)

"Rocky," a predominantly white Border Collie owned by Paul L. Phenix, Jr. of Belding Michigan.

Caora Con's Pendulum's Image as a puppy. Sire: Imported Roy; Dam: Caora Con's Bhan-Tara, CDX. Owned by Caora Con Kennels.

tionally, shepherds have disliked white dogs, claiming they are not as respected as a dark one because the flock mistakes them for another sheep. This folklore seems to have little basis in fact since several top trial dogs in recent years have been predominantly white.

The most important physical traits in the Border Collie are bone structure and movement. Without correct angulation the dog cannot move freely and easily. A dog with straight stifles, shoulders, or hips moves with a stiff, stilted gait. Conversely, the dog with shoulder blades sloping back at almost a 45^0 angle and meeting the upper arm at about a 90^0 angle, with hindquarters of comparable angulation in the hip and thigh bones, will have greater reach and drive. A long stride allows the dog to trot with a minimum of effort.

Gait is of upmost importance when judging a working breed since it is the supreme test of bone structure and function. The Border Collie's stride should be long and fluid so that the dog glides effortlessly over the ground. As the dog increases his speed at a trot his feet converge under the center line of gravity until they follow a single track. A choppy or prancing gait, although pretty to watch, is impractical and causes the working dog to tire rapidly.

Incorrect, straight angulation.

The dog with poor angulation is restricted in movement, has a short, choppy stride, and tires easily.

Correct angulation front and rear
contributes to a long, effortless
stride and smooth action at both
the trot and gallop.

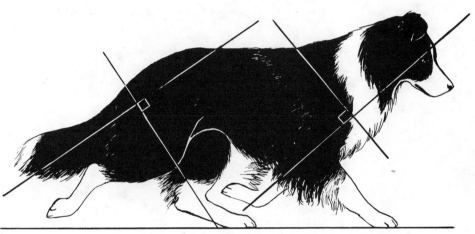

The balanced trot and canter of a
correctly angulated Border Collie.
A good working dog has limbs that
extend freely, and balance to allow
for long hours of work without tiring. The lines show balance.

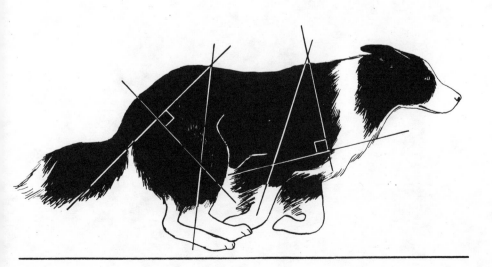

Australian Ch. Tullaview Tarena, a bitch owned by John and Joyce Sullivan of Australia.

Dog shows are a sport. They provide many people an opportunity to get out of the house or take a break from the monotony of their job. At a show you can "talk dogs" with fellow exhibitors and spectators and see what other breeders have to offer. The primary purpose of a dog show, however, is to choose the dog that is closest to the ideal specimen of his breed as described in the breed Standard.

AMERICAN SHOWS

In the United States there are two types of dog shows: "sanctioned matches," are sanctioned by the AKC, but no championship points are awarded; "point shows" are licensed by the AKC, and points toward an AKC championship are awarded to the winners. To become a champion, a dog must earn 15 points, which must include at least two "majors," won under two different judges. A major is three, four or five points earned in competition at a single show. The number of points awarded is determined by the size of the entry. A popular breed will require a larger entry than a more rare breed. The breed competition is divided by sex, and the winners of each sex are awarded championship points and then go on to compete with champions for Best of Breed. The Best of Breed winners next compete for Best in Group (there are seven groups; Sporting, Hound, Working, Terrier, Toy, Herding and Non-Sporting). The Group winners are then in competition for Best in Show.

Border Collies are not allowed to compete for a breed championship in the United States at this time, but may compete for ribbons in the Miscellaneous class. The Miscellaneous class is for breeds recognized by the AKC as purebred but not yet registered by the AKC. The class is divided by sex, and all Miscellaneous class breeds compete together. No points are awarded and the dog can't compete for Group or Best in Show awards. All dogs entered must have an Indefinite Listing Privilege (ILP) Number, entitling them to be shown in the Miscellaneous class and at obedience trials.

Most Border Collie owners in the United States are strongly opposed to full AKC recognition, fearing that people will start breeding for appearance only. If this happens, they fear that delicate herding instinct, which must be tested in every generation would soon be lost. Unfortunately, this loss of working ability has already started to happen in the Australian Shepherd, a closely related breed.

On the other hand, other fanciers of the breed feel that Border Collie owners are entitled to enjoy all aspects of the dog world. They feel

Left: New Zealand Ch. Thunderboy of Clan-Abby, owned by Peter and Judy Vos of Hawkes Bay, New Zealand. He is New Zealand's first Bet In Show award-winning Border Collie at all-breed shows. Here he is shown winning Best of Breed at the 1980 Tux National Dog Show, the biggest show in New Zealand. (Photo: Courtesy of Peter and Judy Vos)

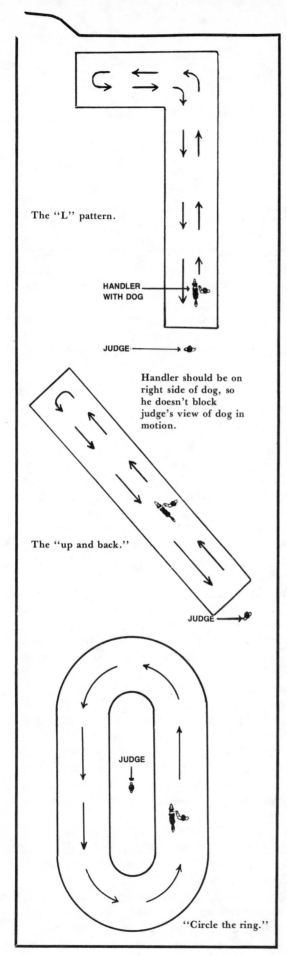

The "L" pattern.

HANDLER WITH DOG

JUDGE

Handler should be on right side of dog, so he doesn't block judge's view of dog in motion.

The "up and back."

JUDGE

JUDGE

"Circle the ring."

that it doesn't matter if there is a show and a working type; that those who want a working dog would buy from a strain of proven working dogs, and alternately those who want a show dog would buy from a strain of winning show dogs.

Since the show ring is supposed to be the proving ground for breeding stock, I personally feel that any dog of a hunting, herding or guarding breed should be required to pass a test of working ability before being awarded a championship. After all, if a person has the time and money to make a dog a champion, he or she most probably can afford to have the dog properly trained to work as well. The dog doesn't necessarily need to win a trial, but I think he should at least be able to put in a competent run. Perhaps a certain number of points for each exercise (like obedience) could be allotted, and a dog who receives a certain minimum number of points given a "qualifying score" and "working certificate."

This system has worked very successfully in Germany and several other European countries. For example, a German Shorthair Pointer has to pass a public test in the field before it can compete in the adult conformation classes, and a German Shepherd dog must pass a Schutzhund (guard and obedience) test. This has made the German-bred Pointer and Shepherd the best in the world. The American breeders have never been able to surpass the German-bred Pointer or Shepherd.

AUSTRALIAN SHOWS

Border Collies are allowed to compete for championship points in Australia. Shows may be conducted by a dog club or an agricultural society. Although any dog three months of age or older may compete, a dog must be at least six months old to earn a Challenge Certificate.

In Australia, as in Great Britain, Challenge Certificates are awarded only at certain shows. The dog winning the Challenge Certificate earns five points automatically, plus a point for each dog over six months he defeats in his sex. The maximum number of points a dog may win at one show is 25, regardless of the size of the entry. Once a dog has accumulated 100 points in at least four different shows under at least two different judges, he becomes an Australian Champion. In addition, a judge has the option of refusing to award a Challenge Certificate and points to any dog he feels is of inferior quality.

BRITISH SHOWS

Border Collies also have championship status in Great Britain. There, a dog must win three challenge certificates under three different judges AND pass a working test under the rules of the International Sheepdog Society to become a "Full Champion." A "Show Champion" must only win three challenge certificates under three different judges. To date, many Border Collies have won the title of "Show Champion," but NO show dog has been able to pass the working test needed to earn the title of "Full Champion." The ISDS requirements are the same as the BCCA's "Working Certificate" except that the gather is 200 yards and the drive is 50 yards. Challenge Certificates are awarded only at Championship Shows. Champions can and do compete against non-champions, and likewise may compete for the Challenge Certificate. Only a few Challenge Certificates are awarded by the Kennel Club each year.

SHOW TRAINING AND GROOMING

Before you enter a show, train your dog to trot willingly on leash on either side of you, and to switch from side to side without fuss. He should not weave or sniff the ground and must also be trained to stand and stay. This training is very important, since Border Collies cannot be "set up" or "stacked" (posed by hand). You can, however, use liver or a toy to "bait" your dog to lift his ears and look alert. Teach him to stand with his feet squarely placed. Also train your dog to move in the following patterns on a leash with you: "L," "T," the triangle, in addition to circling the ring.

To do an "L," make a tight circle in front of the judge, then move the dog in a straight line across the ring, turn in the direction indicated by the judge, and return to your original point. To do the "T," start out as you did for the "L" but continue on until you have completed the top of the "T" and then return. The triangle is also done by moving the dog as you would for the "L," but instead forming a triangle pattern. In all three cases, keep your dog on the side facing the judge. This can be tricky, so practice in advance. As you are returning to the judge, stop about five feet away from him and tell your dog to stand and stay.

Your dog should be moved at a brisk trot, maintaining an even pace and a straight line of travel. Speeding up or slowing down makes his stride look choppy.

Not surprisingly, a trained dog has a definite advantage over a poorly behaved dog in the show ring. Classes in handling techniques are held by many kennel clubs and trainers all over the country. The novice handler will find them invaluable.

In addition, a perfectly groomed dog is an important asset in showing. A clean, well-groomed dog is also considered a courtesy to the judge. Therefore, before you go to a show, make sure your dog is in immaculate form. Clip the dog's toenails, trim the hair evenly on the backs of his hind legs from the hocks down (don't touch his breeches or tail), and trim the hair between his toes and around his feet to make them look small and neat. You should also brush and scrape his teeth and clean his ears. A day or two before the show, he should be given a mild shampoo and rinse to add gleam to his coat. Brush out (don't use a comb or he will lose his undercoat) and remove any loose hair and matts. Finally, just before you enter the show ring, trim the whiskers to obtain a smooth appearance of the muzzle. Now he is ready for a show!

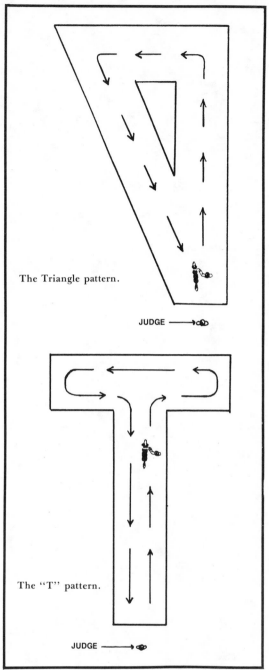

The Triangle pattern.

JUDGE ⟶

The "T" pattern.

JUDGE ⟶

The junior bitch line up at the Sydney Easter Royal Show, 1980. A dog who is trained to stand, stay and walk on leash is easy to show, since it will move where and when the handler wants it to.

GLOSSARY OF DOG TERMS

ACTION—The gaits of the dog—how it walks, trots or runs.

ALTERED—A dog who has had its testicles or ovaries surgically removed. Neutered.

ANGULATION—The angle at which the bones meet at a joint. Applied especially to the shoulder, hip, stifle and hock joints.

APRON—The long hair on the forechest.

ARM BAND—A stiff paper band worn on the left arm at dog shows indicating the dog's entry numbers.

BACK—The vertebrae between the shoulder and tail.

BAD MOUTH—Crooked or mis-aligned teeth, overshot or undershot jaw.

BAD SHEEP—Sheep that try to break, turn, and fight the dog or are uneven, ragged movers.

BAIT—Food used to keep a dog alert in the show ring. Usually cooked liver.

BAITING—Teasing a dog with a tidbit to make him "show" in the breed ring.

BALANCE—The over-all proportions of the dog, including symmetry and proportions of his body.

BARREL CHEST—A dog with ribs that spring out from the spine like a barrel, giving the dog's body a round appearance.

BEEFY—A grossly overdeveloped, chunky dog.

BENCHED—A show where all the entries must remain on display on predesignated benches.

BITCH—A female dog.

BITCHY—An over refined, feminine male.

BITE—The symmetry of the teeth of the upper jaw to those of the lower jaw when the mouth is closed.

BLAZE—A streak of white or mottled color down the center of the head and between the eyes.

BLOCKY—A squarely shaped body or head.

BLOOM—A healthy, lustrous coat.

BLUE MERLE—Blue-grey mixed with a black coat.

BOB TAIL—Born without a tail.

BRACE—Two dogs of the same breed.

BREECHING—The long hair on the inside and back of the thighs.

BRISKET—The lower part of the rib cage between the forelegs.

BROOD BITCH—A female dog used for breeding.

CASTRATED—A male dog who has had his testicles surgically removed.

CAT-FOOT—A short, round, compact foot.

CHAMPION—A dog who has won the prescribed number of points and or challenge certificates, and whose title is verified by the kennel club in that particular country.

CHEEK—The fleshy part on the side of the head below the eyes, and above and behind the mouth.

CHEST—The rib cage and front of the body from the shoulders to the last rib.

CHISELED—A cleanly cut head, particularly beneath the eyes.

CHOCOLATE—A liver brown or mahogany brown coat. The nose in a "true" brown dog is also brown or liver colored. Also called "red."

CLODDY—Thickset and overly heavy.

CLOSE COUPLED—Short from the last rib to the hips.

COARSE—Lacking in refinement; cloddy.

COBBY—Short bodied and compact.

COLLAR—Marking around the neck—usually white.

COMMON—Lacking elegance, coarse. Not typical of the breed.

CONFORMATION—Physical make up of the dog; appearance.

COUPLING—Length of the body indicated by the distance between the hip bones and last rib.

COW HOCKED—Weak hock joints that turn in toward each other and cause the feet to turn outward.

CRABBING—Trotting sideways.

CREST—The upper arch of the neck.

CROUP—The rear portion of the back above the tail.

CRYPTORCHID—A male dog whose testicles have not descended into the scrotum.

DEW CLAWS—An extra or fifth toe on the inside of the legs.

DISQUALIFICATION—An action taken against a dog or exhibitor that bars any further competition and awards at a show or trial. It can be temporary or permanent.

DOMED—An evenly rounded top skull.

DOUBLE HANDLING—Having someone outside the ring or trial course giving the dog signals. Illegal.

DOUBLES—Running dogs as a brace in trial.

DOWN IN PASTERNS—Weak or faulty pastern joints.

DRIVE—A dog with his handler herding sheep, usually through a series of obstacles.

DRIVE—A solid thrusting of the hind quarters, causing a good forward movement.

DROP EAR—Pendulous ears that hang flat and close to the head.

DUDLEY NOSE—A flesh colored nose (pink).

ELBOW—The joint between the upper and lower arm.

ELBOWING OUT—Moving with the elbows protruding away from the body.

EWE—A female sheep.

EXPRESSION—The appearance of the head, eyes, and ears. Shows alertness and intelligence.

FAULT—Any deviation from the breed standard, in either working style or appearance.

FEATHERING—Long hair on the tail, legs, and ears.

FETCH—When the dog drives the sheep toward the handler after the lift.

FLANK—The lower part of the body between the last rib and the hips.

FLANK—To head off sheep.

FLAT-SIDED—A dog whose chest and ribs lack roundness.

FLEWS—Lips that are pendulous and hang at the corners.

FOREARM—The foreleg between the pasterns and elbow.

FOREFACE—The muzzle.

FRILL—Long hair on the chest and neck.

FRINGES—Longer hair on the ears, tail and legs.

FRONT—The forelegs, chest and shoulders.

GAIT—The way a dog moves at a walk, trot or run.

GATHER—To collect scattered sheep into a compact group.

GAY TAIL—A tail carried over the backline.

GOOD SHEEP—Sheep that trot nicely in front of the dog and stay grouped.

GRIZZLE—White hairs on the base coat. Often a sign of aging.

GUIDE DOG—A dog trained to lead blind people.

HACKNEY ACTION—Abnormally high action of the front legs—usually indicating a lack of drive in the rear.

HARE FOOT—A long, narrow, close-toed foot.

HARSH COAT—A stiff, wirey coat.

HAW—The third eyelid (sclera or whites) on the inside corners of the eye.

HEIGHT—The distance from the withers (top of the shoulders) to the ground.

HIP DYSPLASIA—An inherited abnormality of the hip joint that results in varying degrees of lameness.

HOCKS—The joint of the hind leg, between the pastern and stifle.

KINK TAIL—A sharply bent tail.

KNUCKLED OVER—Bent out at the pasterns.

LAYBACK OF SHOULDER—Angle of the shoulder blade in relation to the upper arm.

LEATHER—Ear flap.

LEGGY—Extremely long-legged.

LEVEL BITE—When the upper teeth meet the lower teeth edge to edge.

LIVER BROWN—A deep reddish-mahogany color.

LOADED SHOULDERS—Heavy in the shoulders.

LOIN—Region on either side of the spine between the last ribs and hips.

LOOSE LEASH—A dog moving on an unrestrained leash.

LOOSE ACTION—Erratic movement caused by poor muscular development.

LOW-SET TAIL—A tail that is attached level with or below the back line and is carried low.

LOW-SET EARS—Ears that are set on the sides of the head rather than on top.

LOWER THIGH—Area of the leg between the stifle and hock.

LOOSE-EYED—A dog who lacks concentration while working sheep.

LUMBERING—Moving in an ungainly, cloddish manner.

MANE—Profuse hair on the back of the neck of long-coated dogs.

MERLE—A coat colored a patchy black and grey, or chocolate and light red.

MONORCHID—A male dog with only one testical descended into the scrotum.

MOTTLED—A fine mixture of colored and white hairs, also called roan.

MUZZLE—The front part of the face from the eyes to the nose.

NOSE LEATHER—The hairless, smooth skin at the end of the muzzle.

NOSTRIL—The external openings in the nose.

OCCIPUT—The high point or bump at the back of the skull.

OUT AT THE ELBOWS—Elbows visibly turned away from the body.

OUT AT THE SHOULDERS—Shoulder blades that are loose jointed.

OUT RUN—The path taken by a dog as he gathers sheep. Ideally it is pear-shaped. Also called a "cast."

OVERSHOT—When the upper jaw and front teeth overlap the lower front teeth when the mouth is closed.

PACING—A dog that moves his legs on the same side of the body simultaneously.

PADDLING—A flicking motion of the forelegs denoting poor bone structure and lack of reach.

PASTERN—The bones forming the joint between the lower arm and feet.

PEN—A small enclosure that holds sheep or other animals.

PIGEON TOED—Feet turned inward toward each other.

PLAIN—Nondescript or common-looking.

PLUME—The feathery tail of a Collie or northern breed.

POINTS—The color on the face, legs, and tail. (Usually white in the Border Collie.)

POOR—Out of condition.

PRICK EARS—Ears that naturally stand erect.

PURE-BRED—A dog who is registered in an official stud book for the breed and is of unmixed, pure ancestry.

RACY—Long-legged and slightly built.

RAM—An uncastrated male sheep.

RANGY—Long-bodied and long-legged.

RAT TAIL—A tail devoid of hair.

REACH—The length of the forward stride.

RED—A reddish-brown or mahogany colored dog. Also called "chocolate" or "liver" brown.

RED MERLE—A light reddish-brown or fawn with chocolate patches.

ROACH BACK—A back that arches upward.

ROAN—A fine mixture of colored and white hairs, giving a mottled effect.

ROLLING GAIT—A swaying, ambling action of the hindquarters in motion.

ROMAN NOSE—A nose that is curved outward and upward from the forehead to the nose tip. Usually raised at the stop.

RUFF—The thick hair around the neck.

SABLE—A lacing of black hairs over brown as in the German Shepherd and show Collie.

SCISSORS BITE—When the upper teeth fit closely over the lower teeth like a scissor.

SEMI-ERECT EAR—An ear that is carried from one-quarter to three quarters erect, with the upper part folding forward.

SEMI-PRICK EAR—An ear that is erect with just the tips breaking forward.

SET UP—A dog that has been posed artificially by placing the feet and head in position.

SHED—To separate individual sheep from the flock.

SHELLY—A narrow chest lacking in depth.

SICKLE TAIL—A tail carried with the tip curving up.

SIDEWHEELING—Moving sideways with the feet tracking out of line. Also called "crabbing."

SINGLE SHEEP—Separating a shingle sheep from a flock.

SLAB SIDED—Flat ribbed.

SNIPY MUZZLE—A weak pointed muzzle.

SOUNDNESS—The dog's mental and physical condition.

SPAYED—A female whose ovaries are surgically removed.

SPRING OF RIBS—Degree of roundness to the ribs.

SQUARE—A dog whose height from withers to the ground is the same as his length from forechest to rump.

STACKED—A dog that is set up or posed.

STICKY-EYED—A dog who is fixated to staring at his sheep.

STIFLE—The joint of the hind leg between the upper and lower thigh.

STILTED—A dog that moves with a choppy, stiff-legged gait caused by a lack of shoulder and hip angulation.

STOP—The dip in the nasal bone between the eyes which separates the muzzle from skull.

STRAIGHT HOCKED—Little or no angulation of the hock joint.

STRAIGHT IN PASTERN—Little or no bend at the joint above the foot.

STRAIGHT IN SHOULDER—Little or no angulation between the shoulder blade and upper arm.

STRAIGHT IN STIFLE—Little or no angulation at the stifle joint.

STRONG EYE—A dog who stares intently at his sheep, sometimes without moving.

STRUNG UP—A dog held on a tight leash.

STUD DOG—A male dog used for breeding purposes.

SUBSTANCE—Bone structure throughout.

SWAY BACK—A back that sags in the middle.

TEAM—Four dogs worked together.

THROATINESS—A dog with an excess of loose skin under the throat.

TICKED—Isolated black or colored spots on a white background.

TIMBER—Bone, usually of the legs.

TOP LINE—The back from the wither to the tail.

TRI-COLOR—A black bodied dog with white points and small tan markings above the eyes, on the cheeks, and on the legs.

TUCK UP—A belly firmly tucked under the loins; like a Greyhound.

TYPEY—A dog showing all the distinctive characteristics for the breed.

UNDERSHOT JAW—A dog whose lower jaw protrudes in front of the upper jaw like a Bulldog.

WEATHER—A castrated male sheep.

WALL-EYE—A blue or China eye.

WEEDY—A dog lacking sufficient bone. Spindly.

WELL LET DOWN—Hocks that are well bent and set low.

WITHERS—The peak formed at the base of the neck by the tops of the shoulder blade and vertebrae.

SUGGESTED READING

Border Collie Books

A Lifetime With The Working Collie by Arthur N. Allen; 1979. Hardbound, 112 pages. Available from Arthur N. Allen, Route 3, McLeansboro, Illinois 62859.

Because of Eve by Jim Varnon; Softbound. Available from Jim Varnon, 1715 W. Pleasant Run, Desoto, TX 75115.

Border Collies by Iris Combe; Faber and Faber, London. Hardbound, 196 pages. Available from Hi-Ridge Farm, RR 3, Napanee, Ontario, Canada K7R 3K8.

Key Dogs From the Border Collie Family - Vol. I & II, by Sheila Grew; covers outstanding dogs in the Working Border Collie family who were extensively bred from, and thus had influence on the breed. Available from Hi-Ridge Farm.

One Woman and Her Dog and *The Shepherd's Wife* by Viv Billingham; available from Hi-Ridge Farm.

The Border Collie In Australasia by Peidje Vidler; available from Gotrah Enterprises, 4 Hillview Road, Kellyville, NSW 2153 Australia.

Herding Books

Anybody Can Do It by Pope Robertson; Rovar Publishing Co., 1979. Hardbound, 78 pages. Available from Rovar Publishing Co., 522 East Second Street, Elgin, Texas 78621.

Sheepdog Training: An All-breed Approach by Mari Taggart; Alpine Publications, 1986. Hardbound, 168 pgs. Available from Alpine Publications, Inc., 214 19th St. S.E., Loveland, CO 80537.

The Farmer's Dog by John Holmes; Popular Dogs Press, London. Hardbound, 160 pages. Available from Edgar Gould, Cooperlane Enterprises, Shelburne Falls, Massachusetts 01370.

The Sheepdog: Its Work and Training by Tim Longton and Edward Hart; David and Charles, London, 1976. Hardbound, 119 pages. Available from Parker Farms, Route 1, Box 176, Pearland, Texas 77581.

VHS Video Tape

Border Collies: Getting The Right Start - with Russel Graves; available from Graves Kennels, RR 1 - Box 26A, Hardtner, KS 67057

Starting The Young Dog - with Arthur N. Allen; available from Arthur N. Allen Productions, Rt. 3, McLeansboro, Illinois 62859.

Training the Stock Dog - with Steve Winn; available from Barker Video Productions, 1103 Villa Maria Rd., Bryan, Texas 77802.

Training Books

Behavior Problems in Dogs by Dr. William E. Campbell; American Veterinary Publications, Inc. Hardbound, 306 pages. Available from American Veterinary Publications, Drawer KK, Santa Barbara, California 93102.

Best Foot Forward by Barbara Handler; Alpine Publications, 1984; Softbound, 72 pgs. Available from Alpine Publications, Inc.

Beyond Basic Dog Training by Diane L. Bauman; Howell Book House; Hardbound, 256 pages.

Dog Tricks by Capt. Arthur Haggerty; available from Dog Sports Bookshelf, 940 Tyler St., Studio 17, Benica, CA 94510.

Go Find! by Major L. Wilson Davis; Howell Book House, New York. Hardbound, 159 pages.

How to Raise a Puppy You Can Live With by Rutherford and Neil; Alpine Publications, 1981; Softbound, 136 pgs. Available from Alpine Publications, Inc.

Leaderdogs for the Blind by Margaret Gibbs; available from Dog Sports Bookshelf.

Running With Man's Best Friend by Davia Gallup; Alpine Publications, 1986; Softbound, 118 pgs. Available from Alpine Publications, Inc.

Schutzhund by Susan Barwig; Quality Press, Colorado. 218 pages. Available from Schutzhund, 7550 West Radcliff Avenue, Littleton, Colorado 80123.

Search Dog Training by Sandy Bryson; available from Dog Sports Bookshelf.

Scent; Training to Track, Search and Rescue by Milo D. Pearsall and Hugo Verbruggen, M.D.; Alpine Publications, 1982; Hardbound, 232 pgs. Available from Alpine Publications, Inc.

Tracking Dog Theory and Methods by Glen Johnson; one of the most complete tracking books ever written. Available from Dog World Books, P.O. Box 6500, Chicago, IL 60680.

Training the Competitive Working Dog by Tom Rose; covers tracking, obedience and Schutzhund work. Available from Giblaut Publishing Co., 3333 South Bannock, Suite 950, Englewood, CO 80537.

Your Dog Companion and Helper by Milo D. Pearsall and Margaret E. Pearsall; Alpine Publications, 1980; Hardbound, 208 pgs. Available from Alpine Publications, Inc.

Show Ring

Dog Steps by Rachel Page Elliot; Howell Book House, New York. 95 pages.

The Secrets of Show Dog Handling by Mario Migliorini; Arco Publishing Company, New York. 122 pages.

Breeding

Canine Hip Dysplasia and Other Orthopedic Problems by Fred L. Lanting; Alpine Publications, 1980; Hardbound, 232 pgs. Available from Alpine Publications Inc.

Canine Reproduction; A Breeders Guide by Phyllis A. Holst, MS, DVM; Alpine Publications, 1985; Hardbound, 240 pgs. Available from Alpine Publications Inc.

Dogs and How To Breed Them by Dr. Leon F. Whitney, D.V.M.; T.F.H. Publications.

The Mating and Whelping of Dogs by R. Portman Graham; Arco Publishing Company. 162 pages.

Magazines

American Border Collie Newsletter
P.O. Box 148
Redwood Valley, CA 95470

Border Collie News
c/o Janet E. Larson
RFD #3 Pinecrest Lane
Durham, N.H. 03824

Dog Fancy Magazine
P.O. Box 2430
Boulder, Colorado 80322

Dog Sports Magazine
2912 South Waring Road
Denair, California 95316

Dog World
McLean-Hunter Publishing Corp.
300 W. Adams St.
Chicago, Illinois 60606

Front And Finish
P.O. 333
Galesburg, IL 61401

Off Lead
8140 Coronado Lane
Rome, NY 13440

Purebred Dogs/American Kennel Gazette
51 Madison Ave.
New York, New York 10010

The National Stock Dog Magazine
312 Portland Road
Waterloo, Wisconsin 53594

The Southern Stockdog Journal
P.O. Box 735
Tallassee, Alabama 36078

BIBLIOGRAPHY

Allen, Arthur N. *Border Collies in America.* (Private Publisher) Route 3, McLeansboro, Illinois, U.S.A.

Allen, Arthur N. *Album of Fame.* Route 3, McLeansboro, Illinois, U.S.A.

Allen, Arthur N. *A Lifetime with the Working Collie.* (Private Publisher) Route 3, McLeansboro, Illinois, U.S.A.

American Kennel Club. *The Complete Dog Book.* Howell Book House, New York, U.S.A.

Anable, David. "Behind That Floppy Eared Pet Shop Puppy—A Trail of Misery," *Christian Science Monitor,* Monday, July 7, 1975.

Anable, David. "From Birth Kennel to Pet Shop—What Must Be Done to Make a Puppy's Trip More Humane," *Christian Science Monitor,* Tuesday, July 8, 1975.

Ascroft, Pat N. *The Border Collie.* Times—Longbooks, Isle of Man, Scotland.

Beaumont, Barbara. *The Versatile Border Collie* (Private Publisher) Berkshire, England 1981

Bernstein, Susan, editor. *Dog Digest—The Total Guide to Dog Ownership.* Digest Books, Illinois, U.S.A.

Bice, Clare. *A Dog For Davie's Hill.* MacMillan Co., New York, U.S.A.

Boorer, Wendy. *The World of Dogs.* Hamlyn House, London, England.

Brown, Beth. *Dogs That Work for a Living.* Funk and Wagnalls, New York, U.S.A.

Buchanan, Freda M. *The Land and People of Scotland.* J. B. Lippincott Co., Philadelphia, Pennsylvania, U.S.A.

Burger, Carl. *All About Dogs.* Random House, New York, U.S.A.

Burns, M. and Fraser M. "Progressive Retinal Atrophy in Border Collies," *The American Sheepdog Journal,* March 1975.

Caius, Dr. Johannes. *Of English Dogges* 1576, Republished by Theatrum Orbis Terrarum, Amsterdam, Holland.

Cato and Varro. *De Re Rustica* (English Translation by William Davis Cooper A.M., Lilt D.) Harvard University Press, Cambridge, Massachusetts, U.S.A.

Clement, J. H. and F. D. *The Working Border Collie: A Handbook for Trainers and Handlers.* North American Sheepdog Society, Illinois, U.S.A.

Collie Club of America. *The New Collie* Howell Book House, New York, 1983.

Collie Club of America. *The Complete Collie.* Howell Book House, New York, U.S.A.

Combe, Iris. *Border Collies.* Faber and Faber. London, England, 1978.

Combe, Iris. *Collies of Yesterday and Today.* J. B. Offset Printers, Essex England.

Coppinger, Lorna. *The World of Sled Dogs.* Howell Book House, New York, 1977.

Dangerfield, Stanley and Howell, Elsworth, editors. *International Encyclopedia of Dogs.* McGraw-Hill Book Company, New York, U.S.A.

Dinning, H.H. *The Farmer's Best Friend: A Working Sheepdog.* (Private Publisher) Strathalbyn, S.A. Australia, 1979.

Elliot, Rachel Page. *Dog Steps, Illustrated Gait at a Glance.* Howell Book House, New York, U.S.A.

Faas, Merlin & Larry. *Training Stockdogs.* (Private Publisher) Tempe, Arizona, 1977

Falkner, James. "Jigger," *American Kennel Gazette,* January 1977.

Farnsworth, Marjorie. "Editor's Report," *Dogs Magazine,* September 1974.

Fiennes, Richard and Alice. *The Natural History of Dogs.* Bonanza Books, New York, U.S.A.

Fiorone, Fiorenzo. *The Encyclopedia of Dogs.* Thomas Y. Crowell Co., New York, U.S.A.

Fox, Dr. Michael W. *Understanding Your Dog.* Coward, McCann & Geoghegan, Inc., New York, U.S.A.

Gibbs, Margaret. *Leader Dogs for the Blind.* Darlinger Books, Farfax, Va, 1982.

Graham, Capt. R. Portman. *The Mating and Whelping of Dogs.* Arco Publishing Company, New York, U.S.A.

Grew, Johannes. *Deutsche Schutzhund Schule.* Quality Press., Larkspur, Colorado, 1981.

Hanlyn House. *The Book of the Dog.* Hamlyn House, London, England.

Hart, Edward. *The Hill Shepherd.* David and Charles, London, England, 1977.

Hart, Ernest H. *The Encyclopedia of Dog Breeds.* TFH Publications, Neptune City, New Jersey.

Hartley, C. W. G. *The Shepherd's Dog.* Whitcombe & Tombs Ltd., Wellington, New Zealand.

Hawthorne, Melville. "A Friend in Need," *Animals Magazine,* October 1971.

Holmes, John. *The Farmer's Dog.* Popular Dogs Publishing Co., London, England.

Holmes, John. *The Family Dog.* Popular Dogs Publishing Co., London, England.

Holmes, John. Contributor—*Know How to Train Your Guard Dog,* Pet Library, Ltd., New York, U.S.A.

Humane Society of the United States. "Special Report on Abuses in Pet Industry," February 1974.

Humane Society of the United States. "Close Up Report on Puppy Mills," Pet Shop Report, 1977.

Humphrey and Formula Press. *Dogs of Australia.* Humphrey & Formula Press, Melbourne, Australia.

Humane Society of the United States. "Close Up Report on Puppy Mills," Pet Shop Report, 1977.

Humphrey and Formula Press. *Dogs of Australia.* Humphrey & Formula Press, Melbourne, Australia.

Iley, Tony. *Sheepdogs at Work.* Dalesman Books, North Yorkshire, England, 1978.

Jones, Arthur F. and Hamilton, Ferelith. *The World Encyclopedia of Dogs.* The World Publishing Co., New York, U.S.A.

Kelley D. V. Sc., Ralph B. *Sheepdogs: Their Breeding, Maintenance and Training.* Angus & Robertson, Sydney, Australia.

Kenworthy. *Dog Training Guide.* Pet Library L.T.D., New York, U.S.A.

Klipstine, Emily. "Working Ability in the Border Collie." *The American Sheepdog Journal,* November 1975.

Koehler, William. *The Koehler Method of Guard Dog Training.* Howell Book House, New York, U.S.A.

Lemorieux, Diane. "Border Collies as Sled Dogs," *American Sheepdog Journal,* March 1975.

Lipton, Dean. "Mixed Up Genes and Purebred Dogs." *Science Digest Magazine,* December 1970.

Longton, Tim & Hart, Edward. *The Sheepdog: Its Work and Training.* David & Charles, London, England.

McCoy, J. J. *Dog Training and Care.* Coward-McCann, Inc., New York, U.S.A.

McCulloch, John Herries. *Sheepdogs and Their Masters.* Robert Dinwiddie, Dumfries, Scotland.

McCulloch, John H. *Border Collie Studies.* Robert Dinwiddie & Co. Ltd., Dumfries, Scotland.

McCulloch, J. Herries. *Midget.* Robert Dinwiddie & Co. Ltd., Dumfries, Scotland.

McKenzie, Kenney. "Scottish Mountain Rescue Dogs," *Off Lead Magazine.* March 1976.

Means, Ben. *The Perfect Stockdog.* (Private Publisher) Route 1, Walnut Grove, Missouri, U.S.A.

Migliorini, Mario. *Secrets of Show Dog Handling.* Arco Publishing Co., New York, U.S.A.

Malvany, Mollie. *All About Obedience Training for Dogs.* Pelham Books, London, England.

National Geographic Society. *Man's Best Friend.* National Geographic Society, Washington, D.C., U.S.A.

Octopus Books. *The Love of Dogs.* Octopus Books, London, England.

Ollivant, Alfred. *Bob, Son of Battle.* Garden City Publishing Co., New York, U.S.A.

Osborne, Margaret. *Collies.* W. and G. Foyle L.T.D., London, England.

Pearsall, Margaret E. *Successful Dog Training.* Howell Book House, New York, U.S.A.

Pfaffenberger, Clarence. *The New Knowledge of Dog Behavior.* Howell Book House, New York, U.S.A.

Pickup, Madeleine. *The German Shepherd Guide.* Pet Library LTD., New York, U.S.A.

Rapp, Jay. *How To Train Dogs For Police Work.* Denlinger Books, Fairfax, Va., 1979.

Rine, Josephine Z. *The World of Dogs.* Dolphin Books, New York, U.S.A.

Robertson, R. B. *Of Sheep and Men.* Alfred A. Knoph Co., New York, U.S.A.

Saunders, Roy. *Sheepdog Glory.* Andre Deutsch Limited, London, England.

Shaffner, Carroll S. *Training a Working Collie.* (Private Publisher) Boalsbury, Pa., 1979.

Staff. *The American Sheepdog Journal.* February, March, April, May, June, 1975; April 1976.

Strickland, Winifred G. *Expert Obedience Training for Dogs.* Macmillan Co., New York, U.S.A.

Taggart, Mari. "Border Collie Qualities—Part I and II." *Dog World Magazine.* April and May, 1975.

Terhune, Albert Payson. *The Dog Book.* (Chapter 1 - The Collie), Saalfield Publishing Co. New York, 1932.

Tracy, Anne. "A Good One is Worth Four Hired Hands." *Yankee Magazine,* September 1976.

United States Army. *FM 19-35 - Military Police Working Dogs.* Washington D.C., 18 February, 1977.

Unkelbach, Kurt. *The American Dog Book.* E. P. Dutton, New York, U.S.A.

Varnon, J. D., editor. *Border Collies: The Journal of the Working Sheepdog.* December 77, March 78, May 1978.

Vidler, Peidje. *The Border Collie In Australisia.* Gotrah Enterprises, Kellyville, Australia, 1983.

Weatherwax, Rudd. *The Lassie Method.* Western Publishing Co., U.S.A.

Weatherwax, Rudd & Rothwell, John. *The Story of Lassie: His Discovery and Training.* Duell, Sloan and Pearce, New York, 1950.

Whyte, William. *Sheepdog Trials and the Art of Breaking In.* Whitcombe & Tombs, Ltd., Wellington, New Zealand.

William Benton Publishing Co. *Encyclopedia Brittanica,* Vol. 7, William Benton Publishing Co., Chicago, Illinois, U.S.A.

Wolters, Richard. *Family Dog.* E. P. Dutton & Co., Inc., New York, U.S.A.

Young, Anne. *Collie Guide.* Pet Library L.T.D., New York, U.S.A.

The author with Caora Con's Pennent U.D. (left) and Caora Con Lochinvar C.D.X. (right) and some of their trophies. (Photo: Col. W.A. Johnston)

148

CLUBS

Alabama Stockdog Assoc.
Jack B. Venable
P.O. Box 736
Tallassee, AL 36078

Alberta Stockdog Assoc.
M.L. Tipton
Lone Pine
Alberta, Canada TOG 1MO

American Herding Breeds Assoc.
Linda Rorem
1548 Victoria Way,
Pacifica, California 94044

Blue Mountain Border Collie Club
Rte. 1 Box 105
Walla Walla, Washington 99362

East Tennessee Stock Dog Assoc.
F. Stan Moore
3335 Byington Solway Road
Knoxville, Tennessee 37931

Inland Empire Border Collie Club
L. Whitman
Rte. 2, Box 90
Cheney, WA 99004

Iowa Border Collie Assoc.
Kevin Gute
RFD #3, Box 140
Coon Rapids, Iowa 30058

Kansas Stockdog Assoc.
Dean Fentress
P.O. Box 12
Altamont, Kansas 67330

Mid-West Herding Dog Assoc.
44 West 431 Rt. 64
Maple Park, Illinois 60151-8552

Midwest Stockdog Assoc.
Ester Plaffoot - President
Maplewood, Ohio 45340

Minnesota Stockdog Assoc.
George E. Rodgerson
2354 Chilcombe
St. Paul, Minnesota 55108

Mississippi Stockdog Assoc.
Jim Chandler
Rte. 2, Box 424
Meridan, Mississippi 39305

Missouri Stockdog Assoc.
Donald Hankins
Rte. 2, Box 73
Willard, Missouri 65781

Montana Stockdog Handler's Assoc.
Ellen Hart
Red Lodge, Montana 59068

Mountain and Plains Border Collie Assoc.
Barb Hummel
3339 Wagon Wheel Road
Berthoud, Colorado 80531

North East Border Collie Assoc.
Doug McDonough
Rte. 1, Box 34
Chapachet, RI 02814

North Island Border Collie Club
Sharon Jones
RR #4, Headquarters Road
Courtenay, B.C. Canada V9N 7J3

Oregon Sheepdog Society
Virgil Brown
38847 Gilkay Road
Scio, Oregon 97374

Pennsylvania Stockdog Assoc.
Jack Monsour
RD #1, Box 408
Bedford, Pennsylvania 15522

Redwood Empire Sheepdog Assoc.
Dee Samson
42400 Hwy 128
Cloverdale, California 95425

San Jouquin Valley Border Collie Club
Jack Selgrath
2813 Verdugo Lane
Bakersfield, California 93308

Show me Working Stockdog Assoc.
Dale Lewis
Rte. 1, Box 32
Ashland, Missouri 65010

South Central Stockdog Assoc.
Don A. Brown - President
Rte. 1
Fayetteville, Arkansas 72701

Southern California Working Sheepdog Assoc.
Candy Kennedy
10210 48th Street
Mira Loma, California 91752

Southern Coastal California Sheepdog Assoc.
B.S. Arine
205 Countrywood Drive
Lomoc, California 93436

Texas Sheepdog Assoc.
E.B. Raley - President
Rte. 1
Crawford, Texas 76638

The Australian Border Collie Society
Peter Buckley
Lot 3, Airstrip Road
Pitt Town, NSW 2756, Australia

The Border Collie Club of America
J. E. Larson, Secretary
RFD 3, Pinecrest Lane
Durham, New Hampshire 03824

The Border Collie Club of Great Britain
Mrs. M. Leigh, Secretary
Willow Cottage
Firbeck, Worksop
Nottinghamshire, England

The Southern Stockdog Journal
P.O. Box 735
Tallassee, Alabama 36078

United States Border Collie Club
Sunnybrook Farm
White Post, VA 22663

Virginia Border Collie Club
Bill Crowe
P.O. Box 12
Aylett, Virginia 23009

Washington State Stockdog Society
Cliff Steelman
Rte. 1, Box 105
Walla Walla, Washington 99362

Wisconsin Working Stockdog Assoc.
Jean Kitsembel - President
Rte. 1
Blue River, Wisconsin 53518

INDEX

anal glands, 29
associations
  American Border Collie Assoc., 21
  American - International Border Collie
    Registry, Inc., 21
  Australian National Kennel Council, 22
  Border Collie Club of America, 17
  International Sheep Dog Society, 21
  The Kennel Club, 21
  The Kennel Union of Southern Africa, 22
  The New Zealand Kennel Club, 22
  North American Sheepdog Society, 17,21
  United States Border Collie Club, 21
bleeding, 70
bloat, 71
breeding, 73
  brood bitch, 81
  mating, 83
  stud dog, 83
Breed Standard, 125-135
  American, 126
  Australian, 130
  British, 129
  comparisons, 132
  U.S., 128
broken bones, 71
brood bitch, 81
  heat cycle, 82
  whelping, 87-91
Brucellosis, 85
buying, 22-24
canine strongyloids, 64
cardiac arrest, 70
characteristics, 3
Coccidiosis, 64
Collie Eye Anomaly, 67, 80
commands,
  herding, 50
  whistle, 47, 56
conformation
  evaluation of, 98
constipation, 65
convulsions, 71
cryptorchidism, 83
dermatitis, 66
diarrhea, 65
diseases
  infectious, 60
distemper, 60
driving, 19, 52, 56
drowning, 70
ears
  care of, 28
  congenital deafness, 67, 80
  mites, 65
  training of, 99
eclampsia, 90
eczema, 66
epilepsy, 66, 80
evolution, 11
exercize, 29
eye, 18
  Collie Eye Anomaly, 67, 80
  injury, 71
  lens luxation, 80
  progressive retinal atrophy, 67, 80
famous lines, 13-15
fetch, 55
first aid, 69
flanking, 51, 54
fleas, 64
gathering, 18

genetics
  defects, 80
  in a breeding program, 78
  practical applications, 78
  principles, 74-77
grooming, 27
  equipment, 28
heartworm, 63
heat stroke, 71
hepatitis, 60
herding
  commands, 50
  equipment, 49
  shedding, 58
  training, 49-68
hip dysplasia, 67, 80
history, 9, 10
hookworm, 62
housing, 29, 30
inbreeding, 78
intelligence, 1, 2
leptospirosis, 60
lice, 65
linebreeding, 78
mastitis, 90
mating, 83, 84
medication
  administration of, 72
metritis, 91
milk fever, 90
mites
  ear, 65
  mange, 65
monorchidism, 83
nails
  cutting, 28
neutering, 24
nutrition, 25-27
  of lactating bitch, 91
obedience dog, 6
  training, 43-47
obstacles, 57
old age, 30, 31
Old Hemp, 13, 14
outcrossing, 78
outrun, 52, 55
parainfluenza, 61
parasites
  external, 64, 65
  internal, 61-64
parvovirus, 61
pedigree, 21
penning, 57
poisoning, 70
problems
  chewing, 39
  barking, 40
  jumping up, 40
  chasing cars, 40
  digging, 41
progressive retinal atrophy, 67
puppies
  buying, 23
  immunizations, 94
  newborn care, 93
  nutrition, 27, 95
  orphans, 93, 94
  selling, 95
  temperament evaluation, 96-98
  training, 35-37
  whelping of, 87-90
  worming, 94
pyometra, 91

rabies, 61
registration papers, 21
reproduction
  bitch's heat, 82
  brood bitch, 81
  female system, 82
  male system, 83
  stud dog, 83
respiratory failure, 69
round pen, 51
roundworm, 62
shock, 69
snake bite, 70
socialization, 36, 37
spaying, 24
stud dog, 83
style, 18
tapeworm, 63
tattooing, 30
teeth,
  care of 28, 29
  correct bite, 127
  overshot bite, 127
  undershot bite, 127
temperament, 18
  evaluation of, 96-98
ticks, 64
tracking, 5, 117
training
  ears the, 99
  equipment, 35
  to herd, 49-68
  housebreaking, 35
  obedience, 43-47
  principles, 34
  puppies, 35-37
  for shows, 139
  tricks & games, 38, 39
trials
  American, 115
  British, 117
  Great Britain Sheepdog, 108
  New Zealand & Australia Sheepdog, 112
  obedience, 115-119
  Schutzhund, 121-124
  United States Sheepdog, 102
vaccinations, 59, 94
vital signs, 69
vomiting, 71
wearing, 53
whelping
  box, 88
  equipment for, 87
  problems, 90
whipworm, 63
working ability, 2
  with the blind, 5
  as hunters, 5
  with military, 4
  as sled dogs, 5
  as trackers, 5
  in TV & movies, 6
working certificate, 20